AF352470

Speaking Qur'an

Studies in Comparative Religion
Frederick M. Denny, *Series Editor*

Speaking Qur'an

AN AMERICAN SCRIPTURE

Timur R. Yuskaev

THE UNIVERSITY OF SOUTH CAROLINA PRESS

Published by the University of South Carolina Press
Columbia, South Carolina 29208

www.sc.edu/uscpress

Manufactured in the United States of America

26 25 24 23 22 21 20 19 18 17
10 9 8 7 6 5 4 3 2 1

Library of Congress Cataloging-in-Publication Data
can be found at http://catalog.loc.gov/

ISBN: 978-1-61117-794-7 (hardcover)
ISBN: 978-1-61117-795-4 (ebook)

To Nadya, Adam, and Olivia

CONTENTS

SERIES EDITOR'S PREFACE

Speaking Qur'an is a long-needed historical study and contemporary explication of how Islam's sacred scripture has been studied, obeyed, chanted, and deeply loved by devout Muslims in North America for generations. Now that there is a sizable and richly diverse community of Muslims here, it is important for citizens in both Canada and the United States to learn about, respect, and appreciate Muslims, their beliefs and practices, and their social and cultural ideals and customs as they become authentic citizens in their chosen communities.

Longstanding North American religious communities since the immigration of Europeans and other new citizens have been largely devoted to Jewish and Christian scriptural texts with beliefs, values, and practices shared through the Hebrew Bible with its Mosaic and prophetic teachings, known by most Christians as the Old Testament, which was followed by the New Testament, with the teachings of Jesus and his life. The Islamic Qur'an ("reading, recitation"), believed by Muslims to be the actual words of Allah/God, is also within the expanded communities of what Jews, Christians, and Muslims acknowledge as the "Abrahamic traditions."

Professor Yuskaev provides for his readers a delightfully detailed and civilized tour through historical, spiritual, cultural, social, and contemporary dimensions of how Muslims have developed and are energetically dedicated to serving their faith communities while always being deeply devoted American citizens as well. *Speaking Qur'an: An American Scripture* will be an important choice for high school and college courses, as well as faith communities and the general public for years to come.

Frederick Mathewson Denny

ACKNOWLEDGMENTS

This book is a product of many coincidences, experiences, and exchanges. Some of them were official interviews: a thousand thanks, as always, to Faheem Shuaibe, Abdullah bin Hamid Ali, Sadaf Khan, Sayyid M. Syeed, Benkong Shi, and many other anonymous interviewees, especially my mentor in chapter 3. Beyond this circle are dozens of other conversation partners I encountered while researching and writing what would become *Speaking Qur'an* (including Amina Wadud, whose hospitality and advice I will never forget).

Still beyond that group are hundreds of other interlocutors, mentors, and friends from many walks of life, who helped me learn how to hear American experiences and scriptures. They include, centrally, those with whom I had the privilege to work while serving on staff of the Interfaith Center of New York from 1999 to 2005, long before this book was conceived: Aisha al-Adawiyya, James Parks Morton, Matt Weiner, Alfonso Wyatt, Sarah Sayeed, Ratan Barua, Kusumita Pedersen, Uma Mysorekar, Myo Ji Sunim, Antonio Mondesire, Feisal Abdul Rauf, Bill Leicht, Henry Young, Tamara Greenfield, Craig Miller, Talib Abdur-Rashid, Abd Allah Latif Ali, Muhammad Abd Al-Rahman, David Ball, Louis Cristillo, Musa Drammeh, Alamelu Iyengar, Muhammad Hatim, Ibrahim Abdul-Malik, Mohamed Moussa, Kevin James, Faroque Khan, T. K. Nakagaki, Andrew Stettner, Moushumi Khan, Souleimane Konate, Saeed Phipps, Asha Samad, Sana Shabazz, Abdus-Salaam Musa, Muhain Alidina, Alice Fisher, Shamsi Ali, Amir Al-Islam, Nadeem Kazmi, Munire Terpis, Nurah-Rosalie Cordner, Adem Carroll, Robina Niaz, Debbie Almontaser, George Stonefish, Moustafa Bayoumi, Ashin Indaka, Zain Abdullah, Muhammad Tariqur Rahman, Annie Rawlings, Naim Baig, and many, many others—I cannot name and thank them all, a shortcoming that reflects just how blessed I have been.

The first written inklings of this text appeared during a class with Bruce Lawrence at Duke University, another class at Duke with Ebrahim Moosa, and then, simultaneously, classes and informal exchanges with Carl Ernst, Omid Safi, Thomas Tweed, Laurie Maffly-Kipp, Yaacov Ariel, Lauren Leve, Randal Styers, and many others at the University of North Carolina at Chapel Hill. One of this book's key approaches came from a class with Carol Blair, also at UNC, which I took because of Peter Wright. Charles Kurzman, through a side project, taught me how to collect and analyze American Muslim dialogues.

Many of my recordings of such voices come from the fieldwork I conducted as a recipient of the Social Science Research Council's Muslim Modernities Pre-Dissertation Research Fellowship. My ability to interweave these and other threads with what I heard and read before and after was fine-tuned during the SSRC workshops in conversation with other Muslim Modernities fellows. From there emerged my dissertation, which followed the outline but not the full argument of this book. It was supervised—often with elegant understatement—by Ernst, Lawrence, Safi, Kurzman, and Ariel. I was assisted in the arduous task of translating that initial text into a related but very different book by my colleagues at Hartford Seminary: Mahmoud Ayoub, Yahya Michot, Sami Shamma, Benjamin Watts, Bilal Ansari, Scott Thumma, Usman Khan, Feryal Salem, Khalil Abdullah, Yehezkel Landau, Tricia Pethic, Shanell Smith, Ryan Sawyer, Lucinda Mosher, Jawad Bayat, Steven Blackburn, Kaiser Aslam, Ingrid Mattson, M. T. Winter, Uriah Kim, Heidi Hadsell, and others. My thanks to all, to those who read and commented on chunks of my constantly changing chapters, as well as to those whose conversations, often on alternate subjects, have shaped what materialized in the end. Beyond Hartford's welcoming walls, I am particularly grateful to Juliane Hammer, Martin Nguyen, Rumee Ahmed, and Gregory A. Lipton for offering insightful reflections and much-needed prompting. A special thanks is due to Jim Denton and the patiently meticulous editorial team at the University of South Carolina Press.

The people who set me on my academic and professional path were Lynda Clarke of Bard College (later of Concordia University) and Frederick Denny of the University of Colorado Boulder—as well as many others, such as Lawrence Mamiya and Ihsan Bagby, who invited a twenty-year-old undergraduate version of me to accompany them as they interviewed African American imams in New York City in 1993; a professor of literature at Bard who taught a magnificent class on Nabokov (and who, I am sure, does not remember my name); Mark Lytle and Gennady Shkliarevsky at Bard and Ira Chernus at CU-Boulder (I would not be where I am now without their efforts); and my literature teacher in St. Petersburg, Russia, Elza Bazhenova. To all of them, I am in debt.

Yet my greatest debt is to my family: my mother, father, brother, and grandmothers, and to Nadya, Adam, and Olivia. Words fail me. Silently, continuously, I thank you from my heart.

INTRODUCTION

·······)(·······

The Qur'an is only lines inscribed between two
covers; it does not speak; people only utter it.

'Ali ibn Abi Talib, quoted in Ernst, *How to Read the Qur'an*, 63

The text lives only by coming into contact with another text (with
context). Only at the point of this contact between texts does
a light flash . . . joining a given text to a dialogue.

Mikhail Bakhtin, *Toward a Methodology*, 162

··· | ···

She frowned but did not turn away. She was an elderly Egyptian American Qur'an teacher at a suburban mosque in North Carolina. I interviewed her in the summer of 2008, when I worked as a researcher for a project unrelated to this book, which examined American Muslim responses to terrorism. She was taken aback when I awkwardly asked, "What do you think about some Muslim radicals claiming that their actions are inspired by the Qur'an?" "Well," she said, "my Qur'an never told me to be a terrorist. My Qur'an never told me to kill other people."[1]

As the teacher spoke, her voice stressed "my Qur'an" and "never told me." Her facial expression reminded me of the Qur'anic verse "*'abasa wa tawalla*," or "he frowned and turned away," where God admonishes the Prophet Muhammad for turning away from a blind man who interrupted him during a meeting with a group of notables.[2] I developed the habit of hearing reminders of the Qur'an in the verbal and facial expressions of my conversation partners while conducting research for this book, which I carried out from 2008 to 2010.[3] The ethnographic part of this exploration entailed paying attention to how American Muslims spoke and made the Qur'an resonate with their realities.

I doubt my interviewee was aware of how her response embodied, for this particular listener, a reminder from the Qur'an. The rest of her answer, however, was an unmistakable sign of the problematic place Muslims and their sacred book had come to occupy in the United States in the decade after the terrorist attacks of September 11, 2001. My question touched on a raw nerve of her post-9/11 experience: in this moment, she must have felt that she was, yet again, conversing with a person who connected her religion with terrorism.

Our exchange took place within the context of incessant controversies ensnaring Muslims and the Qur'an. One of those flare-ups occurred in early 2007—one year before the teacher and I spoke—when the first Muslim member of Congress, Representative Keith Ellison (Democrat of Minnesota), was sworn into office. During the ceremony Ellison placed his hand on a copy of the Qur'an. This symbolic act stirred a ruckus of negative voices. Dennis Prager, a conservative columnist, declared that "insofar as a member of Congress taking an oath to serve America and uphold its values is concerned, America is interested in only one book, the Bible."[4] Several other pundits and politicians followed suit, with Representative Virgil Goode (R–VA) declaring that Ellison's "use of the Koran" during the swearing-in ceremony violated "the values and beliefs traditional to the United States."[5] One of many opinions in defense of Ellison's choice was issued by David Kuo, a former deputy director of the White House Office of Faith-Based and Community Initiatives. He poked fun at the outrage: "So the Bible is America's holiest book? Was there a vote? Did Oprah decide? Was it Jefferson?"[6] Of course, in Ellison's case, it was, in part, Thomas Jefferson: the congressman used a copy of an English translation of the Qur'an that had once belonged to the third President. Ellison's adaptation of Jefferson's Qur'an was astute. It provided an immediate retort to his critics by demonstrating that the Qur'an had indeed been part of American history, its tradition of inclusivity, since at least the beginning of the republic.[7]

Still, what makes a religious book American? Surely it is not Oprah's Book Club! After all, the Qur'an is, in some ways, foreign: it originated in a faraway past, it is in a foreign language, and its believers in distant times and places have understood it in ways that are surely quite at odds with current American sensibilities. It even looks unlike most texts that contemporary readers encounter: it is not a textbook, novel, or collection of stories; it is not structured to convey one or a series of unfolding stories from a beginning to an end. Its appearance is different because it is a premodern and oral text (another example of an old oral text is the *Iliad*). Its first existence was as a recitation; the Arabic word *qur'an* literally means "recitation." It is indelibly linked with the figure of the Prophet Muhammad, who received it, fragment by fragment, over the course of twenty-three years, from around 610 to 632 C.E., and recited it to his community in Mecca, Medina, and beyond. The written text of the Qur'an is based on the traditions of oral recitations that originate with the Prophet and his disciples and which were continued through centuries by subsequent generations of religious students and teachers. Also significant is that, for most Muslims, proper understanding of the Qur'an is impossible without simultaneous engagements with other texts, primarily the Hadith, written down—but also memorized and orally recounted—narrations of the Prophet's sayings and actions, as well as works of formal exegesis, or *tafsir*.[8]

Of course, most other American scriptures, like the Bible and the Sutras, are also foreign imports: they, too, originated in distant pasts, have existed as oral and written texts, and are linked to extensive traditions of interpretations, some of which, from contemporary points of view, have been quite awkward—think about patriarchy and slavery, which until very recently in the United States and other places were taken for granted and scripturally supported realities. To post-9/11 critics of American Muslims, however, these facts did not matter. The Qur'an's foreign appearance confirmed to them what they had been implying all along: that Muslims were somehow out of place in the fabric of American life. For American Muslims this widely circulated common sense presented a quintessential post-9/11 Catch-22: without the Qur'an, they could not be Muslim, but their allegiance to it fueled speculations about whether or not they were really American.

My book cuts through this dilemma. It is based on the perspective that the Qur'an, like other imported scriptures, is American because millions of Americans, who in this case happen to be Muslim, have made it so. How have they been making it theirs and, therefore, American? The answer to this question is necessarily lengthy. A simple declaration—"the Qur'an is American"—would not suffice, even if it is enacted symbolically in the U.S. Congress. Crucially, it would not explain *how* it is American. It would also come across as ungainly and, for most of my Muslim readers, jarring—it would go against the grain of their theological sensibilities, according to which every word of the Qur'an belongs to God.[9]

Still, if the Qur'an is God's, how could the Egyptian American teacher say "my Qur'an?" Her articulation was indeed theologically awkward. But it was not unique: I have heard and read variations of this phrase many times.[10] What prompted her expression, which was instinctual rather than formally theological, was her intimate affinity with the sacred text. The pain audible in her voice and visible in her frown was a reaction to a possible affront to the book of God. That anguish was deep precisely because it was *her* Qur'an, and even a hint at its disparagement was a potential offense to her very humanity, which she had been modeling on her sacred text. In this sense, her reaction would resonate with many Muslims, who might recall that 'A'isha bint Abi Bakr, a wife of the Prophet, described him as "the Qur'an walking." To embody the Qur'an, as it was lived by the Prophet, is the height of aspiration for any Muslim .

•••||•••

This book focuses on the human side of scripture. More specifically, it examines American Muslims' cultural translations of the Qur'an. It explores how they have been interpreting their sacred text to make sense of it and their experiences. I wrote it for several overlapping audiences: those who would

3

like to learn about American Muslims, as well as those who are interested in the Qur'an. My subject is at once broad and focused, which prompts me to bridge diverse fields and methodologies. This book, therefore, might be particularly useful to undergraduate and graduate students who study religious people and texts through diverse courses and perspectives, including anthropology, history, religion, and sociology. My colleagues, academics who teach such courses, might also benefit from how this book employs theoretical approaches from the disciplines and fields of rhetoric, history of ideas, memory studies, and religion in public life. As much as possible, I attempted to keep theories behind my analysis just below the surface of the text. Sometimes, however, I chose to highlight them (the first such resurfacing occurs in the introduction, most obviously in section IV). This is because my central inquiries address questions that begin with the word "how," which are difficult to address effectively without some theory.

My approach to the Qur'an is largely anthropological, modeled after the understanding of anthropology as "the systematic inquiry into cultural concepts."[11] In the broad network of scriptural and Qur'anic studies, I aim to contribute to the ongoing shift toward the examination of sacred texts as they are lived and embodied by human beings. Exemplary here are William A. Graham's *Beyond the Written Word*, Vincent L. Wimbush's *Theorizing Scriptures*, and Rudolph T. Ware's *The Walking Qur'an*. Among books that provided the initial impetus to my study are Farid Esack's *Qur'an, Liberation and Pluralism*, which analyzes South African informal Muslim exegeses in the era of the antiapartheid struggle, as well as Allen Dwight Callahan's *The Talking Book*, Bruce Lawrence's *The Qur'an: A Biography*, and Michael M. J. Fischer and Mehdi Abedi's *Debating Muslims*, which emphasize the dialogical nature of human engagements with canonical texts. In the field of American religion, my analysis is particularly indebted to Susan Friend Harding's *Book of Jerry Falwell*. In the area of American Islam, my work belongs to an ensuing wave of scholarship that moves toward the study of American Muslim discourses and intellectual history. Notable here are Kambiz GhaneaBassiri's *A History of Islam in America*, Juliane Hammer's *American Muslim Women*, Zareena Grewal's *Islam is a Foreign Country*, and Moustafa Bayoumi's *How Does It Feel To Be A Problem?*

The subject of American Muslim engagements with the Qur'an is vast. For example, the earliest existing American document that contains a possible Qur'anic exegesis is the autobiography of Omar Ibn Said (1770–1864), a West African Muslim who found himself enslaved in the Carolinas.[12] He wrote it in Arabic in 1831, around the time of Nat Turner's rebellion. He framed the story of his life by first writing down from memory the Qur'anic chapter 67 (*"al-mulk"* or "Sovereignty"). This sura—"sura" is the Qur'anic term for a "chapter"—states that God is the ultimate master of all creation. And Ibn Said likely used it to make sense of his American experience of slavery, his forced submission to a human master in a foreign land. While Qur'anic, his response was also American: it resonated with broader African American religious discourses of his time. Some twenty years later, for instance, Reverend Jeremiah Wesley Loguen, a former slave and a Methodist minister, would echo Ibn Said's declaration by proclaiming at an antislavery meeting in upstate New York, "I owe my freedom to the God who made me."[13]

Ibn Said's written commentary on his American life was understandably indirect. Writing by slaves at that time was typically seen as subversive; after Turner's uprising it became prohibited. That might have been a reason why he rendered his interpretation as a mere scriptural hint. From a broader perspective, however, his choice also demonstrates that Muslims have been bringing the Qur'an to comment on their lives in a variety of ways. Some of them are officially recognized as exegeses, or works of *tafsir.* Other types of interpretation, the absolute majority, are too elusive to be classified. And all of them are cultural translations: they bring texts from the past into the present. Because of this, any interpretation, formal or otherwise, is also a work of memory.

Muslims everywhere memorize, recite, and quote the Qur'an routinely. While recitation of portions of its text is a necessary part of their daily prayers, the Qur'an's influence goes further: just as many Christians insert biblical phrases into their everyday speech, many Muslims habitually intersperse their words with Qur'anic words and phrases, such as *"in sha' allah"* (literally, "if God wills," often translated as "God willing"), which comes from Qur'an 18:24. Such utterings are the same everywhere. Yet, every time they are spoken, they acquire distinct meanings derived from the context of their speakers: "if God wills" only makes sense when it is attached to a specific situation. The same holds true for formal recitations of the Qur'an, whose purpose is to faithfully and precisely replicate how the text has been recited by generations of Muslims, going all the way to the Prophet.[14] As with everyday expressions, such canonical recitations become meaningful to their human speakers and hearers within their contexts.

I witnessed an example of this process in January 2009 during my research at a large Muslim congregation in western New York, which coincided with one of Israel's massive military assaults on the Gaza Strip, "Operation Cast Lead." Members of this American community were absorbed in the event, monitoring it via satellite channels and online—and some through phone conversations and e-mails with relatives in Palestine. They discussed it incessantly, sharing a collective shock and grief over the killing of many hundreds of human beings, overwhelmingly civilian, during this three-week campaign, which began abruptly, on Saturday, December 27. However, the leader of this congregation, its imam, did not make any public announcements about it for six days. One of the reasons for it was that his time to speak would come exactly in six days, during his weekly Friday sermon. Another reason was that he needed to prepare himself and his community for how to speak about it. For instance, since 9/11, this congregation had developed close relationships with neighboring synagogues, and its imam did not want an international conflict to devastate their local friendships. Moreover, the community itself was not monolithic: some 40 percent of it were Arab Americans, many of whom thought that the crisis in Palestine was the most important issue of the moment; others, while sharing this pain, had other concerns as well.

Just because the imam did not make any official statements about the crisis does not mean that he did not comment on it. Every day he kept leading collective prayers and reciting the Qur'an, and his commentary was embedded in what and how he chose to recite. Day after day he kept highlighting passages that spoke to the intertwined sacred histories of Muslims and Jews. By speaking from the Qur'an and without adding a word of his own, he reminded his congregation that Jews and Muslims belong to the same tradition of revelation, which comes from the same divine source. One of the Qur'anic utterings he repeatedly brought in, however, had—on the surface—nothing to do with Muslims or Jews, or the modern political entities called "Israel" and "Palestine." It was sura 94, *"al-sharh"* ("Consolation"). Many Muslims know it by heart, because it is one of the Qur'an's shortest suras and is typically memorized in childhood. It had been revealed to the Prophet Muhammad in Mecca, before he was forced to migrate to Medina, at a time of serious hardship. Its consolation was directed to him. So how could it comment on a twenty-first-century conflict and speak to some Muslims in western New York?

During a month I spent in the area, I began most of my days by joining a group of men at this congregation in their dawn prayers. On one such morning, during the first week of Operation Cast Lead, I saw the answer to how the Qur'an becomes a local sacred text. As the imam was reciting sura 94 yet again, I furtively looked right and left to see the faces of men praying next to me—and saw tears. They wept while hearing in Arabic the lines they had heard thousands of times before: "Yet hardship will bring ease. Indeed hardship must bring ease."[15] Their tears signaled that, in that moment, they heard the Qur'an speak to the anguish they felt during those days. This was a moment when they—with their senses—were engaged in a heartfelt and embodied dialogue with the book of God.

···III···

Mikhail Bakhtin, a linguist whose thought is central to my analysis, observed that "all language is collective" and dialogical. It is saturated with contextually specific meanings shared by participants of particular collectives, which change depending on when, where, and in whose company they are.[16] Words—and sacred texts—acquire different shades of meanings in different settings. This means that the overwhelming majority of moments and cases of the Qur'an becoming an American text are barely noticeable. This book, therefore, is a series of compromises that make this subject more accessible, for my readers and me.

My first compromise is that I largely, but not completely, stay away from less tangible cases of the Qur'an's American cultural translations, such as Ibn Said's elusive exegesis or interpretations that appear as mere recitations. (The two examples, by the way, are related: Ibn Said's was a written-down recitation and, as such, it was an interpretation expressed exclusively as an evocation.) I also sidestep the subject of the Qur'an's technical translations, books that aim to transmit it into written English in its entirety. I avoid such seemingly obvious examples of cultural translation for two reasons, which have to do with my goal of highlighting American contexts of the Qur'an as a living text. First, the genre of written translation, by its nature, conceals the agencies and contexts of translators. Although some of them try to overcome this inherent limitation of their art, their successes are at best marginal—sometimes literally so, because their observable commentaries typically appear in the margins or in the footnotes of their books, which are officially never theirs to begin with.[17] My second reason for omitting such works is more significant: written translations also conceal the agency and contexts of their audiences.

Instead, I analyze more obvious examples. At the center of my book are interpretations developed by four prominent American Muslim public intellectuals: Fazlur Rahman (1919–1988), a Pakistani-American academic; Amina Wadud (b. 1952), a feminist scholar and activist; Warith Deen Mohammed (1933–2008), an African American community leader; and Hamza Yusuf (b. 1960), arguably the most popular American Muslim preacher of the post-9/11 era. These personalities were highly influential and represented diverse, yet interrelated, streams in American Muslim discourses. What matters most for my analysis, however, is that Rahman was a writer, Wadud was both a writer and a preacher, and Mohammed and Yusuf were almost exclusively preachers. This selection of case studies, therefore, allows me to analyze writing and preaching as two distinct modalities of cultural translation.

My examples limit my exploration to the period between the mid-1960s and the end of the first decade of the twenty-first century. The first marker in this chronology is 1965, the year of the Immigration Act, which made it possible for millions of non-Europeans to immigrate to the United States. Over time, they transformed this country and, in the words of Diane Eck, a scholar of American religious diversity, created "a new religious America," where being Protestant, Catholic, or Jewish was no longer the only acceptable way of being American.[18] Among these immigrants there were millions of Muslims, who joined the ranks of previously existing communities and established new and more numerous institutions. Along with this institutional growth came dramatic expansion in the depth and range of Muslim intellectual production. The year 1965 was also the year of the assassination of Malcolm X, a watershed event in the history of African American Muslims, whose contributions have always been crucial in broader American Muslim life. On the other side of this timeline is the first decade after September 11, 2001, during which American Muslims emerged as their country's new problematic minority, a status they inherited from other religious and ethnic groups, such as American Catholics and Jews, as well as African and Asian Americans.[19]

The disadvantage of this chronology is that it leaves out countless other stories. It is balanced out, however, by the fact that American Muslims in this era of globalization were formulating their Qur'anic interpretations while being in constant contact with international Muslim conversations. At the same time, their expressions of specifically American concerns were now more pronounced as well. In part it was because they relied on the discursive legacies of previous generations of their American coreligionists, those who had been brought here as slaves or arrived as immigrants in the late nineteenth and early twentieth centuries. Another reason behind it was that this was also the period when other religious minorities had gained—or were, contemporaneously with Muslims, acquiring—the recognition as integral participants in American life. This was the period when religious diversity, as a concept, became an American common sense. This combination of factors allows me to approach American Muslim discourses in light of both global and local trends, as well as the experiences of other American religious groups.

···IV···

Rahman, Wadud, Mohammed, and Yusuf were public intellectuals, which means that their efforts had practical orientations. Through their written and oral rhetoric, they taught their readers and listeners how to make sense of themselves as Muslims. Key in this process was how they directed their readers and listeners to remember the Qur'an. Yet, every remembering is a *re-membering*—a *re*-collection, *re*-arrangement of the past by those who bring it back to life in light of their own contexts and times. In addition to their American settings, therefore, what these four interpreters shared was that they were modern human beings who translated the Qur'an, a premodern text, across time to make it resonant with their modern audiences.

The concept of time is central in any contemporary exegesis of a premodern scripture. Interpreters render such texts understandable by infusing their words with connotations they share with their audiences, including their perceptions of time. Embedded in this process are cultural translations

8

across time-bound concepts, those of premodern texts and their modern believers. Most often, however, this aspect of interpretation goes unnoticed—for what is more commonsensical and, therefore, unremarkable than time? And yet, there is nothing more contextually specific than common senses.

Consider here an example of an almost identical articulation of time by two individuals, Vladimir Nabokov and Fazlur Rahman, who did not know one another and had few things in common, except for being contemporaries and therefore, in a sense, co-sharers of time. In his 1951 autobiography, *Speak, Memory*, Nabokov, a secular (at least on the surface) Russian novelist and poet, described time as a "colored spiral in a small ball of glass."[20] Some thirty years later, Rahman, an Indian-born religious scholar, depicted time as a spiral as well: it was a "spiral," he insisted, and "not a cycle."[21] He made this statement in *Major Themes of the Qur'an*, published in Chicago in 1980.

The two writers had different reasons behind their formulations. Nabokov conjured this image to make sense of his personal experience of the passage of time. Rahman used it to explain the Qur'an in "terms adequate for the needs of contemporary man." The scriptural notion of time, he wrote matter-of-factly, was not cyclical, because "cyclic motion is incomparable with any purposefulness; it belongs more to the world of merry-go-rounds."[22] What he meant by "purposefulness" was progress, which was a predominant twentieth-century way of thinking about human history.

Rahman's description of the Qur'anic notion of time as resonant with the modern idea of progress, however, was not as self-evident as he presented it to be. It is just as likely that this seventh-century—and therefore premodern—text's conception of time is cyclical (at least in its notion of human historical time). The Qur'an's recollections about past events direct its audiences toward cultivation of piety—and being pious is always in the present. The Qur'an tells stories from the past to express recurring patterns of human behavior. Crucial among those, it keeps reminding its listeners and readers, is the human propensity toward forgetfulness—most important, people's tendency to forget about their dependence on God. Therefore, it depicts human beings and societies as going through cycles of remembrance and forgetting. During particularly rough stretches of such cycles, God sends reminders through prophets, messengers, and other inspired people. Yet, as time passes, forgetfulness returns.[23] Even the community of Muhammad, whom the Qur'an calls "the best community," are constantly warned about the danger of disremembering, because they are merely human and thus not immune from forgetting.[24]

All this may suggest, as the historian Fred Donner put it, that the Qur'an is basically an ahistorical text: it is aimed at its audiences' present, and thus the "very concept of history is fundamentally irrelevant to [its] concerns."[25] Of course, it depends on what one means by the term "history." Another historian, Chase Robinson, stipulated that the Qur'an does have a historical component to its style and content. He examined how the Qur'an recalled events of the past specifically for its first audiences, the contemporaries of the Prophet Muhammad. These recollections, he proposed, delineated a history. But it was a "different kind of history," which was told orally and with the goal of establishing a tradition. This type of an oral telling of history, Robinson explained, rhetorically created a place for the new society of believers: it confirmed to them that they were descendants of Abraham and other prophets, and taught them that they were inheritors of the lessons that God had already taught to Jews, Christians, and others. Viewed from this perspective, the Qur'an is a document that shapes a "tradition transmitted orally"—because oral recollections that establish a lineage tend to appear in "hourglass" shapes, with stories "clustering around formative (frequently legendary) origins and more recent generations (usually fathers and grandfathers)."[26]

Robinson's characterization of the Qur'anic method of history telling was a twist on the thought of Paul Ricoeur, a French philosopher. From Ricoeur's perspective, memory is a broad category that includes both written and oral modes of remembering. All memory, whether oral or written, confronts the fundamental contradiction: it represents in the present the past that obviously no longer exists. How writers and speakers perform such representations, however, is fundamentally distinct. As William Graham, another follower of Ricoeur, explained, "where [oral] memory collapses time spans, writing tends to fix events temporally and heightens the sense of their distinctiveness as well as their 'pastness,' or separation from the present and the individual person."[27]

Writing distances the past from its readers because it fossilizes it as an image through conglomerations of written words. Most important, however, is that writers perform their remembrances in isolation from their readers, and readers consume such works in their own separate times and places. This means that writers and readers typically do not remember together: they are not engaged in direct and simultaneous dialogues—except when a writer reads out loud her or his text in front of an actual audience. In such moments, writers stop being writers and become storytellers. This metamorphosis represents the difference between writing and speaking memory. Public speakers, including storytellers and preachers, carry out remembrances right in front of their audiences; even recorded versions of live speeches cannot fully compromise this sense of immediacy. At the same time, in oral performances, listeners are never passive because listening is, by its nature, instantaneously dialogical. Through such dialogues, speech reinfuses the past into the present more naturally.[28]

The Qur'an is an oral text. Its existence has been primarily as a recited, listened-to, and retold composition, where sound is inseparable from meaning. When it comes to books, this is a peculiarly premodern characteristic. One of the signs of modernity is the emergence of printed books and mass literacy, which spurred the practice of reading texts silently. Before then, the act of reading was different—it actually entailed pronouncing words out loud.[29] Because of this, Rahman's stipulation about the Qur'an's progressive, and spiral-like, presentation of historical movement through time says more about him—and Nabokov and other moderns—than it does about the Qur'an. To explain what this means, I have to refer to yet another historian, Reinhart Koselleck, whose seminal work, *Futures Past,* offers a retrospective retelling of what moderns and premoderns meant by the term "history."

Koselleck's central insight is straightforward: human beings derive "their terminology" of speaking and thinking "about history, [and] specifically historical time," from "[their] nature and their surroundings."[30] When these change, so do their perceptions of time. Modern technologies of telling and managing time—which swept most of the world in the nineteenth and twentieth centuries—were instrumental in the emergence of modern ways of living and management of nature, including human nature. Premodern human beings told time and scheduled their lives through physical nature, by relying on daylight and the change of seasons. They, unlike us, were not surrounded by clocks. We, unlike them, embody artificial time, time calculated through instruments. Our days begin, for example, when schools, shops, and factories open at particular times dictated by clocks and other machines. Therefore, we have a different *sense* of time. And the word "time," although it can be found in various premodern languages and texts, to us means something different from what it did before the advent of modernity: "time" looks the same—it is composed of the same letters or symbols—but it is sensed differently.[31]

In addition, according to Koselleck, premodern perceptions of history followed two basic and interrelated models. The first way of making sense of the past, present, and future was based closely on an organic model: premodern people perceived history as moving along recurring rounds of growth and decline, akin to the movement of agricultural cycles. It is possible that the original Qur'anic concept of time belonged to this category. The second model perceived historical time as a process of decline from some spectacular peak, such as the time of God's tangible intervention in human history, as in the coming of Christ or the revelation of the Qur'an.[32] According to this perspective, if an improvement was noted in some element of the human condition, it did not encompass much, and from a practical angle what mattered most was the overall inevitability of decline. This notion is reflected in a saying of the Prophet: "The best people are those living in my generation, then those coming after them, and then those [of the generation] coming after."[33] As the generations of Hadith collectors recalled the Prophet's statement about his own and the next three generations, they made sense of it in ways that reflected Koselleck's second type of premodern time telling. The Qur'an, understood as God's final revelation, was the summit of human history. After it, as time passed, humans would be increasingly removed from it, and the task of the following generations would be to resist decline, which in the end would occur anyway, until the coming of the messiah.[34]

Of course, the actual story is more complicated, which is why Koselleck's two models are interrelated. While speaking about decline, Muslim premodern thinkers were also teaching about the process of constant renewal. Through this combination, they re-membered the notion of decline into a powerful teaching tool that highlighted the indispensability of renewal.[35] This, in turn, underscored the importance of Muslim religious authorities, who served as guides to the revelations' proper rememberings and reimplementations. Their merger of the cyclical and decline models of time transformed it into a spiral as well— of a downward variety, of course.

From this perspective, it appears that Rahman, based on his modern perception of time, merely reoriented the traditional, premodern spiral into a modern one: it had a similar underlying logic, where revelation and its renewed remembrance were key, except now this logic supported the sense of time as moving progressively into better futures. And, like his premodern predecessors, he wrote about time pedagogically, as a strategy of teaching practical lessons. For an exegesis to be practical, it has to be resonant with its time-bound contexts and understandings. Rahman's engagement with the question of time, therefore, was not unique: other modern Muslim interpreters of the Qur'an, including those whose works I explore in this book, do it routinely—even when they do not address it directly; even when they do it naturally, without reflection—whenever they explain the Qur'an for their modern audiences.

···V···

What I just wrote previews of some of my book's analysis: all of its case studies address the question of the Qur'an's translation across time. Chapter 1 delves into Rahman's writings, most centrally his *Major Themes of the Qur'an*, to explore challenges interpreters face when they attempt to make the scripture resonant with sensibilities and dilemmas of their modern audiences. In addition, it places Rahman's work within the context of the post-1965 history of Islam's cultural translation into an American religion, an ongoing process that obviously had begun much earlier. Chapter 2 examines Amina Wadud's exegesis, found in her books and sermons. It zeroes in on a practical issue, the concept of gender equality, which highlights why strategies of crossing time matter. Gender, after all, is a modern concept, which, like time, has the tendency of appearing constant. As Wadud put it, although at the time of the Qur'an's revelation "gender was not a category of thought," by the end of the twentieth century it became unavoidable: the "absence of such a category of thought," she observed, "was not sexist at the time of revelation, but it is palpably so today."[36] Wadud's choice of the words "sexist" and "palpably" hints at the purpose of my exploration of her work, which goes further than gender per se: it considers the notion of gender equality as an integral component of her American Muslim contemporaries' common sense of justice, including, for many of them, the sense of what it meant in the Qur'an. Similarly, chapters 3 and 4, which focus on Warith Deen Mohammed and Hamza Yusuf's sermons, examine deeper connotations in American Muslims' Qur'an-based discussions on race and politics. In chapter 3 that deeper subject is the African American concept of redemption, which W. D. Mohammed articulated as Qur'anic and without which the Qur'an cannot be a harmoniously African American scripture. In chapter 4, it is the dynamics of cultural politics, the give-and-take between religious and civic values, where American Muslim articulations of their scripture are obviously vital.

Throughout the book, I aim to highlight the dialogical nature of American Muslims' engagements with the Qur'an, which they have carried out in conversation with other, past and present, Muslim authorities. In chapter 1, the dialogue I feature is between Rahman and Muhammad Iqbal (1877–1938), an Indian poet and public intellectual. Chapter 2 examines Wadud's exegesis as a continuation of the interpretive methodology charted by Rahman, with help from Iqbal. Chapter 3 offers a case study of a sermon by one of W. D. Mohammed's close disciples, Imam Faheem Shuaibe. Chapter 4 incorporates close analysis of reflections by some of Yusuf's regular listeners.

The subject of all these chapters is American *tafsir*. Literally, *tafsir* means "explaining" the Qur'an. I use it in this straightforward sense, which broadens its scope significantly—and which may appear unusual for some of my Muslim and academic readers, who are used to seeing this word applied to works of formal exegesis, written texts produced by specialists, *mufassirun*, who adhere to particular, highly specialized rules. Typically, when authors of formal *tafsirs* analyze a given scriptural passage, they can comment on its possible meanings only after providing evidence of the time and occasion in which it was revealed, noting its variant readings and determining whether or not that passage had been overruled by another scriptural uttering (a process called *naskh*, abrogation).[37] If such a procedure is not followed, other scriptural authorities are readily available to dismiss the offenders as not real exegetes. Thus, Jalal al-Din al-Suyuti, a fifteenth-century Egyptian interpreter, famously dismissed the philosophically oriented *tafsir* of Fakhr al-Din al-Razi, a thirteenth-century Persian, as having "everything [in it] except *tafsir*."[38] Suyuti's opinion made sense: it was a case of one Muslim authority casting aside the work of a competing exegete. Less understandable, from my perspective, is the academic tendency to dismiss and therefore fail to investigate a wide array of informal and differently produced Qur'anic interpretations. One of my goals, therefore, is to prompt my colleagues to look beyond such officially recognized *tafsirs,* in any setting.

The people whose exegeses I explore did not produce formal *tafsirs* and avoided this term when they described their work—which, among other things, helped them circumvent the bitter contestations over who could serve as exclusively authoritative voices of the scripture. Rahman and Wadud wrote their explanations of the Qur'an in a different, contemporary and academic, genre that allowed them to navigate around the rules of formal *tafsir.* Their writings communicated the Qur'an's meanings to wider audiences, beyond the narrow circles of professional exegetes, which is why they had broader significance. W. D. Mohammed and Yusuf did not call what they did *tafsir* either (although Mohammed's students used it), because they merely preached; Wadud, of course, was also a preacher. Their preaching, however, was exegetical. And it was precisely because they explained the scripture though preaching that their oral *tafsir* was influential: it was highly flexible and immediately resonant with their listeners. As such, it belonged to the vast vernacular field of spoken articulations of the Qur'an.

At the core of this book is an approach to the Qur'an as a spoken text. This idea is not new. William Graham's *Beyond the Written Word* is my study's most notable precursor. His book, however, contains a telling—and, for me, productive—discrepancy. Graham emphasized that religious scriptures often serve as "the sacred spoken word." He explained that scriptures become "spoken" when they are recited and retold in official and everyday speech, as in preaching. He illustrated this broad definition with examples from Protestant Christian preaching. But then, when it came to the Qur'an, he addressed it primarily as a "recited text": he stopped short of exploring it as a spoken, rather than recited, scripture.[39] My book goes beyond the recited Qur'an. It examines how the Qur'an becomes a spoken text when it enters Muslims' everyday speech, which is shaped in dialogues with their authoritative speakers, such as preachers.

The Qur'an speaks only when it comes into contact with other speakers. Its text, which is marked by its orality, highlights how it functioned as a discourse during the time of its revelation, or, academically speaking, formation. One of its central stylistic features is polysemy, an ability to convey multitudes of meanings through a single word or phrase. During the Qur'an's formative period, its polysemy served to connect it with collective memories of its first listeners. The Qur'an aimed to reform their lives, which meant that they had to *hear* it, understand its lessons as speaking to the very depth of who they were. This is why the Qur'an addressed them through a language it shared with them, a type of Arabic specific to their time and place. This language went beyond shallow definitions of linguistics: it embodied their concepts and common senses, which, by articulating them anew, it attempted to reshape.[40]

To truly speak, in any context, the Qur'an has to touch upon what cannot be said easily. That is why this book examines both immediate and deeper American Muslim notions—or, rather, senses—of justice, race, and politics, which are always specific to their time. I suggest that contemporary public speakers, those who speak Qur'anic words and stories and harmonize them with their audiences' experiences, engage their scripture's polysemy and lend new lives to its orality. In this process, the Qur'an, through the speech of its human agents, speaks a local language, addresses local concerns, and participates in local discourses.

Oral *tafsir* is a mode of speaking—and therefore embodying—the Qur'an. Yet, to understand the strategies of cultural translation embedded in modern speaking of a premodern text, one must pay attention to written interpretations as well. This is because writers are more thorough than preachers: they do not have the freedom to gloss over points that are either too obvious or thorny, which preachers do routinely. This is why, although this book is about the Qur'an as an American spoken sacred text, it begins with explorations of the Qur'an's written articulations.

Chapter One

TIME

······ ✗ ······

View the world otherwise, and it will become other.

Muhammad Iqbal, *Javid-Nama,* no. 2019

Repeating is neither restoring after-the-fact nor re-actualizing:
it is "realizing anew." The creative power of repetition is contained
entirely in this power of opening up the past again to the future.

Paul Ricoeur, *Memory,* 380

···I···

Fazlur Rahman was born in 1919 in prepartition India, in a family that had deep roots in Islamic scholarship. After completing his M.A. in 1942 from Punjab University in Lahore, he moved to England in 1946, and in 1949 received his Ph.D. from Oxford. From 1950 to 1958 he taught at Durham University in England and from 1958 to 1961 at the Institute of Islamic Studies at McGill University in Montreal. In 1962, after sixteen years abroad, he returned home, to the new nation of Pakistan, to serve as the director of the Central Institute of Islamic Research, whose mission was to interpret "Islam in rational and scientific terms" that met "the requirements of a modern progressive society."[1] In this capacity he provided support to the modernization reforms of Pakistan's ruler, General Ayyub Khan, whose opponents ultimately forced Rahman to resign and immigrate to the United States in 1968, after one of his English-language books, *Islam,* was translated into Urdu. The central charge against him had to do with the Qur'an: he was accused of denying its uncreated and divine nature—arguably a tone-deaf reading of what he actually proposed. The longest and most productive phase of his career took place in the United States, where, while teaching at the University of Chicago from 1969 until his passing in 1988, he solidified his reputation as a Muslim scholar of global importance.[2]

Rahman's impact was most pronounced in the academic study of Islam. At the University of Chicago, he was the teacher to dozens of students who became well-known scholars of Islamic studies in the United States and Canada. Through his books and students, he contributed to a dramatic transformation in how Islam came to be studied at American universities and colleges.[3] Yet what was his influence among American Muslims? I asked this question often during my research. A typical answer came from Sayyid M. Syeed, a longtime leader in the Islamic Society of North America (ISNA), which in the late twentieth and early twenty-first centuries was the largest Muslim American organization. Like many people who knew Rahman personally, Sayeed considered him an intellectual giant and remembered him fondly. But, he noted, echoing many other respondents, "regretfully, [Rahman's] influence [was] limited to academics."[4]

Syeed's evaluation was understandable: unlike other prominent American Muslim intellectuals of his day, such as Seyyed Hossein Nasr (b. 1933) and Ismail Raji al-Faruqi (1921–1986), the Iranian American and Palestinian American philosophers, Rahman was rarely seen or heard at the gatherings of American Muslim organizations. One possible reason for this was that ISNA, like many other American Muslim institutions of this era, had significant South Asian constituencies, and many people in these groups allied themselves with the ideology of one of Rahman's opponents in Pakistan, Abu al-Aʿla Mawdudi (1903–1979), an exegete, journalist, and the leader of Jamaat-e-Islami, the Indian subcontinent's predominant Muslim political movement. Therefore, Rahman and this group stayed out of each other's way. This made his influence less visible. But it does not mean that it did not exist.

In many ways Rahman's position in American Muslim history is akin to the role of Jacques Maritain (1882–1973) in American Catholicism. Like Rahman, Maritain was a foreigner, in his case French, and an academic. In the 1940s and 1950s, he taught at Princeton University and was known as a global Catholic intellectual. He was a philosopher and a student of Henri Bergson, whose name will appear in this chapter. His central contribution to international Catholic discourses was in articulating "more nuanced understandings of the challenges posed by modernity."[5] In the post–World War II context, when the Catholic Church had to overcome widespread misgivings about its affiliation with antidemocratic regimes, he formulated the language of Catholic participation in democratic societies. This global proposition became American through the efforts of Maritain's local followers, such as John Courtney Murray (1904–1967), a Jesuit priest, theologian, and public intellectual, who used Maritain's insights to develop a new vision and language of American Catholic politics.

In a way similar to Maritain's, Rahman's influence in American Muslim discourses was embodied in the works of local intellectuals such as Amina Wadud, who followed in his footsteps (see chapter 2). Here, I will situate Rahman in the American Muslim context of the post-1965 era and then examine his American masterpiece, *Major Themes of the Qur'an,* a book he published in Chicago in 1980. In the 1980s and 1990s, *Major Themes* was perhaps the most widely used text on the Qur'an at American colleges and universities. Its impact was more than academic. For many young American Muslims, it served as their first significant introduction to the Qur'an. What made it appealing was how naturally it harmonized the scripture with their sensibilities, including their concepts of justice and ethics (which, like the notion of time, tend to appear constant but, historically speaking, are not). The significance of *Major Themes* for my study, however, is broader than the tracing of Rahman's influence on those who acknowledged it directly. His exegesis was unique in one specific way: its author was also a historian. Because history was for him a central interpretive tool, his work highlighted what most exegetes typically skip: the dilemmas that arise when a premodern text is translated into a meaningful guide for its modern believers. An understanding of what this entails is imperative for all of this book's case studies.

···II···

In the year 2000, twelve years after Rahman's death, a group of American Muslim academics and activists published a book, *Windows of Faith: Muslim Women Scholar Activists in North America*. Its aim was to "give evidence of, and voice to, the diversity of expressions that constitutes contemporary Muslim women's scholarship and activism in the United States."[6] The range and depth of its articles certainly fulfilled this goal. But it did something else as well. Its language, both in terms of its conceptual vocabulary and internal logic, demonstrated the depth of Rahman's influence on American Muslim discourses of the last two decades of the twentieth century. Indicative of this was an article by Nimat Hafez Barazangi, a Syrian American professor at Cornell University. One of Barazangi's arguments was acutely controversial: she challenged her Muslim colleagues to embrace the term "feminism." As is often the case with daring propositions, she presented it as grounded in uncontested sources, which, to her, were the Qur'an and Fazlur Rahman. She proposed that "the basis of feminism lies in the Qur'an" because the principles of feminism correspond with "the Qur'anic concept of justice." She added that it was not her intention to "read history backward," that she was "merely reinterpreting what Rahman stated: The basic principle in the Qur'anic view of Islamic justice is the equality between sexes."[7]

A telling illustration of Rahman's broader influence is an autobiographical vignette by Ingrid Mattson, a Canadian convert to Islam who spent much of her career in the United States and from 2006 to 2010 was the first female president of ISNA. On the website of Hartford Seminary in Connecticut, where she was a professor of Islamic Studies from 1998 to 2012 (and where I happened to teach as well), she chose to introduce herself in the following way:

> In the summer of 1987, I was riding the train out to British Columbia to start a tree-planting job in the mountains. I had just finished my undergraduate degree in Philosophy and had only recently begun my personal study of Islam. I came across Fazlur Rahman's *Islam* in

a bookstore a few days before my trip. Reading that book as I traveled across the Canadian prairies, I made the decision to apply to graduate school in Islamic Studies. . . . Going a step further, I wrote a letter to Rahman. . . . I dropped the letter in a post box somewhere in the Rockies and forgot about it until I returned east in August. There I found a hand-written note from him, inviting me to come to the University of Chicago to study with him. Rahman died before I arrived in Chicago, but it was his book and his encouragement that inspired me to start on the path to scholarship that I have found so rewarding.[8]

Islam, the book that inspired Mattson, was the same text that stirred the controversy that forced Rahman to leave Pakistan. Mattson's recollection glossed over this fact. In a way her sidestepping of this issue was natural because she encountered *Islam* in Canada. First published in England in 1968, its 1979 edition by the University of Chicago Press was one of the most widely assigned textbooks on Islam in North American colleges and universities. So it is not surprising that a recent graduate from a Canadian university just happened to "come across" it while not being cognizant of its somewhat controversial status in Pakistan. When Mattson recalled that story in the late 2000s, however, the situation was different. At that time, some twenty years after the incident she narrated, she was serving as the president of ISNA, whose membership was overwhelmingly South Asian. Her statement, therefore, risked ruffling feathers among some of her organization's older members. Yet, many years after Rahman's passing and beyond that specific constituency, his name was now safe and acceptable enough to be presented by the president of the largest North American Muslim organization as a kind of an *ijaza,* or a certificate that a student of a respected Muslim scholar receives to demonstrate the validity of his or her intellectual lineage.

While the passage of time and Rahman's academic accomplishments contributed to the transformation of his image, more significant was that his overall arguments, reflected in *Islam* and other works, were quite at home in broader American Muslim discourses of the time. What he shared with many Muslim immigrants of his generation was the language of Islamic reform. As Kambiz GhaneaBassiri, a historian of American Islam, explained, for many American Muslim activists of Rahman's generation, the "adherence to Islamic beliefs and practices was not only a religious duty but a transformative experience."[9] For many of them, religiosity was tied to political activism. This combination was reflected in their conceptual vocabulary, which took on such modern political notions as "nation" and "progress" and reformulated them as Islamic and even Qur'anic. They often derived the language of their religious and political activism from the works of Mawdudi and Sayyid Qutb (1906–1966), an Egyptian writer, exegete, and one of the ideological fathers of the Muslim Brotherhood, the Arab world's parallel to Jamaat-e-Islami. Although there were many differences between Rahman and these two Muslim thinkers, what they had in common was an understanding of modern Islamic reforms as necessitating a return to Islam's original texts, the Qur'an and Hadith, which, they felt, had to be interpreted anew and often in contradiction to established exegetical traditions. In this context the overall direction of Rahman's interpretation of the Qur'an was not particularly contentious. America, for many of Rahman's immigrant Muslim contemporaries, held the promise of a new beginning. It was a modern nation, where they could build a new Muslim community that would be free from the politics they left back home. Besides, Rahman's interpretation had another element in common with Mawdudi and Qutb: like them, he explained the Qur'an thematically, which was an acutely modern methodology. Qutb, for example, who was originally a literary critic and journalist, borrowed his methods from the literary studies of his day.[10]

Of course, such resonances would not matter had Rahman been still absorbed in local Muslim politics. By immersing himself in the academy, he avoided unwelcome political exposures. This was reflected in the decidedly academic style of his writing: his works came across as objective and above the politics of the day. Yet even this element was not unusual among immigrant Muslim intellectuals of his generation. Another person who maintained the same seemingly detached approach was Seyyed Hossein Nasr, who was often perceived as a direct opposite to Rahman. Another commonality Rahman and Nasr shared was that they highlighted the serious nature of the challenges faced by individual Muslims and their societies in the postcolonial era. Rahman's solution was to formulate new and decidedly modern strategies of rethinking Islam, including the Qur'an. Nasr's response was different: he rejected modernity itself. He wrote and spoke about it as a civilizational disease, accompanied by hypermaterialism and secularism. He argued that Islam was a "traditional" religion, which to him meant premodern. Because of this heritage, it and other old traditions—such as Catholic and Orthodox Christianities, as well as some forms of Judaism, Buddhism, and Hinduism— had the depth of knowledge necessary to overcome the modern predicament. Like Rahman, he wrote academic and more popular books, which addressed secularly educated Muslims around the globe and especially in the West.[11] Their disagreement was profound: while Nasr viewed modernity as godlessness, Rahman embraced what he saw as its positive streams.

In spite of this, both of these authors shared yet another stylistic commonality: they avoided writing about politics and concentrated instead on "essential" meanings of Islam. In Nasr's books the phrase that conveyed such principles was "integral Islam." Another term he and Rahman used frequently was "normative Islam." While what they meant by these phrases was somewhat different, their rhetorical choice of stressing—and thus defining—some core aspects of Islam was pedagogically productive in a similar and telling way. During their careers in Iran and Pakistan, both Nasr and Rahman were close to the political centers of power that intruded into the domains of religious authorities. In Iran and Pakistan their "integral" and "normative Islam" reflected their attempts to avoid direct confrontation with guardians of orthodoxy and their institutions. In the United States, however, these same words had a different utility. They resonated with how many American immigrant Muslims of the post-1965 era spoke about themselves—because they were a very diverse conglomeration of people, who did not agree on what was "orthodox" but needed to work together. To Rahman and Nasr's immigrant Muslim audiences, "normative Islam" was a godsend. In 1968, for example, the year Rahman immigrated to the United States, the Muslim Student Association included among its members individuals from thirty-six countries, and described itself as an organization of "Muslims first, Muslims last, and Muslims forever."[12] This sort of pan-Islamic rhetoric was not unique to the MSA. It was shared by many national and local groups: many mosques established in this period, for instance, included both Sunni and Shi'i Muslims.

"Normative"—as opposed to the stern-sounding "orthodox"—Islam appealed to some converts as well. This was the time when many Americans—and Canadians—were searching for spiritual alternatives and were finding them in Buddhism, Hinduism, and Islam. For some of them Rahman and Nasr's essentialist language provided an opening into an Islam that was at once exotic and relatable. In this respect Mattson's remembrance of Rahman's *Islam* was quite telling. He had written it, after all, for Western audiences, as well as for secularly educated Muslims all over the world. Its language appeared unfettered by local politics, either in Pakistan or North America. Practically speaking, it presented a vision of Islam that was essential enough to be readily translatable into new sets of local realities.

···III···

Wendy Cadge, an anthropologist specializing in contemporary American Buddhism, noted that "[with] the exception of Native American religions, Mormonism, and a few other religions started in the United States, American religious history is a story about how religions started in one place are carried along global networks and constructed and reconstructed in new ways on American shores."[13] The story of Islam becoming an American religion is complex. It is undeniable, however, that Muslim intellectuals have been pivotal in this process. By serving as authoritative voices of Islam, they contributed to its cultural translation into an American reality. Their role was in formulating conceptual vocabularies and grammars of American Muslim

discourses, which helped their readers and listeners make sense of themselves as Americans and Muslims.

In the post-1965 period, this process of cultural translation unfolded in
three overlapping stages. In the first movement of this progressive spiral,
Islam's cultural interpreters—typically immigrants, like Rahman and Nasr—
distilled foreign Muslim discourses from such places as Pakistan or Iran
into general notions of "normative Islam." Following this development, their
American students and audiences, who included immigrants, African Americans, and others, appropriated such "normative" ideas and developed their
own, more tangibly American interpretations. After this they were able to
address global concerns not as generic "normative" Muslims but as Muslim
Americans. Key in this process was American Muslim institutional life: the
transformation in the rhetoric of public intellectuals was tied to the development of locally resonant institutional practices and articulations, which
became particularly pronounced after 9/11.

This dynamic is reflected in the works and words of two American imams,
Muhammad Abdul Rauf (1917–2004), a prominent Egyptian American Muslim leader, and his son, Feisal Abdul Rauf (b. 1948), a New York City–based
imam who gained national renown in 2010 during the controversy surround-
ing the establishment of Park 51, a Muslim community center a few blocks
from the World Trade Center in Manhattan, which some called "The Ground
Zero Mosque."[14] Abdul Rauf the elder was a contemporary of Fazlur Rahman.
Unlike Rahman, he was prominently engaged in the building of American
Muslim institutions. Yet, like Rahman and many Muslim leaders of that generation, he often talked about Islamic essentials. For instance, during the 1957
opening ceremony of the Islamic Cultural Center in Washington, D.C., in
whose founding he played a key role, he declared, "May this Islamic Center
in Washington serve its purpose of shedding the light of truth about Islam
as a universal religion, as a way of life, and as a culture which is essentially
creative and humane."[15] His son, Feisal Abdul Rauf, often wrote and spoke in
a similar vein—until September 11, 2001. Before 9/11 he wrote *Islam: A Search
for Meaning* and *Islam: A Sacred Law.* In these books one could detect subtle
connotations that hinted at the author's American cultural location. To notice them, however, one would have to read between the lines, because their
overall language was of "normative Islam." After 9/11 he wrote *What's Right
with Islam Is What's Right with America* and *Moving the Mountain: Beyond
Ground Zero to a New Vision of Islam in America,* which formulated an explicit
vision of an American Islam.

Feisal Abdul Rauf's transformation was part of a broader shift in American Muslim articulations, which occurred in the aftermath of 9/11. I will explore one such example in chapter 4. What is important to note here is that,
while his and many other American Muslim intellectuals' emphasis on the

American character of Islam was novel, their overall language was not altogether new. Many African Americans had established such articulations earlier. But even those who would begin to speak and write in this way after 9/11 followed the logic that can be traced to the earlier, pre-9/11 period. Many of them arrived at speaking and writing about "American Islam" through the language of "normative Islam." The notion of "normative Islam" allowed them to put distance between their own interpretations and the discursive streams that had developed in other contexts. In the post-9/11 era, they filled that gap with the phrase "American Islam."

In this respect Rahman's role as an American Muslim cultural translator was momentous. But it was not obvious. At about the same time as his *Major Themes*, for example, another American Muslim intellectual, Ismail Faruqi, published a text, *Toward Islamic English,* that aimed explicitly to serve as a blueprint for how American Muslims had to speak. He presented in it, after a short introduction, a glossary of Arabic terms, which, he argued, English-speaking Muslims had to adopt to be properly Muslim. The impact of Faruqi's book, however, was limited: its audience was narrow, and it was too technical—a dictionary of sorts. Dictionaries, however, do not shape languages. It is, rather, spoken languages, and their ongoing transmutations, that prompt constant upgrades of dictionaries.

Rahman's *Major Themes* was different and its influence more lasting. It addressed a broad audience, Muslims and non-Muslims, academics and otherwise. For Muslims specifically, it provided a path through which they could revitalize Islam in new contexts. And it did this is a way that was at once direct and subtle: rather than teaching vocabulary, it instilled a conceptual grammar, an invisible logic of contemporary Muslim thought. Step by step, it engaged its audience in a particular method of reading and interpreting the Qur'an. It embodied a carefully developed logic designed to enable its Muslim readers to articulate new ways of speaking and thinking about their past and present as they worked toward a better future.

···IV···

"The Qur'an," wrote Rahman in the first sentence of the first chapter of *Major Themes,* "is a document that is squarely aimed at man." Its goal, he argued, was to enable humans to live their lives successfully, toward a successful end. For each individual, it meant cultivation of God-consciousness, or *taqwa.* For God-conscious societies, it entailed striving toward the attainment of "a moral social order on earth." Because of this practical orientation, the Qur'an, in Rahman's reading, was not a theological treatise but a book of signs. It "does not 'prove' God," he explained, "but 'points to' Him from the existing universe." To guide humans toward God, the Qur'an, in his view, presented a cosmology, a depiction of the universe, whose aim was to remind them about their "unique position in the order of creation."[16] Therefore, he structured his book to direct his readers toward recognizing how the Qur'an communicated with them: he began it with a chapter on God and then immediately proceeded with essays about human beings and societies, nature, processes of God's revelation, eschatology, the problem of evil, and, only at the end, the history and lessons of the first community of Muslims.

From the beginning, Rahman identified the goal of his book: it was an intervention into how the Qur'an should be read in the modern era, which to him went beyond the discipline of *tafsir*. The "innumerable Muslim commentaries on the Holy Book," he observed, "often take the text verse by verse and explain it." This customary approach, however, "cannot yield insight into the cohesive outlook on the universe and life which the Qur'an undoubtedly possesses." He further explained that most interpreters of his time "lack[ed] . . . a genuine feel for the relevance of the Qur'an today" and "fear[ed] that such a presentation might deviate on some points from traditionally received opinions." These two characteristics, he argued, prevented his colleagues from presenting the Qur'an "in terms adequate to the needs of contemporary man." His book, on the other hand, responded "to the urgent need for an introduction to major themes of the Qur'an." Such thematic reading, he proposed, was "the only way to give a [contemporary] reader a genuine taste of the Qur'an, the Command of God for man." Rahman described his "procedure . . . for synthesizing themes" as "logical rather than chronological," which was a clear indication of his trespassing on the rules of traditional *tafsir*. He further insisted that he used interpretation "only [when it was] necessary for joining together ideas," and added, "Apart from this, the Qur'an has been allowed to speak for itself."[17]

Rahman's style was at once academic (in the modern sense of this word) and religious. His writing—expressed in the passive voice and "logical" presentation—came across as "normative." It concealed the agency of the man who "allowed [the Qur'an] to speak for itself." This posture of objectivity reflected Rahman's position as an in-between intellectual, one trained in both Muslim and secular traditions of Islamic Studies, and because of this he could evaluate and utilize what he deemed to be their most productive approaches. Western academic study of Islam was useful to him and, he hoped, to his Muslim colleagues as well because it provided the tools necessary for rethinking the historical contexts of Muslim texts. Of course, he urged his coreligionists to apply such tools carefully, so as not to disrupt the vital dimensions of the Islamic intellectual traditions. *Major Themes* reflected this line of thought. In it Rahman attempted to reread the Qur'an with the help of the methods developed by Western academics—as they had been applied to the historical exploration of the Bible, for example—in a way that was also faithfully Muslim, because the Qur'an to him was "the Command of God."

Such a delicate balancing act was characteristic of Rahman's overall scholarship. A telling example of it is the book Rahman published in Pakistan in 1965, *Islamic Methodology in History*. Its subject was the Sunna, or Muslims' collective memory of the life of the Prophet Muhammad. Rahman took seriously Western academic critiques of the historicity of the hadith literature, the scriptures that communicate the Prophet's Sunna, while refusing to allow such evaluations to devalue the Muslim traditions of engagement with the Prophet's legacy. He conceded that many accounts of Muhammad's words and acts were misremembered by generations of Hadith collectors. But that, he argued, did not negate the value of the Hadith for discovering the "normative" message of the Sunna. As a professional historian, he knew that human memory is not exact and that contexts always influence how the past is remembered. His solution to this fundamental feature of memory was to search for the themes that would be consistent throughout the Hadith. Such themes, he proposed, represented the Sunna as a "concept," which reflected the ethical principles behind the Prophet's actions and words.[18]

Major Themes built upon *Islamic Methodology*. In both books Rahman did not just interpret the scriptures, but theorized about the tools of their interpretation. Like many other exegetes, he read the Qur'an and Hadith in tandem. But whereas customary exegeses used the Hadith to comment on and verify meanings of individual Qur'anic passages, he reversed this order and used the Qur'an to authenticate the Hadith. Rahman's basis for this reversal was academic: the Qur'an, to him, was an accurate recording of the revelation, while much of the hadith literature was not. In addition, *Islamic Methodology* and *Major Themes* employed a particular methodology of re-reading the scriptures. In *Major Themes* it became more developed and yet less obvious—perhaps because too detailed an explanation of its author's role as an interpreter would have distracted its readers from paying attention to how the Qur'an spoke "for itself." This was likely the reason why Rahman reserved the technical explanation of his method for a subsequent book, *Islam and Modernity: Transformation of an Intellectual Tradition*, which he published in 1982. It was there that he finally gave his method a name: he called it a theory of "double movement."[19]

Rahman's "double movement" is akin to a choreographic composition, an outline of a dance. It is a method that encourages other interpreters to follow a particular pattern of movement, to step carefully into the past and then into the present, and then keep repeating variations of these moves over and over again, because the present and therefore perceptions of the past change constantly. The first movement in this dynamic outline entails stepping into the past to understand the "micro and macro" contexts within which the Qur'an was revealed.[20] This requires a historically sensitive examination of how the Qur'an made sense to its initial audience, the Arabic speakers of seventh-century Mecca and Medina. It necessitates a study of their history and language, including their contextually specific understandings of words and concepts. The second step is equally contextual. It entails cultural translation of the Qur'an's lessons into the logics and words understandable to modern human beings. To do so, interpreters have to be attuned to what is sound to their own contemporaries; they have to study the realities of their audiences. Otherwise, how would they make sense of the Qur'an for those who need it now? This task of constantly moving across time is so complex that Rahman imagined his "double movement" as a collective endeavor: the first step is "primarily the work of the historian, [while] in the performance of the second the instrumentality of the social scientist is obviously indispensible."[21]

The general parameters of Rahman's proposition were not entirely new. On the surface his methodology resonated with the standard premodern method of interpreting the Qur'an through the Hadith. Like other exegetes, Rahman relied on what Muslims call "occasions of revelation": records, contained in the Hadith, of particular situations within which individual segments of the Qur'an were revealed. He also employed *naskh,* or abrogation, the process through which interpreters have been traditionally sorting out contradictions among passages that had been revealed to the Prophet at different times between 610 and 632 C.E.[22] Yet, Rahman did not just use such tools; he redesigned them almost completely.

His reformulations relied on the approach he had already developed in *Islamic Methodology,* where he interpreted the Hadith not as a collection of individual records but as the Sunna, a coherent representation of the Prophet's life and message. Similarly, he did not interpret the Qur'an one passage at a time, as most of his premodern counterparts did. Rather, he read it as coherent whole—somewhat in the way literary critics analyze novels. This too was not a new perspective. The emphasis on the coherence of the Qur'an's overall message had been present in some medieval exegeses as well, such as the *tafsir* of the twelfth-century Persian scholar al-Zamakhshari. In the modern period it was developed into a methodology of interpretation by the Pakistani interpreter Amin Ahsan Islahi (1904–1997) and the Iranian Shi'i scholar Seyed Mohammad Hossein Tabatabai (1904–1981). Rahman's competitors, Mawdudi and Qutb, followed this understanding as well.[23]

What Rahman did with both the occasions of revelation and *naskh*—in light of his reading of the Qur'an as one coherent text—was immensely productive. He refashioned the occasions of revelation into a concept, which verified that the Qur'an was forever relevant: during its period of revelation, it responded to specific and changing situations, and it continued to speak in subsequent settings as well. Behind the Qur'an's chronologically revealed statements, Rahman perceived a coherent network of narratives. As the Qur'an was gradually and dialogically revealed, he argued, it communicated—in various ways that were tied to specific contexts—a set of core ethical lessons. He called these lessons the Qur'an's "major themes."

Based on this understanding, Rahman transformed *naskh* into a particularly time-sensitive tool of cultural translation. His *naskh,* unlike the one his predecessors had used, was thoroughly thematic. By emphasizing "major themes," he deemphasized those scriptural lessons that, to him, were not so central. Surely, he did not neglect any passages. But he read them thematically in light of more "major" passages and ideas. In this way he reformulated the Qur'an as a whole into a "normative" text whose meanings went beyond the specifics of many of its individual utterings. In this process he culturally translated both the Qur'an as a whole and its individual passages. Technically speaking, from the customary definition of *naskh,* he abrogated nothing. In his interpretation even those passages that had been nullified by some of his colleagues were still communicating. But they did so thematically and thus spoke, across time and cultures, to Rahman's contemporaries on occasions when they needed the revelation.

Rahman, of course, did not call what he did *"naskh"* because, technically, it was not it—just as his *tafsir,* narrowly speaking, was not a *tafsir.* While it is possible to interpret his versions of *naskh* and *tafsir* as mere contemporary upgrades of their premodern versions, such a perspective would not be entirely sound. What drove Rahman's effort was a reality that, to him, was commonsense: his and his contemporaries' contexts were modern, and the modern period of human history is fundamentally different from what had transpired before. This was the reason for his redesigning of the very art of interpretation—to the extent that its tools, even if he were to give them "traditional" names, would still have to be modern. Without such modern devices, Rahman hinted, the Qur'an could not speak and make sense to modern humans. Or, as he put it, "[To] the extent that we achieve both moments of this double movement successfully, the Qur'an's imperatives will become alive and effective once again."[24] This phrasing was uplifting, but one does not "become alive . . . once again" without being otherwise previously.

Rahman's "double movement" was his attempt to answer the most vital dilemma of any modern engagement with the Qur'an, which is too commonsense to be noticeable and hence is almost always ignored. It stems from the modern sense of time, which assumes that history—societal or individual progression through time—is irreversible: today is never like yesterday; things always change and can never be repeated; history is not a circle. His "double movement" was a response to a temptation that afflicts many religious and other nostalgic people who want to somehow revert to the past of their mythologies—such as the supposedly wholesome American 1950s or, for Muslims, the time of the Prophet Muhammad. Repeating the past, Rahman was certain, was impossible, and he saw those who employed such rhetoric as intellectually immature and irresponsible. His own interpretation was a cultural translation of a particularly productive kind. He did not merely translate Qur'anic words, phrases, and concepts into a contemporary language, but he also choreographed a series of steps for future human engagements with the Qur'an.

Rahman's *Major Themes* invited other interpreters to keep engaging in faithful and responsible dialogue with the eternal revelation. Their attempts to hear "the Qur'an speak for itself" would take place in their own contexts, in response to their own struggles—such as overcoming the logic of dehumanization embedded in the peculiarly American notions of something called "race," or striving to live justly according to a sense of justice in which gender inequality is felt as somehow essentially unjust. Practical connotations of "race," "justice," and other commonsense concepts, it must be remembered, change constantly: we often forget that the right to vote, an inviolable right of every American citizen, did not apply to women until 1920 and that before the Equal Credit Opportunity Act of 1974 all American banks denied credit or loans to married women because, in the banks' common sense, financial decisions belonged to husbands. The real significance of Rahman's interpretation was that it charted a course for the Qur'an's future rereadings. His Qur'an was the Qur'an of the future, perhaps even more than the Qur'an of the distant past or the ever-disappearing present. Of course, in the commonsensically modern fashion of his time, he perceived "the future" as being somehow always better than "the present" and "the past."

···V···

The following passage illustrates how Rahman carried out his "double movement" in *Major Themes*. It translates the Qur'anic concept of *taqwa*, which literally means a "fear of God," into the twentieth-century vocabulary of "human rights." I quote it at length to give, as Rahman would put it, "a genuine feel" of the style and logic of his argument:

> The essence of all human rights is the equality of the entire human race, which the Qur'an assumed, affirmed and confirmed. It obliterated all distinctions among men except goodness and virtue (*taqwa*):
>
>> Oh you who believe! Let not one group of men among you deride another, for they may be better than them; nor one group of women deride another, for they may be better than them, no slander each other, nor call each other names—how bad it is to call [each other] bad names after all of you became Believers . . . So fear God—indeed, God is forgiving and merciful. O people! We have created [all of

28

you] out of male and female, and we have made you into
different nations and tribes [only] for mutual identification;
[otherwise] the noblest of you in the sight of God is the
one most possessed of *taqwa* [not one belonging to this or
that race or nation]; God knows well and is best informed.
(49:11–13)

The reason the Qur'an emphasizes the essential human equality is
that the kind of vicious superiority which certain members of this
species assert over others is unique among all animals. . . . It is also
true that the distance between human potentialities and their actual realization displays a range exemplified by probably no other
species of living beings. . . . To offset all these artificial but powerful
sources of discrimination between man and man, it is necessary that
man constantly reminds himself that we "are all children of Adam
and Adam was of dust" (as the Farewell Pilgrimage address of the
Prophet has it). . . . With perfect justification have the lawyers of
Islam emphasized four fundamental freedoms or rights—life, religion, earning and owning property, and personal human honor and
dignity. . . . Through its more specific social reforms, the Qur'an
aimed at strengthening the weaker segments of the community: the
poor, the orphans, women, slaves, those chronically in debt. In understanding the Qur'an's social reforms, however, we will go fundamentally wrong unless we distinguish between legal enactments
and moral injunctions. Only by so distinguishing can we not only
understand the true orientation of the Qur'an but also solve certain
knotty problems with regard, for example, to women's reform. This
is where the Muslim legal tradition, which essentially regarded the
Qur'an as a lawbook and not the religious source of law, went so
palpably wrong.[25]

The structure of this passage embodies Rahman's "double movement."
It begins with a statement about the guidelines, or dynamic principles, that
the Qur'an had established for the sake of the human progression toward
God-conscious forms of societal life. He called these principles, which appeared jurisprudential, "the Qur'an's social reforms." He noted, however
briefly, the Prophet's experiment with actualizing these "social reforms" in
his community: this was likely his reason for quoting Muhammad's last sermon. And then he delivered a lesson to contemporary Muslims by contrast-
ing, through an example from "the Muslim legal tradition," what they had
done previously with what they must do from now on.

What this excerpt also provides is a sense of Rahman's rhetoric, his art of
persuasion. The text of the Qur'an, in Rahman's translation, is framed by his

introduction and explanation. Through this arrangement some of the apparently Qur'anic words come across as naturally in sync with the conceptual vocabulary of Rahman's readers.[26] In fact, for a book where the Qur'an is "allowed to speak for itself," it is remarkable how this seventh-century text incorporates in its vocabulary the language of the post–World War II era, the time of the United Nations, overthrow of colonialism, and the American civil rights movement. In Rahman's rephrasing the Qur'an speaks about "freedom" and "rights." These words appear Qur'anic, but, technically speaking, they were not—at least not in the sense of the network of connotations that was commonsense to Rahman's audiences in the 1980s. For his readers these words would resonate, for instance, with the language of the Universal Declaration of Human Rights and its insistence on the fundamental right of all human beings, men and women of all races, to be "free and equal in dignity and rights."[27]

Another telling example is Rahman's late-twentieth-century rendition of an excerpt from Qur'an 2:228, which he translated as "for women there are rights [over against men] commensurate with the duties [they owe men]—but men are one degree higher."[28] The beginning of this Qur'anic uttering, in Rahman's interpretation, would appear promising for the readers accustomed to including women's rights under the umbrella of the concept of "rights." Yet, for such readers the end of this passage would likely be quite problematic. This was precisely the kind of incongruity that necessitated for Rahman a "double movement." He proposed, therefore, that this Qur'anic ruling was quite "normative" but not in the way that many of the custodians of "the Muslim legal tradition" would think. Rather, he said, the passage as a whole reflected "the usual procedure of the Qur'anic legislation": "Generally speaking, each legal or quasi-legal pronouncement is accompanied by a ratio legis explaining why a law is being enunciated. To understand a ratio legis fully, an understanding of the sociohistorical background (what the Qur'anic commentators call 'occasions of revelation') is necessary. The ratio legis is the essence of the matter, the actual legislation being its embodiment so long as it faithfully and correctly realizes the ratio; if it does not, the law has to be changed."[29]

Based on this perspective, Rahman argued that the first half of Qur'an 2:228 was "normative": it instituted that women had rights. But then he upped the ante by producing the ratio legis behind all Qur'anic legal rulings that involve men and women: "Religiously speaking, men and women have absolute parity."[30] Women's rights, therefore, must be determined by their status as human beings who, "religiously speaking," have "absolute parity" with men. This trumps all else. Thus, Rahman concluded, the passage's depiction of a hierarchy between men and women—"men are one degree higher"—could be safely de-emphasized, in effect abrogated, because it was specific to the context of seventh-century Arabia. If the Qur'an is approached as the source of law and not "as a lawbook," then the premodern notions of human hierarchies, based on gender or any other factor, must not be carried over into how the Qur'an is applied in modern settings.

This example illustrates the practical nature of Rahman's "double movement." One of its outcomes is easily discernable: it makes *ijtihad,* the process of constant renewal of Islamic jurisprudence, inescapable. However, his methodology's less obvious, yet more momentous insight had to do with the very nature of time and history. The reason why so many Muslim scholars had failed to relate the Qur'an to "the needs of contemporary men," Rahman argued, was because they feared "to deviate . . . from traditionally received opinions." Those opinions came from premodern settings, when perceptions of history and the progression of time had been strikingly different from what would become commonsense in the nineteenth and twentieth centuries. Premoderns saw history as either repeating itself in cycles or moving, along a downward spiral, toward an inevitable decay. Moderns, on the other hand, tend to perceive the movement of time as inherently progressive.[31] In other words, the deeper consequence of *Major Themes* is that it challenged its readers to engage the Qur'an as human beings who are aware of their limitations, including their historical location in modern time, which keeps distancing them from the time of the revelation. In this way Rahman made the Qur'an "speak for itself" not just in the new, post–World War II vernacular but in the very grammar, the invisible logic, of his readers' sense of the world. Without such updated grammar, how could the Qur'an continue to speak and make sense?

···VI···

Behind Rahman's exegetical movement was the thought of the Indian poet and philosopher Muhammad Iqbal.[32] Rahman belonged to the generation of South Asian Muslims for whom Iqbal was the preeminent voice of renewal. He and Iqbal had much in common: they both came from devout Muslim families, received thorough religious and secular education, were enamored with the Qur'an, and spent significant parts of their formative years abroad (Iqbal studied law and Persian literature in England and Germany). They also shared the belief that the future of Muslims depended on how they could embody the Qur'an's message in the modern era of history. For the sake of that future, they taught their audiences how to remember the Qur'an anew by engaging their collective memory.

Maurice Halbwachs, the French philosopher who coined the term "collective memory," perceived it as inseparable from language, which he understood as something deeper than mere vocabulary: "[It] is the language, and the whole system of social conventions attached to it, that allows us at every moment to reconstruct our past. . . . People living in society use words that they find intelligible: this is the precondition of collective thought. But each word (that is understood) is accompanied by recollections. There are no recollections to which words cannot be made to correspond. We speak of our recollections before calling them to mind."[33]

How did Rahman, in conversation with Iqbal, attempt to shape his readers' collective memory and language? Like all teachers of memory storytellers, writers, or historians—Rahman and Iqbal projected through their rhetoric a common ground between themselves and their audiences, which for each of them were distinct. The fundamental purpose of memory is to make the present comprehensible by rendering the past meaningful.[34] Rahman and Iqbal used the past pedagogically, to direct the movement of Muslim thought and practice from a common past into a better future.[35] They re-membered the past not merely to indicate what had been possible before but to make sense of the present and articulate new ways of thinking, without which, they thought, a better Muslim future would never come. How they taught was also, to an extent, similar: they attempted to instill in their audiences particular biases, or seemingly commonsense perspectives—because biases are "what makes events knowable in the first place."[36]

Rahman's methodology of interpreting the Qur'an through its principles was a method of remembering. It was a strategy of teaching a common sense of "normative Islam," which opened a way toward a future beyond the past and present realities of his Muslim readers. Their realities, for him, were too political, in the pedestrian sense of this word: they reflected "all these artificial but powerful sources of discrimination between man and man." His role was to reiterate that we "are all children of Adam and Adam was of dust." His readers' task was to understand and embody this message, which was at once Qur'anic and Prophetic. Therefore, he reminded them about the Qur'an's characterization of humans as unique creatures, who, unlike most other beings, had the capacity to consciously implement the lessons of God's revelation. The catch, however, was that this capacity was potential: it was an ideal toward which humans, as individuals and societies, had to constantly progress. The Islam of real human history highlighted to him "the distance between human potentialities and their actual realization." His "normative Islam" was a goal, which Muslims had to strive constantly to realize.

Rahman taught his "normative Islam" through emphases, not negations. This he learned from Iqbal, whose term for "normative Islam" was "Muslim culture." Both Iqbal and Rahman recollected the past, most centrally the past of the Qur'an, to emphasize its essential themes. They taught and related this message to their audiences by remembering anew the eternal lessons of "normative Islam" and "Muslim culture," the background knowledge that their readers and listeners already possessed or were supposed to remember. Theirs, therefore, was a commonsense approach. Yet, how they carried it out was different, because Rahman was an academic writer, while Iqbal was a poet. What Rahman chose to emphasize from the Qur'an paralleled Iqbal's selections. But the purpose of his pedagogic remembrances was distinct. In *Major Themes* he borrowed Iqbal's insights and then customized them to suit his agenda, which was to shape a modern discipline of Qur'anic exegesis that, in his view, had to be both state-of-the-art academic and faithfully Muslim.

Iqbal's influence was profound throughout Rahman's career. Particularly impactful was the poet's philosophical masterpiece, *The Reconstruction of Religious Thought in Islam,* a book based on a series of lectures Iqbal delivered in English at several Indian universities in 1929. For example, Rahman began his *Islamic Methodology* by echoing Iqbal's differentiation between mystics and prophets, as expressed in *Reconstruction.* And he ended that book by defending Iqbal's theory of *ijtihad.* The defense, however, came with a caveat—he offered some key technical corrections. This move was indicative of Rahman's overall approach to Iqbal. While referencing Iqbal, he typically corrected him from his own perspective, as an academic specialist in Islamic history, philosophy, and jurisprudence. Such corrections silenced—or half-silenced—those elements of Iqbal's thought that Rahman found counterproductive.

His hushing of Iqbal, however, went even further. Those not familiar with Iqbal's works would find it almost impossible to detect his influence in Rahman's books, because he mentioned Iqbal very rarely: in *Major Themes,* he revealed Iqbal's presence just once.[37] This avoidance is understandable in some cases. For example, Rahman envisioned that the primary audience of his *Islamic Methodology* would be "traditionally-minded Muslims" in Pakistan, including some clerics, or the *'ulama.*[38] For that particular audience, his reliance on Iqbal might have been an additional turnoff. But why did he need to conceal Iqbal's name in *Major Themes,* which he wrote long after immigrating to the United States and for more general English-speaking audiences, including, of course, Muslims?

Sheila McDonough, one of Rahman's students, recalled that he "wrestled intellectually with Iqbal all his life." He loved Iqbal's poetry but was also cautious about its potential to "distract Muslims from the seriousness of moral purpose."[39] Poetry, to him, was a valuable but perilous art, because it surpassed reason: it could make its consumers too "drunk" on its energy, drunk enough to act before thinking. Therefore, for Rahman, Iqbal's status as the national poet of Pakistan was problematic: his poetry was used to fuel raw nationalism, which Rahman saw as antagonistic to the egalitarian message of the Qur'an. McDonough also remembered that Rahman was wary about Iqbal's reliance on the philosophy of Friedrich Nietzsche, in part because of its association with nationalist ideologies.

Poetry and Nietzsche, however, were the surface indicators of Rahman's much deeper anxiety about Iqbal. A major reason for it was that Iqbal's poetry was mystical, and Rahman, like many Muslim intellectuals of his time, including Mawdudi and Qutb, was uncomfortable with Sufism, the Muslim mystical tradition: he saw it as a medieval vestige, problematic for "contemporary man." Iqbal's association with Nietzsche was also just the tip of the iceberg around which Rahman navigated with caution. It reflected just how thoroughly intertwined Iqbal's insights were with the philosophical and scientific discourses of the late nineteenth and twentieth centuries. This was readily apparent in Iqbal's *Reconstruction,* which presented the seventh-century Qur'an as a text that crossed the boundaries of time, geography, and culture, and hence was a modern scripture as well. To make this point, Iqbal explicitly interpreted it with the help of insights he derived from the leading Western intellectuals of his time, including Albert Einstein, Sigmund Freud, Henry Bergson, and Alfred Whitehead, a British mathematician and philosopher who influenced Bergson. While making this argument, Iqbal utilized his fluency in Muslim and non-Muslim intellectual traditions. He did not hide his position as an in-between intellectual but rather used it to illustrate his argument, which called on Muslims to remember the Qur'an anew in order to break beyond the habits of their thought.

Rahman, of course, was a similarly in-between individual. However, he chose to display his in-betweenness differently, especially when it came to his "normative" Qur'an. Besides, had he emphasized his dependence on Iqbal, he would be hard pressed to avoid the impression that he too was influenced by such figures as Nietzsche or Freud, an intellectual pedigree he did not want to inherit. Therefore, he quoted Iqbal rarely. In *Major Themes* he erased Iqbal's name almost completely.[40] Yet, his conceptual grammar, the underpinning logic through which he "allowed [the Qur'an] to speak for itself," was unmistakably Iqbalian.

···VII···

How can one detect Iqbal's influence in *Major Themes?* One does so by paying attention to Rahman's vocabulary and trying to detect what informed it. An obvious place to start is with the word "God." Rahman described God as "an organic unity."[41] In *Reconstruction* Iqbal also defined God as an "organic unity." While Rahman did not acknowledge the source of his phrase, his echoing of Iqbal was likely not accidental because it was tied to how he and Iqbal presented the very purpose of the Qur'an. For Iqbal it was "to awaken in man the consciousness of that of which nature is regarded as symbol."[42] For Rahman, it was "to shake [human beings] into belief" through reminders about the signs of the divine in nature and human history. "Organic," for both authors, was an indispensible word because it evoked nature and, most important, the process of naturally occurring constant change, which they saw as essential to the entire creation, including processes undergirding human civilizations. The constant movement of and in nature was for both of them a sign of God's ceaseless creativity. The concept that communicated change was time. Yet, how Rahman used the word "organic" and the connections it generated was acutely distinct—because Iqbal read the Qur'an as a poet and translated it into a text of creative inspiration, while Rahman, inspired by Iqbal, translated it into a "normative" and practically applicable "document."

Iqbal's inspirational use of "organic" was far-reaching and, indeed, mystical: he employed it to guide his audiences toward overcoming what he saw as a debilitating perception of an impenetrable boundary between human beings and God. Based on the Qur'an, he understood God and human beings to be unique, because God is creative and humans are created to be creative as well. Nature, to Iqbal, embodied God's "systematic mode of behavior," or God's creativity. For humans the arena of such creativity was in their knowledge—the knowledge of the universe, human self, and God, or the "mystic knowledge." To Iqbal these seemingly different realms, Godly and human, were interrelated. He pointed toward this interweaving by peppering—seeding really—his text with the word "organic." Nature, he stated, was "organic to the Ultimate Self [God]," and human knowledge, mystical or otherwise, was "organically determined" as well.[43]

Iqbal described God and nature as "organic" because, to him, they were alive. He articulated their realities as characterized by "change . . . without ceasing," "a constant mobility, an unceasing flux of states, a perpetual flow in which there is no halt or resting place." Similarly—but not identically—he perceived and expressed constant change as the very character of human life, both physical and inner: in the human mode of being, he declared, "there is nothing static."[44] This, to him, was the essence of the unique connection between humans and God: human knowledge of the universe, he insisted, is not mechanical; it is alive, "organic," and creative. It is precisely this creativity that gives us the unrivaled capacity to perceive deeper meanings behind constantly moving natural realities, including the "ultimate Reality," or God.

Behind this assertion stood the entire network of Iqbal's philosophy, which creatively interweaved Western philosophical discourses with expressions of Muslim mysticism and the Qur'an. He derived his vocabulary of constant change and movement from Bergson, Whitehead, and Einstein. The latest breakthroughs in Western philosophy, physics, and mathematics confirmed to him what the Qur'an had said all along. Doesn't Qur'an 10:6, in Iqbal's translation, say that "in the alternations of night and of day in all that God created in the Heavens and in the earth are signs to those who fear Him"? And isn't the notion of God's ceaselessly creative movement the obvious connotation behind Qur'an 55:29, which states, again in Iqbal's translation, "every day doth some new work employ Him"?[45]

Indeed, Iqbal added, God's creative movement is of a unique kind, impossible to grasp through the ordinary human perception of time: human beings, in the conventional sense, are finite, and their habitual sense of time provides limited perception of the constant and infinite flow of God's creative activity. Yet, Iqbal proposed, within the human self there is an "appreciative side of the self," which is truly creative and thus can move toward the grasp of the "organic" reality of God. Relying on Bergson's phraseology, he explained that human beings progress toward realizing this side of themselves by examining their "conscious experience," especially "in the moments of profound meditation," when "we sink deeper into our deeper self and reach the inner centre of experience." In such moments, he argued, "the states of consciousness melt into each other," and while "there is [still] change and movement . . . this change and movement are indivisible." Therefore, "the time of the appreciative self is a single 'now.'"[46]

This insight was central to Iqbal. He derived his phrasing from Western psychology and Muslim mysticism: his was at once the conceptual language of Bergson and the Persian poet Jalal ad-Din Rumi (1207–1273). And it was within this network of meanings that Iqbal's "organic" made sense: it was a word that transcended and transgressed boundaries. Its meanings were polysemous—distinct, yet resonant and interrelated—just as the creative nature of God was distinct from and yet resonant with the creative nature of humans. It was this resonance that enabled humans—not all, but those who remembered the divine—to consciously act in resonance with God's commands and move toward grasping God as well. For Iqbal such "organic" movement was the purpose of the Qur'an. In *Reconstruction* he urged his readers to overcome their self-imposed limitations, to pursue the life of constant creativity, and, in the process, shape their own nature and history. This was how he made sense of history as well. History, for him, embodied human beings' "organic"—or divinely inspired—creativity; this creativity, in turn, made the movement of history progressive, its future always new, never repetitive.

Rahman was inspired by this vision and translated it into his own reading of the Qur'an, but only to an extent. Echoing Iqbal, for example, he insisted that "God and nature are not two different factors." Like Iqbal, he explained that there is a "more ultimate causation," imperceptible to human beings' conventional senses, which bestows "upon natural processes in their entirety a significance and intelligibility that natural processes viewed in themselves do not yield." "This higher causation," he further clarified, "is not a duplicate of, nor is it in addition to, natural causation. It works within it, or rather is identical with it—when viewed at a different level and invested with proper meaning." Could it be that by "different level" Rahman meant something similar to Iqbal's idea of "appreciative self," which some human beings, very rarely, realize "in the moments of profound meditation"? Rahman moved close to saying just that—but he was careful not to go too far. Like Iqbal, he wrote that "inner perception" is essential in attaining deeper knowledge.[47] Yet, unlike Iqbal, he stressed that even such unique human knowledge is essentially limited.

This careful dance around Iqbal's mysticism reflected Rahman's deep discomfort with Sufism: mystics, in his estimation, had a history of moving too close to pantheism, the belief that the creation is somehow identical with the Creator. And, to make sure that his readers "keep clear of pantheism and relativism, the most attractive and powerful of all spiritual drugs," he was careful to avoid the term "organic" in one place where "organic" would be most natural—when he defined the nature of nature. Like Iqbal and the Qur'an, he called on his readers to marvel at nature: it is "so well-knit and works with such regularity that it is a prime miracle of God." But then he described it as "gigantic machine."[48] Rahman's word "machine" was characteristically non-Iqbalian and quite foreign to the Qur'an: it was a patently modern way of describing creation.

Rahman's innovative terminology reflected his proposition about a central principle of the Qur'an, the notion of the "fundamental disparity between God and His creation," according to which, "whereas God is infinite and absolute, every creature is finite." Therefore, he observed, "All things have potentialities, but no amount of potentiality may allow what is finite to transcend its finitude and pass into infinity.[49]

This was distinct from what Iqbal conveyed by the word "organic." Iqbal's inspirational dictum was that the destiny of "man" was "a unity of life." In his poetic philosophy life was "organic." Like nature, it was constantly evolving. And what human beings had to overcome, he argued, was precisely the perception of the creation as a machine. Such perception, to him, was produced by the "mechanizing effects" of modern everyday life, "of sleep and business." For Iqbal nature was not a machine because God was not a machine either. He related it to human beings by stating that "nature is to the Divine Self as character is to the human self." Both God and "man" to him were individualities/egos, as in ego and the Ultimate Ego. Both were organic, in polysemous ways. Both were living, which to him meant constantly moving, creating, and reshaping themselves. Indeed, what made human creative thought—even of the finite variety—possible for him was the "Infinite Thought of the Ultimate Ego."[50] In Iqbal's interpretation, therefore, the true promise of the Qur'an to humanity was in its reminder about human beings' essentially creative nature, which held the potential of freeing them from their machine-like mode of existence and propelling them in the direction of overcoming their finality, toward a mystical union with God.

For Rahman, however, this proposition was too impractical and potentially too inebriating. Practically speaking, he insisted that when the Qur'an "is allowed to speak for itself," without accompaniments from Bergson or even Rumi, it "expresses the most fundamental, unbridgeable difference between the nature of God and the nature of man." It is, therefore, a "dangerous silliness" for humans to "equate and identify finite beings with the Infinite one."[51] (Iqbal, of course, did not equate humans with God: he wanted them to work constantly on their creative potential, which he identified as a movement toward—and not a static state of—the reunion with "the ultimate Reality.")

···VIII···

Charles Taylor, a Canadian Catholic philosopher, argued that what makes contemporary human beings modern—like the writer and readers of this book, or Rahman's and Iqbal's readers and listeners—is that we live in "secular time."[52] To articulate and relate the Qur'an to modern audiences, contemporary interpreters, like Rahman, have to somehow address this reality—even if they do it "pretheoretically," as Taylor would put it, even if they do not or cannot explain that this is what they do—because it is unavoidable.

To see how Rahman carried out such translation, it is worth paying attention to Iqbal. Iqbal's *Reconstruction,* as well as his poetry, urged his readers to overcome their ordinary perception of time, to become attuned to the time of eternity. In a sense, his emphasis on religious, as opposed to profane, or everyday, understanding of time was characteristically Muslim and Qur'anic, expressed by many premodern and modern Muslim authorities. As Abu Hamid al-Ghazali (d. 1111), a preeminent medieval religious thinker, pointed out, for example, the very sound of the Qur'an, when it is recited, is filled with sadness: it expresses God's sorrow over the typically sorry state of human beings, who tend not to notice God and eternity behind the everyday flow of their lives.[53] Yet, Iqbal also added that the profane time of the modern age is "mechanizing." And it is this "mechanizing" quality that makes modern permutations of profane time, the time of our everyday experience, "secular."

From Iqbal's perspective, all that imposes such "secular time" upon human beings—and disciplines their sensibilities to be, in a sense, mechanical—is unnatural and therefore ungodly: the way modern humans live their lives, he argued, takes them constantly out of sync from the natural flow of life, the "organic" time of "the ultimate Reality." Yet, as a scientifically attuned intellectual of the post-Darwinian age, he was certain that evolution was an undisputable fact. Therefore, for him, the movement of time, including human history, was irreversible and progressive. At the same time, as a religious person, he refused to think of time and evolution, either in nature or human history, as merely "secular."

As the French sociologist Bruno Latour had put it, the basic feature of modern scientific perceptions of time and other phenomena is that they relegate God, and therefore eternity, to "the sidelines."[54] In *Reconstruction* Iqbal attempted to solve a peculiarly modern dilemma hinted at by Latour: the dichotomy between the "secular time" and the religious time of eternity.[55] But how could Iqbal express his solution, which relied on the word "organic," for his listeners and readers, most immediately Indian Muslim university students in the late (and roaring) 1920s? Like most modern human beings, their "mechanizing" flow of life accustomed them to perceive eternity as "unchanging" and "secular time" as an expression of constant change?[56] Iqbal's answer was to teach his audiences—like most influential writers and speakers, he had multiple audiences—to perceive eternity otherwise. Eternity, he declared, is "organically" related to the time of unceasing change, because it is constantly in flux as well.

How did Rahman, in the footsteps of Iqbal, address the dichotomy between secular and religious senses of time? In large part, his answer was Iqbalian. Rahman's methodology of leaping across time, his "double movement," relied on Iqbal's interpretation of the Qur'an as a revelation that pointed toward eternity and, because of this, spoke to and within constantly changing realities. At the same time, Rahman was cautious about Iqbal's mysticism. He was concerned with practicalities of Muslim life and was wary of the intoxicating effects of poetic visions. This is why he deemphasized some of Iqbal's most far-reaching formulations. Particularly productive here was Rahman's sober take on Iqbal's idea of "history," which was at the core of his "double movement." The significance of this move, however, went beyond Rahman's methodology of interpretation: it allowed him to present the Qur'an as the scripture of ethics, as opposed to a mystical or theological text.[57] This outlook informed the practical nature of Rahman's methodology, which contributed, in turn, to a wide array of subsequent interpretations of the Qur'an, including those by American Muslims.

Rahman agreed with Iqbal's perception of the character of the Qur'an's presentation of history: it was, for both of them, didactic; it has been constantly reminding its listeners about stories from the past pedagogically—in order to change the very course of human history. Like Iqbal, he also understood the Qur'an as a text of rational and logical guidance: it spoke across time and could be applied in dramatically different historical contexts precisely because it was logical.

This is what Iqbal attempted to demonstrate by highlighting the Qur'an's "constant appeal to reason and experience, and the emphasis it lays on Nature and History as sources of human knowledge." What made this statement uniquely Iqbalian was its emphasis on the grand concepts of "Nature" and "History," as opposed to the more mundane "nature" and "history." He capitalized "History" for the same reason he capitalized "Nature": because, like nature, history for him was an arena of God's creativity and thus constantly evolving. As a mode of human knowledge, "history" for Iqbal was not a secular social science but an ongoing endeavor aimed at discovering "History," by which he meant the divine creative movement behind the human history. Borrowing from Bergson, he characterized this divine "History" as evolving in "pure time," which "is not a string of separate, reversible instants; it is an organic whole in which the past is not left behind, but is moving along with, and operating in the present."[58] That is why, perhaps, Iqbal never used the phrase "Muslim history." Instead he kept speaking of "Muslim culture"—because "Muslim culture," to him, was cumulative; it belonged in the present and the future as much as in the past.

Iqbal's goal was to inspire Muslims to break beyond the limits of their realities and perceptions, to become makers—cocreators, together with God—of their history. He urged his audiences to remember their "Muslim culture" and recognize that it had been moving in the right direction all along, despite all sorts of political and other setbacks. The direction for this movement, Iqbal proposed, was set by the Qur'an, which had opened "our eyes to the great event of change," and by the Prophet, who had translated the revelation into the human reality of his time. Beyond the Prophet, Iqbal remembered Muslim thinkers such as the philosopher Ibn Miskawayh (d. 1030), who articulated a concept of evolution, the poet Fakhr al-Din 'Iraqi (d. 1289), who advanced a notion of multiplicity of time and space, and the historian Ibn Khaldun (d. 1406), who envisioned a theory of patterned progression of history. These and other personalities confirmed to Iqbal that Muslim history, or rather "culture," was really, underneath it all, about creativity and knowledge: it moved progressively toward ever deeper engagement with the universe of God and the Qur'an. Or, as he put it, the past of "Muslim culture" demonstrated that "all the lines of Muslim thought converge on a dynamic conception of the universe."[59]

Iqbal's reading of the past was inspiring because it was optimistic. The legacy of "Muslim culture" served for him as an illustration of what could become possible in his and his audiences' present and future. Thus, he spoke the language of the state-of-the-art Western intellectual discourses of his time not because he wanted to catch up with the West—the center of the colonial world, whose political periphery his listeners and readers inhabited—but to position Muslims at the forefront of humanity's historical evolution, which, to him, was about creativity and knowledge. He delivered his *Reconstruction* in anticipation of "the day [that] is not far off when Religion and Science may discover hitherto unsuspected mutual harmonies."[60] And then he called on his audiences to remember that the Qur'an had already harmonized the seemingly distinct realities, those of humans and the eternal, the "ultimate

Reality." This remembrance was counterfactual and forward looking. It ran counter to his listeners and readers' ordinary sense of history, which relegated them to the sidelines of the modern world. It inspired them to "view the world otherwise" and, in the process, transform themselves and become makers of the next move in history's never-ceasing progression. This was indeed a powerful and timely articulation: it emerged in the midst of the global anticolonial struggle and shaped the language of a Muslim counter-vision of history and progress.

Rahman, however, was a professional historian, not a visionary poet. His understanding of history was academic and practical: it unfolded entirely in the finite human time. In no way would he "equate" the history of humans with the "History" of "the Infinite one." Unlike Iqbal, Rahman perceived much of the Muslim past in terms of stagnation, a view he shared with most professional historians of his generation.[61] Contributing to his outlook was the fact that he worked in an era distinct from that of Iqbal's *Reconstruction*—after the Islamic Republic of Pakistan had become a somewhat messy reality and after the pre–World War II enthusiasm about scientific knowledge, which Iqbal shared with many of his contemporaries, became soured by the atomic bomb and other forms of industrialized mass slaughter. What Rahman observed, therefore, was "the fact that man is still plagued by moral confusion . . . and that his moral sense has not kept pace with his advance in knowledge."[62]

In *Major Themes* Rahman's central example of the sluggishness of the Muslim past revolved around the Qur'anic word *qadar*, which literally means "fate" or "destiny." Medieval Muslim thinkers, he argued, had misunderstood what it meant and imagined it as depicting a static type of predestination. Their interpretation—which, in his view, created a culture of "traditional placidity"—was shaped by their reading of the Qur'an through the lenses of "strong fatalistic doctrines in the world-views of certain highly sophisticated peoples, particularly the Iranians." Aside from it being, to put it mildly, quite sweeping, Rahman's characterization connoted a methodological criticism. It suggested that his predecessors had not carried out the first move of his "double movement": they did not examine what the term *"qadar"* had meant in the historical context where the Qur'an had been revealed. It "actually means," he explained, "'to measure out.'" God creates, he stated, in an orderly way, and everything in creation "bears . . . the mark of 'being measured.', i.e., having a finite sum of potentialities." Therefore, for Rahman, *qadar* indicated "potentialities" of movement and change that God instilled in humans. Here, Rahman's interpretation was very much Iqbalian, except for his insistence that human "potentialities" were "finite."[63]

Rahman's dynamic understanding of predestination had two repercussions. First, it allowed him to break through the limits of the customary depiction of Muslim history as stagnant. Second, it enabled him to stress the development of what he called "moral sense," or ethics. From the perspective of ethics, human history, to him, was evolutionary, characterized by the constant movement of progress. This, he argued, was the authentically Qur'anic concept of history, which he advanced by reading the scripture thematically:

> In discussing evolution and discontinuity of civilizations, we have already said that although the Qur'an often speaks of the discontinuity of civilizations, i.e., of making a fresh start with an altogether "new generation" of people [Qur'an 6:6; 23:31, 42; 38:3], it is on the whole optimistic about the future because "the inheritance of the earth is given to good people."[64] A word also must be said about the legacy of civilizations for their successors. Here again there is a tension between two opposite directions. On the one hand, the history of civilizations is cumulative and evolutionary because while the "foam on the top of a torrent disappears, that which is beneficial to mankind [the alluvium] settles down upon earth" (13:17). This means that while the negative side of men's conduct departs, the constructive side does leave a positive legacy for mankind. On the other hand, the evil legacies of earlier peoples do affect the quality of performance of later ones. In a sense, every civilization is a forerunner of or an example for later ones; hence the tremendous responsibility of the future generations. It is not clear whether this influence is due to the fact that later civilizations actually learn of the earlier ones—and try to vie with their foolish deeds—or whether their legacy becomes embedded in the unconscious of the later ones and becomes, as it were, part of their moral genes—in which case it is cumulative and the entire historic movement is like a spiral, not a cycle.[65]

In this passage, Rahman was not certain about the exact reasons behind the evolution in history—perhaps because, for him, such reasons were fundamentally beyond human comprehension. What was clear, however, was his stress on "good people" and "moral genes." This is why the proper understanding of *qadar* to him was key: it communicates "the doctrine of the power of God," which "issues forth in the merciful creativity of God, in terms of 'measuring' things, producing them 'according to a certain order or measure,' not haphazardly or blindly." This "measuring" is a reflection of God's mercy, which, Rahman stated, is the most important Qur'anic theological principle. Divine mercy, for him, was part of the "Qur'anic concept of God as an organic unity." The other elements of it were "orderly creativity, guidance, [and] justice."[66] All of these elements—or, rather, streams and, hence, themes—come across, in Rahman's interpretation, as "measured," because their orderly appearance allows human beings to grasp and strive to embody the dynamic principles of God's just commands.

Rahman explained that the key Qur'anic concept that designated such a mode of living, constant discipline of mindfulness, was *taqwa*, or God-consciousness. In his interpretation, God's mercy and human beings' *taqwa* were two movements where the divine and human agencies worked in tandem. Through merciful communication—in scripture, nature and history—God discloses the potentialities of human beings. Therefore, by constantly attempting to be God-conscious, human beings can progress toward developing who they truly, ideally, should be. *Taqwa*, in Rahman's interpretation, signifies a "unique balance of integrative moral action," through which human beings could live in accordance with God's "just and merciful guidance." This type of living, he stressed, is both individual and collective. What drives human history, he explained, is the ongoing civilizational and societal movement toward more balanced, ethical, and "organically" God-conscious collective life. That is why, Rahman insisted, "a central aim of the Qur'an is to establish a viable social order on earth that will be just and ethically based."[67]

This vision was, once again, resonant with Iqbal's *Reconstruction*. Rahman's distinction, yet again, was in his choice of emphases. While discussing *taqwa*, he highlighted, for example, the "moment of balance where both sides [divine and human] are fully present, not absent, integrated, not negated." But, quite tellingly, he did not call such moments "mystical." In addition, unlike Iqbal, he stressed that the "unique position" of human beings in the creation was due not so much to their potential of knowing—truly knowing—God, but to their ability to discern God's guidance and make moral decisions. Therefore, to him, the ongoing historical evolution of human societies unfolded not in some grand "History" but at the more down-to-earth plane of human "history," where each "new generation" attempted to strike anew the balance of "moral integrative action," while certainly building upon the legacy of previous generations. This, Rahman proposed, was "the knowledge of history" that the Qur'an communicated "for man."[68]

Rahman's reading of the Qur'anic concept of "the knowledge of history" resonated with the discipline of history he was accustomed to—the academic, and hence largely secular, discipline of studying the past. This correspondence enabled him to fashion the academic study of history into an exegetical contraption. Yet, beyond this methodological intervention, which was very significant, Rahman's articulation of the Qur'anic mode of telling and teaching history had a more consequential practical edge: it resonated with societal, as opposed to spiritual and inspirational, "needs" and sensibilities "of contemporary man." This is because, as Charles Taylor noted, modernity, the period of history inhabited by Rahman and his readers, is certainly secular—"not in the frequent, rather loose sense of the word, where it designates the absence of religion, but rather in the fact that religion occupies a different place, compatible with the sense that all social action takes place in profane time."[69]

In light of what I have just outlined, there is indeed a significant difference between Rahman and Iqbal. Rahman's own evaluation of Iqbal's legacy provides insight into why he was so cautious about the poet's influence, and yet could never escape it:

> The result is that in so far as Iqbal's teaching has been influential—and it has been so deeply and far-reachingly influential that spiritually it has been the chief force behind the creation of Pakistan—it has thrown its overwhelming weight on the revivalist side and has been largely construed in an anti-rational direction. The doctrine of activism and dynamism advocated by Iqbal has found such a tremendous response that the very considerable intellectual effort of which it was the result has been made to commit suicide in process. Iqbal's philosophical legacy has, therefore, not been followed, partly because of what he has said but largely because he has been both misunderstood and misused by his politics-mongering followers. His *Reconstruction of Religious Thought in Islam* has remained a purely personal statement of Islamic Faith, and has not so far been able to function as a datum-line from which further developments could take place. In the event of such a real development taking place, the genuine insights of Iqbal into the nature of Islam will have to be carefully disentangled from the contemporary philosophical interpretations of science, especially the excessive assimilation of the natural to the spiritual.[70]

Based on this, Rahman's *Major Themes* was likely an attempt to transform Iqbal's insights into a practical "datum-line." Central here was his rendering of Iqbal's idea of constant movement into a measured methodology of Qur'anic exegesis.

···IX···

Major Themes exemplifies the first movement in the constantly ongoing process of Islam's translation into an American religion, at least as it unfolded in the post-1965 era. Rahman articulated in it a "normative" voice of the Qur'an: his, after all, was a book that merely "allowed the Qur'an to speak for itself." Of course, to sound "normative," it could not come across as obviously influenced by recognizably extra-Qur'anic discourses. Is this why Rahman silenced Iqbal so thoroughly? Was it because Iqbal's name was too closely associated with Pakistan? Was it because Rahman's direct acknowledgment of his debt to Iqbal would have jeopardized the "normative" appearance of his "procedure . . . for synthesizing [the Qur'an's] themes," which he used "only as necessary for joining together [the Qur'an's own] ideas"? Perhaps. Another, more consequential, explanation is that he did not conceal Iqbal at all but rather expressed himself in his own language, which echoed Iqbal's formulations—because the poet's vocabulary and logic, the grammar of his thought, resonated so "organically" with Rahman's own common sense.

At the end of the day, I do not know why Rahman hushed Iqbal. What I do know is that Rahman was instrumental in American intellectual history of the late twentieth and early twenty-first centuries because he was resonant in that particular context (and not only because numerous prominent local scholars and activists acknowledged his influence directly). It was this resonance, more even than Rahman's methodology of exegesis, that allowed his American readers, like Mattson, to infuse his "normative" ideas with their American meanings.

A case in point is the scholarship of Azizah al-Hibri (b. 1943), a Lebanese American legal scholar, who specialized in U.S. constitutional law and Islamic jurisprudence and was one among many American Muslim academics and activists influenced by Rahman. What she borrowed from him was not just his "double movement" but the underlying trajectory that informed his exegetical choreography: the notion that the Qur'an is a text that communicates to its believers divine, and therefore dynamic, ethical principles. Rahman called these principles "themes" precisely because they were dynamic or, as Iqbal first expressed it, "organic." He argued that they had the precedence over and had to inform any time-bound human formulations of Islamic law. In other words, whereas for over a thousand years Muslim jurists had presented the Qur'an as a book of law, Rahman went around their authority and stated that it was the book of Muslim ethics. For al-Hibri this insight was productive: by borrowing Rahman's emphasis on scriptural ethics, she was able to argue that the American foundational legal texts, such as the Constitution, were essentially, thematically, compatible with the texts that informed Islamic jurisprudence because they spoke, however distinctly, to the same dynamic ethical principles.[71]

Al-Hibri's line of argument is significant for my analysis not only, or primarily, because it echoed Rahman's logic but because it resonated with how myriad other American Muslim speakers and activists of the post-1965 era articulated themselves. Most often without Rahman's direct influence, they kept reiterating the notion articulated by al-Hibri—that their Muslim beliefs were harmonious with their American principles because of their ethics. For example, two of this book's central characters, W. D. Mohammed and Hamza Yusuf, had no direct relationship with Rahman. Yet, when Mohammed searched in the Qur'an for answers to his listeners' questions, which were often uniquely African American, he found them in his scripture's ethics. Of course, he did not use the word "ethics." But he spoke of it nonetheless whenever he highlighted the morals of the Qur'anic lessons he preached. Yusuf, unlike Mohammed, spoke the word "ethics" explicitly, especially after

9/11, when his American Muslim listeners longed to hear an affirmation of their belonging within the fabric of their country's life. His reliance on ethics is particularly telling. Throughout his career, he presented himself as a "traditional" Muslim, who came to reverse "modernist" trends advocated by people like Rahman. And yet, when it came to his own cultural translations of the Qur'an, he conjured "ethics"—a word that does not appear in the Qur'an—as a central theme of the Qur'anic message.

Such resonances, especially indirect ones, highlight the importance of Rahman in American Muslim discourses. They have broader significance as well. Rahman's *Major Themes* made tangible a simple fact that most interpretations—formal and informal, written and oral—conceal habitually: that any text, including scripture, has to be constantly rearticulated so as to be sound outside of its original historical context. To be sound, to make sense of and in new settings (and therefore to have any promise of changing them), a scripture's consequent verbalizations have to be resonant (which does not mean identical) with what is common sense, at each particular moment, to its current believers. In modern contexts the Qur'an has to be constantly translated to speak to deeply ingrained, modern cultural logics, which did not exist or did not make quite the same sense during the time of its revelation.

Additionally, what Rahman's "double movement" reveals is that such rearticulations entail distilling and synthesizing anew the Qur'an's original formulations. He called the yields of this process "themes." Most other interpreters, in this book and beyond, do not speak of "themes" and instead choose to talk about the scripture's "lessons," "messages," and sometimes "principles." Or, they may choose not to assign any term to what they articulate and instead merely speak reminders from the Qur'an that highlight a particular scriptural word, phrase, or story. Like Rahman's "double movement," however, every such act of highlighting translates the Qur'an across time: it focuses on an uttering from the Qur'an and then places it in light of—and in dialogue with—the present experiences of its believers, including their senses of justice and ethics, which are always contextually specific.

Chapter Two

JUSTICE

I owe my freedom to the God who made me and who stirred me to claim it
against all other beings in God's universe.

Jermain Wesley Loguen, as quoted in George, "Widening the Circle," 156

Men kill me
How they think the earth of green and gold and God is all for them

Mohja Kahf, "Men Kill Me," 61

Amina Wadud, originally named Mary Teaseley, was born in 1952 into
the family of a Methodist minister. A single mother of five children—a
fact she insists that all her biographers must include—she is a scholar, ed-
ucator, and activist, roles that are inseparable from her experiences as an
African American and Muslim woman.[1] She grew up in Washington, D.C.,
and converted to Islam in 1972, while pursuing a B.A. at the University of
Pennsylvania. After college, she married, had children, studied and taught in
Libya, returned to the United States, divorced, lived on welfare, and worked
as a schoolteacher in Philadelphia. Later on, as a doctoral student at the University of Michigan, she began her academic engagement with the Qur'an
and traveled to Egypt to learn Arabic. Between 1989 and 1992, she taught at
the International Islamic University in Malaysia, where she joined Sisters in
Islam, a fledging study circle of Muslim women that would become Malaysia's leading women's rights organization. She returned to the United States
in 1992 to teach at Virginia Commonwealth University, where she worked
until 2008. Since then she held a number of academic positions in the United
States and abroad, including in Indonesia.

As a scholar Wadud was widely known among American Muslims in
the 1990s and early 2000s for for her interpretations of the Qur'an, exemplified by her seminal book *Qur'an and Woman: Rereading the Sacred Text
from a Woman's Perspective,* which was originally published in English in
Malaysia in 1992, republished in the United States in 1999, and later translated
into Arabic, Dutch, Indonesian, Persian, Spanish, and Turkish. As an activist
she gained even broader fame—and, to some, notoriety—after leading and
preaching at a mixed-gender Friday service in New York City in 2005. That

was not her first experience of preaching a Friday sermon: she did this, albeit in a different format, in August 1994 in Cape Town, South Africa. Yet, while her preaching in South Africa remained somewhat less known, the New York incident gained her an unprecedented international fame. All of a sudden, news outlets all over the Muslim world reported on the action of a woman who dared to break the taboo on women leading men in prayer.[2] In later recollections Wadud regretted that her preaching had been discussed mostly because of its political symbolism and that few people had paid attention to what she actually preached.[3]

This chapter looks beyond such somewhat shallow politics and instead explores her exegesis, expressed in her writings and sermons. Wadud's *tafsir*, of course, has been deeply political. Throughout her career she has been an academic and an activist, and in both roles she has carried out her struggle for women's rights in the light of the Qur'an. Like many academics of her generation, she was inspired by Fazlur Rahman and contributed, perhaps more than others, to the transformation of his "normative" interpretation into a markedly American one. What made it possible was her activism: it was this practical drive that allowed her to propel Rahman's scholarship beyond the academy. By merging exegesis with activism, she reshaped Rahman's logic of ethically rereading the Qur'an into a transformative force in American Muslim life. In this way, without ever mentioning Iqbal, she has also continued the trajectory of the Iqbalian activist spiral.

Wadud was among the first American Muslim intellectuals to articulate the idea of gender equality as inseparable from the Qur'anic principle of justice. By the end of the first decade of the twenty-first century, this notion became part of American Muslim common sense. This highlights the extent to which contextually specific concerns shape local, in this case American Muslim, enunciations of scriptures. For Wadud, such a central issue has been gender justice. Based on her experience, she insisted that it was as a global challenge, which is why in one conversation with me she expressed unease about the American angle of my analysis: I told her that I was examining her work as belonging to an American tradition of Qur'anic exegesis; she thought that this approach was too limiting. Indeed, she was right, and her impact has been global. Yet, in her writings and speeches, the second word in the phrase "gender justice"—that is, "justice"—was inseparable from a particular network of meanings tied to African American history and her experience as an African American woman. This observation has broader significance: in the United States discourses about women's rights cannot be divorced from contextually specific conversations about other aspects of justice, including race and politics. This chapter, therefore, foreshadows what is to come in the remainder of this book. In addition, and crucially, its simultaneous focus on one intellectual's written and oral interpretations serves to highlight some key distinctions between writing and speaking as discrete modes of engagement with the Qur'an.

···ǁ···

Mohammed Arkoun, a French philosopher, defined the Islamic tradition as a "logosphere," by which he meant "the linguistic mental space shared by all those who use the same language with which to articulate their thoughts, their representations, their collective memory, and their knowledge according to the fundamental principles and values claimed as a unifying weltanschauung [experience and view of the world]." A logosphere represents human beings who cultivate a "tradition of thought" and whose authority depends on a continuation of established understandings, or what Arkoun called "thinkables." When contexts change dramatically, however, new realities and therefore new ways of thinking emerge.[4] From this perspective, Wadud's exegesis exemplifies a process through which a new thinkable developed. It speaks to how the notion of gender justice became for many American Muslims an unequivocal element of the Qur'an's overall concept of justice. It also demonstrates how that thinkable came about through synthesis of global and local discourses: in this case, an amalgamation of originally South Asian discourses, most centrally by Rahman and Iqbal, and expressions of justice rooted in American history and experience.

In a 2006 interview, Wadud recalled that her lifelong engagement with the Qur'an began with a deep dilemma, which was grounded in her experience and sense of justice: "When I entered Islam and began to live among Muslims in other countries and participate in events in the United States, the most horrific things were being said and done in regard to women in the name of the religion and I found this to be incongruent with my notion of God. So I purposefully decided that I am going to find out what is the position of women in Islam and if it was in fact what I was seeing—the marginalization, the silence, the abuse—then I just cannot be Muslim because I could not perform my love for God within those restrictions."[5]

Qur'an and Woman was a result of Wadud's search for gender equality in Islam. In the late 1990s and 2000s, this book became the best-known written American interpretation of the Qur'an. Wadud wrote it during her sojourn in Malaysia. While based on her Ph.D. dissertation, it was enriched by her experience as an activist. Its goal, she proposed, was to encourage interpretive readings of the Qur'an by women and from the perspective of women. Her interpretation, she argued, confirmed that the Qur'an offered women an "undeniable liberation," at the time of its revelation and in "the modern context."[6]

Wadud wrote the book for Muslim audiences around the world, while quite naturally devoting particular attention to her American and Malaysian readers.[7] Her attention to the readers' contexts came across, for example,

49

in her comparison between English, Malay, and Arabic languages, through which she illustrated the impact of Arabic as a "gender-specific language" on the tradition of Qur'anic exegesis. To highlight the time- and-context-bound nature of language, she further brought up the image the "tropics of Malaysia." Her point was straightforward: for the scripture's original audience, its depiction of the paradise as a bountifully irrigated garden appeared strikingly beautiful in part because to them it was exotic; had the Qur'an been revealed in a different setting, perhaps it would have emphasized heaven's different qualities.[8]

While these examples reflected Wadud's attention to her Malaysian audience, most of her contextually specific references were American and African American. Some of them were explicit. She mentioned, for instance, the U.S. Declaration of Independence to point out that its central phrase "all men are created equal" could be understood differently in various historical contexts: its original wording belonged in the era when patriarchy was an unquestioned reality; over time, however, its meaning expanded to include women as well as men. Through this illustration she stressed that many of the concepts embedded in the Qur'an had be continuously revisited as well.[9] Yet, most of her references to her own contexts were less explicit. For example, she continuously returned in her book to the issue of slavery. The fact that she did not connect it directly to her own cultural heritage is understandable: she wrote, after all, for a broad and international audience. But, in light of the weight she gave to the importance of contextually specific experiences, such suggestions were perhaps even more poignant, precisely because they were indirect.

Wadud's attempt to reach as wide a Muslim audience as possible was also evident in how she chose to present her analysis: throughout the text she refrained from using the term *ijtihad.* Such avoidance was remarkable since her book was an exercise in rethinking Muslim jurisprudential interpretations of the Qur'an. In a typical statement, she explained, "The existence of so many exegetical works *(tafasir)* indicates that, with regard to the Qur'an, the interpretation process has existed and will probably continue to exist, in a variety of forms. It is essential that the natural adaptive nature of interpretation, from individual to individual and from time and place to time and place, should continue unabated until the end of time—on the one hand, because it is natural, and, on the other hand, because only through continued interpretation can the wisdom of the Qur'an be effectively implemented. This implementation will be specific to the varying experiences of human civilization."

In this passage, *ijtihad* was implicit. Wadud's stress on "continued interpretation" in light of "specific . . . experiences" paralleled Rahman's modernist approach. Yet she phrased it in a way that did not come across as too modernist. She described her work as a mere contribution to the discipline of *tafsir,* an "intellectual legacy that is more than fourteen centuries old."[10] Her goal was to demonstrate that women had to become integral to this tradition. Therefore, she wrote as an equal contributor to it and was careful not to come across as an outside agitator.

This likely influenced her selection of conversation partners, the Muslim authorities whose works she most often referenced. She explicitly stated that she engaged with the insights of such authors as Qutb and Mawdudi. Her invocation of their names was particularly productive: in the early 1990s, it projected a veneer of tradition, because, at that time, they were often perceived as advocates for a global Muslim revival in the name of the Islamic tradition and not as outright modernists like Rahman. Of course, these two thinkers' approaches also happened to be methodologically modernist and, therefore, compatible with her analysis, particularly since they both interpreted the Qur'an thematically. Above all, what the four authors, Mawdudi, Qutb, Rahman, and Wadud, shared was the tendency of interpreting the Qur'an without paying much attention to the Hadith. Theirs was the method of *qur'an bi-l-qur'an,* or the process of interpreting the Qur'an by the Qur'an alone.[11]

Here Wadud trod an ambiguous line, which indicated her modern grappling with the inherited tradition of exegesis. On the one hand, she interpreted the Qur'an by the Qur'an in a way that emulated Rahman's "double movement." On the other, she was careful not to push the envelope too far. In the introduction to the book, she explained that she intended for it to serve as a contribution to the study of the Qur'an specifically, which in time would need to be expanded to include the Hadith as well: "[This book] is about exactly what it says it is about—the Qur'an, and woman, as a concept. Although part of a larger concern about understanding Islam and women, it has a particular focus within a specific intellectual discipline of Islamic thought. Each specialty must be developed distinctly before they can be combined together to gain a fuller picture. Hence, the special focus on the Qur'an . . . is appropriately restricted for optimal efficacy of this consideration."

To validate her affinity with the Muslim interpretive tradition, she further explained, "I accept the role of the prophet both with regard to revelation, as understood in Islam, and to the development of Islamic law on the basis of his Sunna or normative practices." But, she added, echoing Rahman, "I place greater significance on the Qur'an. This is congruent with the orthodox understanding of the inerrancy of Qur'anic preservation versus historical contradictions within the hadith literature."[12] Through this move, while affirming her allegiance to the broader tradition of exegesis, she also effectively denied one of its key methodological tools: the possibility of the Hadith abrogating the Qur'an, a widespread practice among classical exegetes that many modern interpreters came to view with suspicion.[13] Further reflecting her ambiguous position, which stemmed perhaps from her desire to appeal to those who disagreed with Rahman, she indicated that her interpretative approach followed an "orthodox understanding." And yet, adding another Rahmanian twist, she paired the suspicion of the historical validity of the hadith literature with the stress on the ethical reading of the Qur'an: "Furthermore," she declared, "I would never concede that the equality between women and men demonstrated in the Qur'an could be removed by the prophet."[14]

What Wadud inherited from Rahman was the method of searching for the Qur'an's ethical principles. Such principles, in her and Rahman's view, were eternal. Because the Qur'an communicated them thematically, however, they were dynamic, not static, and had to be applied differently in various settings. This insight was central to Rahman's and Wadud's translations of the Qur'an from a premodern into a modern text. In *Qur'an and Woman* Wadud applied it to her own context and agenda. She interpreted the revelation's central themes as markers of the ongoing movement toward a more just societal life, which to her was inseparable from progress toward gender equality. Reading the Qur'an by the Qur'an, she examined its statements on women in light of its other passages, which, in her view, corresponded with its major themes. Following Rahman, she identified *taqwa* and social justice as the scripture's most consequential themes.[15] Reaching beyond Rahman, she also insisted on the centrality of the interpreter: she emphasized the importance of who interprets the Qur'an for Muslims and argued that interpretations of the scripture for women must be carried out by women.

···III···

Wadud presented her exegetical methodology as "hermeneutics of *tawhid*," a term that emphasized the central theme of the Qur'an, the notion of God's Oneness, as well as the idea of the coherence of the scripture's overall communication: "the unity of the Qur'an," she explained, "permeates all its parts." This understanding allowed Wadud to sift through the Qur'anic statements that she perceived as addressing particularities of its original context and interpret them through passages that connoted the scripture's eternal concepts. Like Rahman, she argued that the Qur'an had established the principle of an essential equality of all human beings, irrespective of their gender, class, race, or any other qualifier. She based this dictum on the notion of the "equity of [God's ultimate] recompense," the Qur'anic depiction of how God evaluates each human being's actions. Paraphrasing the Qur'an and Rahman, she insisted that for God "the only distinction [between each man or woman] is on the basis of [their] *taqwa*," or God-consciousness.[16]

This assertion was Wadud's interpretation of Qur'an 40:39–40. Its wording relied on the translation of the Qur'an by the Indian Muslim scholar Yusuf Ali, which by the early 1990s had become widely popular among English-speaking Muslims around the globe, including in the United States. In Ali's translation these two verses state, "O my people! This life of the present is nothing but (temporary) convenience: it is the Hereafter that is the Home that will last. He that works evil will not be requited but by the like thereof: and he that works a righteous deed—whether man or woman—and is a Believer—such will enter the Garden (of Bliss): therein will they have abundance without measure."

To Wadud this passage was crucial because it was inclusive: the Qur'an clarified here that it addressed men and women equally, and that God evaluated their actions equally as well. She proposed that it also reflected the broader Qur'anic principle of justice, which overruled the text's other, male-centered statements. In this regard Wadud generally followed Rahman's exegesis. Her next point, however, was a step outside of Rahman's playbook. She observed that the revelation consistently speaks of God as creating everything in pairs, as in Qur'an 51:49: "And of everything We have created pairs: That ye may receive instruction." To her, such natural order of creation was yet another Qur'anic sign of the principle of equality between female and male human beings. Equipped with these two themes—the pairing within the creation and the essential equality of women and men—she moved toward a reinterpretation of two singularly challenging verses, Qur'an 2:228 and 4:34.

Qur'an 2:228 is troublesome for many contemporary Muslim readers because it states that "men have a *daraja* over" women. Ali translated *"daraja"* somewhat neutrally as "a degree of advantage." This translation was his interpretation, an exegesis of sorts, which sidestepped what was problematic about this verse: is this "degree" an eternal condition, a marker of some natural hierarchy between genders? Wadud provided an answer, an exegetical counter-reading of Ali's translation, a rendition of the Qur'an many of her readers took for granted. She read the Arabic Qur'an by the Arabic Qur'an, searching in it for examples where the same or similar terms, such as *"faddala,"* or "preference," are used to assign hierarchy. What she found was significant in light of her understanding of the concept of *taqwa*. She noted that in the Qur'an "most often *daraja* is obtained through an unspecified category of doing 'good' deeds (20:75, 6:132, 46:19)."[17] Such deeds, performed with *taqwa* by women and men, are equally valuable in the eyes of God. She argued, therefore, that the practice of giving broad significance to Qur'an 2:228—or even suggesting, however opaquely, that it is somehow neutral—was scripturally and ethically incorrect: it assigned "a degree of advantage" to men as an eternal societal norm. To Wadud this practice contradicted the Qur'an's balanced approach to the weighty principles of *taqwa* and justice. Based on this, she argued that the *daraja* of men over women is not a universal principle and that alternative interpretations, more sensitive to the Qur'an's overall message, were urgently needed in contemporary contexts.

To further destabilize potentially misogynistic readings of the verse, she examined it within its immediate textual setting. She observed that this verse addressed the issue of divorce and the rights of wives and husbands specifically. Following Rahman's method, she constructed her argument as based on the reading of both the micro- and macro-contexts of the revelation. She highlighted that this verse explicitly used the word *ma'ruf* ("what is known") to demonstrate that it mandated the conditions of the divorce procedure, and the rights of men and women, within the context of what was known or "conventionally accepted" at the time of Muhammad. The implication, of course, was that once conditions change, so do the "known" norms.[18] Therefore, consequent ethical and legal enactments of this Qur'anic verse, in her view, had to resonate with the notions of rights developed later. This meant that in modern settings the Qur'an's "known" norms had to be in sync with modern sensibilities regarding women's rights.

Wadud carried out a similar analysis of Qur'an 4:34, which states, in Ali's translation: "Men are the protectors and maintainers of women, because Allah has given the one more (strength) than the other, and because they support them from their means. Therefore the righteous women are devoutly obedient, and guard in (the husband's) absence what Allah would have them guard. As to those women on whose part ye fear disloyalty and ill-conduct, admonish them (first), (next), refuse to share their, beds (and last) beat them (lightly); but if they return to obedience, seek not against them means (of annoyance): for Allah is Most High, Great (above you all)."

The words that Ali placed in parentheses were his exegetical additions to the verse. His interpretation corresponded with the predominant Muslim exegetical trend, premodern and modern, which softened the harsh phrasing of this Qur'anic uttering. In Ali's rendering the Qur'an no longer said *"adribuhunna,"* or "beat them," but "beat them (lightly)." For Wadud, such tempering of the Qur'anic language rang hollow, because it attempted to conceal just how dissonant Qur'an 4:34 was with the revelation's egalitarian message. This jarring disharmony necessitated deeper reinterpretation, which had to first address the patriarchal sensibilities reflected in the scripture's overall language.

From the perspective of engaging with the patriarchal language of the sacred text, most problematic for Wadud were two of the verse's other words: *"qawwamuna,"* which Ali translated as "protectors and maintainers," and *"faddala,"* which he rendered as "has given." What does it mean for men to be "protectors and maintainers of women"? And what does the Qur'an imply by "Allah has given" men "more (strength)"? Is this phrasing contextually specific, particular to the societal realities of seventh-century Arabia, or is this an eternal rule? Wadud's interpretation of Qur'an 4:34 was based on Rahman's thematic and ethical reading of the scripture for late-twentieth-century contexts. Such an approach was necessary, she argued, because the thorny issues of patriarchal language "cannot be resolved if we look narrowly" at this verse alone.[19] In addition, she relied on the exegesis of the verse carried out by another interpreter, Azizah al-Hibri, who was also influenced by Rahman.[20] With Rahman and al-Hibri's assistance, Wadud performed an ethical abrogation of the verse's difficult words. But she also added to this interpretive mix her own emphasis on the Qur'an's depiction of nature as being created in a deliberately balanced way. By combining ethics with the Qur'anic idea of balance, she effectively declawed any possible legal applications of Qur'an 4:34 in contemporary settings: irrespective of what *"adribuhunna"* might have meant in the minds of the Qur'an's first audience, she declared, it could not be applicable across the board—because the Qur'an speaks here primarily about maintaining a balance between spouses. Therefore, in her view, any consequent interpretations of Qur'an 4:34 had to be based on the principles of familial ethics and balance. Crucial to her was the fact that the institution of family had evolved throughout history and modern family structures were very different from their premodern varieties. Thus, following al-Hibri, she noted that *faddala* in Qur'an 4:34 was conditional on financial and other support a husband provided to his family.

To highlight the importance of varying contexts in determining how this verse should be read by contemporary Muslims, Wadud wondered whether it would be applicable in situations where women served as primary breadwinners for their families? Her question was based on her experience as an African American woman. She observed that contemporary African American women often serve as heads of households, frequently as single mothers. The dichotomy between the context of the Prophet's society and contemporary African American realities prompted her to formulate a broader answer to Qur'an 4:34, which she based on her understanding of Qur'anic ethics. Her solution was to put aside any thought of "beating" and focus instead on the transformation of "marriages of subjugation" into marriages of equal partnership. She argued that thematic analysis of the Qur'an, which must be faithful to its ethics, made it possible to move beyond its text's historically determined male-centered formulations. Instead, she called on her readers to trace the "trajectories of social, political, and moral possibilities" present in the Qur'an, which reflected its deeper ethical lessons.[21]

Wadud implemented such tracing by performing a sort of *naskh*, an informal type of abrogation. In her reading the process of abrogation evident in the Qur'an itself, with some verses correcting others, underscored that it responded to and aimed to transform its immediate context. In new settings, therefore, the Qur'an had to be read anew, in light of its ethical principles.

Wadud carried out her ethics-based abrogation by examining what she called the "languaging" of the Qur'anic text. To do so, she returned once again to the example of Qur'an 40:39–40, which in her understanding reflected the process through which the Qur'an established gender-inclusive references in spite of the male-centered language—and patriarchal common sense—of the cultural environment in which it had been revealed. The Qur'an's own practice of overcoming the limitations of the language of its first audiences was to her an indication of the trajectory of its ethical message of gender equality. It is this message, this progress toward equality, that she insisted must be translated across time and applied in contemporary contexts. Based on this, she appealed to her fellow inhabitants of the modern Muslim logosphere: "If the aim of Islamic society is to fulfill the intentions of the Qur'an with regard to the rights, responsibilities, potentialities, and capacities of all its earnest members, then those who truly believe in the Qur'an would eventually wish for the woman the opportunities for growth and productivity which they demand for the man."[22]

··· I V ···

Qur'an and Woman translated the Qur'an into a modern text by placing it in conversation with contemporary contexts and sensibilities. It was a written translation, a printed book. There is, however, significant distance between books and life. What made Wadud's exegetical contribution to American Muslim life distinct was its pronounced practicality. As she noted in the introduction to the 1999 American edition of *Qur'an and Woman,* she had written it at a time of transition, from being a student to becoming an activist-scholar.[23] By moving into the practical struggle for the equality of women, she took her own—and Rahman's—interpretations out of the enclosure of printed texts. Her activism translated the Qur'an of gender justice into a living text that would encourage the work of many American Muslims, such as the Syrian American poet Mohja Kahf, whose lines opened this chapter.[24]

Wadud's preaching built upon her written exegesis. It was her oral *tafsir.* Her experience as an African American woman was crucial here as well. She explained this in her 2006 autobiographical text, *Inside the Gender Jihad:* "I have never been a Muslim except as an African-American. . . . African-American Islam is unique especially because of the history of African-Americans. I am part of the awesome legacy of the soul and survival of African slaves brutalized by the dehumanization of the institution of slavery in its peculiarly cruel American racist form."[25]

Throughout her life, Wadud reflected on the experience of her parents. Her mother, who "was the glue that kept our family together," inspired her to pay attention to the complexity of gendered power dynamics in families and broader society. Her father, "a devoted man of God," served for her as an example of a preacher she would one day become. She explained that "the origin of [her] three decades of work on Islam, justice, and gender was the awesome light of belief" that she had inherited from her father, "a man of faith and a Methodist minister who was born and died poor, black, and oppressed in the context of racist America."[26]

Wadud's uncompromising stance in defense of the principle of equality was rooted in her experience and African American history. In Rahman, she found an exegetical methodology. Yet what propelled her scholarship and activism was the legacy of African American scriptural interpretations that spoke in the face of oppression, "I owe my freedom to the God who made me." It is not surprising then that Wadud's interpretation of the Qur'an was constantly mindful of the liberating promise of the human relationship with God. This was the central theme of the sermons she gave in 1994 in Cape Town, South Africa, and in 2005 in New York City.

Wadud's two best-known sermons took place in different contexts and distinct stages of her life. She delivered her Cape Town address at the Claremont Main Road Mosque, a major center of Muslim antiapartheid organizing in the 1980s and early 1990s. She was invited to speak there by local activists, who saw the struggle for racial equality as inseparable from the overall movement toward a more just society. Because she was a guest, however, she could not structure the event in a way that resonated fully with her vision. The plans to invite her as a preacher for a Friday congregational prayer were met with significant opposition from neighboring Muslim communities and within the Claremont mosque itself. While there were other occasions when women spoke in front of male and female audiences at South African mosques, this was the first time a woman would stand in front of a congregation of men and women and deliver a sermon. Many saw this act as violating the canon of Muslim ritual life. The organizers of the event, therefore, came up with a solution: instead of a formal sermon *(khutba),* her talk was structured as a pre-*khutba.* After she spoke, a male speaker gave a very short sermon in Arabic and led the congregation in prayer. In this way her sermon was presented as not violating ritual customs, while still furthering the authority of Muslim women.[27]

Wadud's New York City sermon was different. This time, she made sure to serve as the preacher and the official leader of the prayer. Of course, politics were unavoidable in this context as well, except that here the repercussions were quite broad—local, national, and international, Muslim and otherwise. The 2005 sermon was a watershed event in Wadud's career. In the 1990s her *Qur'an and Woman* was the go-to book for a wide circle of American Muslims interested in the issues of gender equality. It was not controversial, or rather, those who saw it as problematic were few and largely not heard. The situation changed dramatically after 2005. With that sermon Wadud made her interpretation of the Qur'an manifestly practical by stepping fearlessly into the role of an authority who (re)established a legal precedent. After this event she was no longer known primarily as an author of a printed exegesis. Through personal example she urged Muslims to exercise gender equality in all spheres of life, including their ritual life.

This challenge was indeed controversial. During my research for this book, which took place in the late 2000s and early 2010s, I was careful to listen to my American Muslim conversation partners' opinions about Wadud. They were often reticent. Yet, when I asked them what they thought about her work before 2005, I heard overwhelmingly positive opinions. Of course, it took a bit of reminding to prompt them to recollect Wadud's legacy as a whole, and not as it became overshadowed by their evaluations of her 2005 prayer. Aside from eclipsing memories of the past, controversies bring to the fore the extent to which discussions on some important subjects become impossible to ignore. The turmoil that erupted after Wadud's prayer highlighted the fact that the issue of female leadership in the American Muslim communities was now, in 2005, at the forefront of local Muslim debates—because of the changing realities on the ground. By the first decade of the twenty-first century, it was typical to see women serving on the boards of mosques or in other leadership structures of all sorts of American Muslim institutions. Even more widespread was the phenomenon where women constituted the majority of volunteers in various organizations, from neighborhood centers to mega-mosques, and from student groups on campuses to national organizations. As Hadia Mubarak, the president of the Muslim Student Association at Georgetown University in the early 2000s, put it: "Everywhere it is the sisters who are holding up organization—even doing the heavy lifting."[28]

In this respect the story of American Muslims mirrored the trends among other American religious groups. For example, Wendy Cadge's comparative study of recent immigrant and convert Buddhist communities in the United States in the 2000s traced a similar trend: Buddhist women, immigrants, and converts were becoming more involved, in various ways, in their religious organizations. Cadge observed that in both immigrant and convert communities, as "in most religious organizations in the United States, women are involved in [temples and other institutions] in greater numbers than their proportions in the Thai and American populations in the United States would predict."[29]

Jewish and Christian communities underwent similar evolutions as well. Wadud's activism, aimed at full equality of Muslim women in ritual life, paralleled, for instance, the movement toward ordination of women among Protestant Christians and Reform and Conservative Jews.[30] Behind this development was a monumental shift in the economic and social distribution of power between men and women, which came along with industrialization, urbanization, mass education, and other factors. After World War I and, even more so, after World War II, women's roles in American society changed dramatically. By the early twenty-first century, the phenomenon of women serving as primary breadwinners in their families and de-facto heads of households became widespread. Along with all such changes came transformations in the common sense of justice, where gender equality became an immediate and commonly expressed concern. This was true of American Muslims as much as it was for other Americans. An example of this development was the election of Ingrid Mattson as the president of ISNA in 2006, less than a year after Wadud's New York City prayer—and, it is worth remembering, two years before Hillary Clinton's first attempt to become the president of the United States.

Of course, many religious women and men do not change their traditions, rituals, customs, and language overnight. Rather, they tend to change the meanings of the words and concepts they inherit while claiming full allegiance to their religious heritage. The titles of "rabbi," "priest," or "chaplain," for example, acquired different meanings once women joined these religious professions. Such transformations also involve people who resist dramatic types of change, such as the ordination of women. A telling illustration of this is the transformation of the institution of "rabbi's wife" in American Judaism. In the United States, Jewish women and men continuously transformed what this position meant in the late nineteenth century and throughout the twentieth century. By the 1970s many rabbis' wives deemphasized or rejected this title. At the same time, many others, particularly in Orthodox Judaism, used it to expand, in practical terms, the sphere and quality of women's authority and power.[31] American Muslim women followed this general trend, including the wide variety of ways in which they reshaped their roles in the community, with some calling for full equality in all aspects of Muslim life but with most choosing different—yet no less consequential—transformative paths.

What is equally important, particularly for the history of American Muslim discourses, is that by the 2000s the realities of increased power of women in Muslim institutional life made it requisite for American Muslim public speakers to reflect this shift in how they spoke, how they addressed their audiences, and how they explained their realities and scriptures. While Wadud's 2005 prayer was controversial, much of what she said in her sermon was not, because it resonated with broader transformations in American Muslim realities.

··· V ···

Wadud's 1994 Cape Town sermon was, in a sense, a crystallization of *Qur'an and Woman*. It addressed the ethics of proper Muslim marriage, where both partners must be fully equal to each other. Wadud based this dictum on Qur'an 30:21, which in that sermon she translated herself: "And among His signs is that He has created from your own selves mates. And He has made between the two of you love and mercy." The phrase "love and mercy" was her translation of the Qur'anic word *"rahma."* Much as in her written interpretations, in this example of her oral *tafsir*, she interpreted the Qur'an by the Qur'an. She called on her audience to ponder the meaning of the word *"rahma,"* to recognize that it signified the Qur'anic ideal of mercy, and to strive to implement it in their family relations: *"Rahma* is supposed to be one of the characteristics of how we engage in surrender in our marital lives. We should not take the other person for granted. We should always extend loving care and mercy for him or her."[32]

On a theological note, Wadud presented the human ethics of mercy as a reflection of God's work in nature, human and otherwise. She urged her listeners to remember that the Qur'an refers to God as *"al-Rahman, al-Rahim."* Like many other Muslim interpreters and preachers, she connected the word *"rahma"*—which is related to *"rahman"* and *"rahim"*—with *"rahm,"* which means "womb."[33] This connection between the divine reality of mercy and the human experience of pregnancy contributed to her formulation of the ethical vision of Muslim living. To be Muslim for Wadud was not just to be "surrendered" to God, as the ordinary translation of the Arabic word *muslim* suggests, but rather to live one's life as an ongoing process of "engaged surrender"—just as mothers surrender to the awe-inspiring process of creation that unfolds within their bodies. She coined the phrase "engaged surrender" to stress the agency of human beings, women and men, whom God gave the freedom to decide, in every moment of their lives, to either follow the path of God-conscious living or rebel against it. Wadud reminded that the Qur'an speaks of God as representing the ultimate *rahma:* "He is Mercy. He is the Ultimate mercy. Both His names of mercy, *rahman* and *rahim,* come from the same root word as *rahm:* the womb. Allah thus engages us continually to understand the nature of our surrender."[34]

Reflecting publicly on her own experience of pregnancy and childbirth, Wadud stated that women's natural surrender in the process of creation of new human life is a sign of God's mercy. Here, based on her experience, she offered a novel exegesis of Qur'an 94, which Muslim preachers often quote (like the imam from western New York, whose prayer I mentioned in the introduction). She translated this short sura and then provided her exegetical reflection: "In Surah Inshirah (chapter 94) Allah says: 'Have we not opened up your heart and lifted/removed from you the burden which weighed so heavily on your back. And raised you high in dignity. And behold with every hardship comes ease. Indeed with every hardship comes ease. Hence, when you are freed from your distress; Remain steadfast and unto your Sustaining Lord turn in love.' Allah gives us the mother in pregnancy and childbirth as a living picture of this idea of engaged surrender."[35]

This verse is ordinarily interpreted as relating to the Prophet. Wadud, however, took the central to the sura theme of God's mercy and connected it specifically to women's experience of "engaged surrender," as they embody it during pregnancy and childbirth. As a female interpreter, she lent this sura a new reading that rendered it viscerally relevant to those who shared her gendered experience. In this instance the Qur'an, through her translation, spoke directly to women and made their experience a divine sign for all human beings, female and male. This example demonstrates that Wadud's 1994 sermon offered more than a mere summation of *Qur'an and Woman.* That sermon was a lived experience—an experience of engaging and speaking with the Qur'an, which Wadud shared with her audience. Through words and physical presence, she actualized her scholarly stress on the importance of the agency of women as the Qur'an's interpreters. Surely, a male preacher could have said something similar to Wadud's notion of "engaged surrender," but he would not be able to infuse it with the same kind of visceral relevancy.

Wadud's 2005 sermon in New York was in many ways similar to her 1994 Cape Town address. Its general thrust resonated with her previous written and oral exegeses. As in her Cape Town *khutba,* she reminded her audience about the need to live their lives while cultivating conscious relationships with the divine. Once again, she stressed that when it comes to this relationship, all humans are equal. Yet, throughout the sermon, she spoke in a way that reflected deeper, more developed, and in many respects more daring articulations of her trajectory of ethical activism.

Wadud began her *khutba,* for example, with a subtle modification of the customary opening supplication Muslim preachers use to initiate their sermons. Ordinarily, a preacher would open his talk by stating that he bears witness that there is no God but one God and that Muhammad is His messenger and Prophet, and by asking God to bless Muhammad and his companions. Wadud, however, added an additional plea: for the blessing of Muhammad's wives. With this opening note, she immediately reminded her audience that women had been principal agents in Muslim history from the very beginning.

Another significant move in that sermon was Wadud's explicit enactment of what she had described in *Qur'an and Woman* as the Qur'an's "languaging," or its tendency to transform the meanings of words in ways that move human beings to reconsider their ordinary understandings and practices. Once again she centered her *khutba* on the relationship between God and human beings. As though echoing Iqbal's dictum, "view the world otherwise, and it will become other," she spoke of God in terms that contravened the masculine perception of the word *"allah"*: throughout the sermon, she called God "He," "She," and "It." This was, to her, a new act of "languaging," which she did not perform in Cape Town. She initiated this process in the opening of the sermon, where she translated the verse that most Muslims know, or at least are supposed to remember, Qur'an 2:255, which is customarily referred to as The Verse of the Throne: "Allah, there is no god but the God, (and) He/She/It is the Ever Living, the Self-Subsistent Fount of All Being." Immediately she linked this passage to Qur'an 33:35, a verse that explicitly names women and men "who surrender" as the people for whom "Allah has prepared . . . forgiveness and vast reward." This connection between God, who is beyond the earthly notions of gender, and human beings as equal recipients of the divine grace allowed her to position herself as an authoritative voice in Muslim discourses. "I stand before you," she testified, "in all my imperfections and weaknesses confessing that I bear sincere love of Allah and love for all of Her *ayat*/signs."[36]

As an equal partner in Muslim engagements with God, she pointed to the Qur'anic sign, which, she emphasized, indicated the Qur'anic principle of equality between men and women. She reminded her audience about Qur'an 4:1, which states that God "has created you from a single *nafs* [soul/self] and created from it, its mate: and spread the two, countless men and women." This pedagogic reminder about the essential equality of humans as creatures of God was the basis for her act of serving as a leader of a Muslim congregational prayer. It was also the ground from which she called on her listeners to live as human beings. She reminded them that their high standing in the creation was given to them by God and that no societal constraints could take this status away: "This unity of origin," she preached, "reflects two important implications, both extensions of the fundamental principle, *tawhid:* 1) of course Allah is One, Allah is Unique, Allah is united and Allah unifies (all things in creation); 2) no human being is ever the same as Allah, able to know or understand all of Allah's intention for the creation of humans, or the entire cosmos. Yet all human beings have been granted the potential to experience at-one-ment with Allah for fleeting moments in the creation, and eternally fi-l-akhira (in the Ultimate and Permanent End)."[37]

··· VI ···

There was more to Wadud's sermons than controversy. Paying attention to what she actually said highlights the extent to which American—and global—Muslim discourses of the 1990s and 2000s increasingly incorporated in them some sense of gender equality. Of course, what kind of a sense it was at a particular time was different for various groups within diverse Muslim communities. Yet, even the elements of Wadud's rhetoric that for many were likely quite uncomfortable—such as her gender-inclusive referencing of God—resonated in some crucial ways with the broader dimensions of the Muslim discourses contemporary to her. The way Wadud phrased it was perhaps too challenging for many to hear, because the text of the Qur'an uses the pronoun "he" when it speaks of God. Still, the tendency to speak differently in light of new realities of gender relations became increasingly widespread in the American Muslim logosphere of her time.

Wadud contributed to the ongoing changes in this logosphere was by introducing ever more daring—yet carefully phrased—articulations of the new thinkables, which had been already present, in various forms, in the experience of many American Muslims. Had her *Qur'an and Women* not resonated with broader American Muslim conversations, it would not have been such a widely discussed and overall well-received text. As years went by, she did not merely repeat what she and others had already said but continued to push boundaries toward more ethical—and, in her view, more Qur'anic— thinkables. Throughout the 1990s and early 2000s, she kept honing her techniques of "languaging," which contributed to further developments in American Muslim articulations. Her constant exegetical and practical challenging of the status quo inspired many Muslim activists in the United States and abroad. But what underscores her influence was how much even her detractors came to speak and write in ways that resonated with her phrases and logic. The echoes of her language were particularly pronounced among her American Muslim critics. While many foreign Muslim sources reacted to her 2005 prayer with bafflement and rejection, typical reactions by many American Muslim public figures were more circumspect—in part because they did not want to come across as dismissive of the sensitivities Wadud shared with their own constituents.

A telling example here was an article, "An Examination of the Issue of Female Prayer Leadership," by Imam Zaid Shakir, an *'alim* (religious scholar, a Muslim equivalent of a Christian cleric or a Jewish rabbi), at Zaytuna Institute in the San Francisco Bay Area. I will examine the rhetoric of Shakir's colleague at Zaytuna, Shaykh Hamza Yusuf, later; but for now, it is important to say that in the mid-2000s Zaytuna was the most prolific American Muslim educational organization among a network of groups that presented themselves as "traditional," which meant a variety of orientations marked by fidelity to the historical legacy of Muslim engagements with sacred texts. Shakir published his article a few days after Wadud's prayer on the website of another *'alim*, Shaykh Abdullah bin Hamid Ali, who would later join Zaytuna's faculty as well.

In the 2000s, together with Hamza Yusuf, Shakir was the most recognized *'alim* at Zaytuna, which included among its teachers male and female *'ulama* (plural of *'alim*), and male and female students. Given Zaytuna's emphasis on the authority of the *'ulama*, it is not surprising that a central point in Shakir's response to Wadud's prayer was a rejection of its Islamic legitimacy. He presented it as an unwarranted innovation in Muslim ritual life. But this was not his whole message. Overall, he agreed that there had been injustices perpetrated by Muslims and that gender inequality was an injustice:

It should be clear that a woman leading a mixed gender, public congregational prayer is not something sanctioned by Islamic law . . . . Her leading the Friday congregational prayer is even more unfounded. . . . Saying this, we should not lose sight of the fact that there are many issues in our community involving the neglect, oppression, and in some instances, the degradation of women. Until we address those issues, as a community, in an enlightened manner, we are open to criticism, and will likely encourage various forms of protest. . . . Perhaps, if the men of our community had more humility, we would behave in ways that do not alienate, frustrate, or outright oppress our women. . . . When we live for our Lord it becomes easy to live with each other. If in our personal relationships we can come to embody the spirit of mutual love, mercy and affection, encouraged by our Prophet, peace and blessings of God be upon him, we will be able to live together in harmony, and make a beautiful and lasting contribution towards the uplift of men and women alike.[38]

Muslims and others who are attentive to the dynamics of power in gender relations might be uncomfortable with Shakir's formulation. They might notice that he presented Wadud's prayer as a form of "protest" by a woman who was "frustrate[d]" and "alienate[d]." Such phrasing came too close to a sexist stereotype of a difficult and rebellious woman: anyone who drives a car in the United States likely has encountered a bumper-sticker response to this stereotype: "Well-behaved women seldom make history." In addition, Shakir articulated his message in a way that appeared to leave little room for the authority of women. The agency of change, in his phrasing, came across as belonging in the hands of men like Shakir who pronounced what was and was not "sanctioned by Islamic law," while obscuring his own agency as an interpreter behind his statement's grammar, its passive voice.

Yet, an overly critical reading of Shakir's statement would miss what was perhaps most important about it. Yes, he wrote it as a male religious leader. But in this role—as patriarchal as it might appear—he directed his criticism at men, not women. As a male 'alim, he shamed men to be more humble. In this way he articulated an ongoing transformation of the Muslim male religious authority, which in the new American settings of the time had to be expressed as sensitive to women's rights. This was particularly pronounced in his use of the word "we," which signaled that he addressed men and women. He concluded his opinion with a call for "the uplift of men and women alike." His "alike" here was key: it indicated a degree of sensibility of gender justice, as distinct as it perhaps was from Wadud's.

This document reflected Shakir's own process of "languaging." It represented his endeavor to speak in a way that resonated with his audiences' sense of fairness. Among his readers and listeners were his female colleagues, students, and administrative staff and volunteers at Zaytuna. But his audiences were also national and international. A popular preacher, he was often featured as a keynote speaker at American Muslim gatherings, and his speeches were popular on the Internet as well. His audiences were made up of constituents who belonged to a wide array of Muslim organizations, where women were prominently represented not just in numbers but in terms of organizational and financial power, as professionals, volunteers, and donors. Such practical power translated into how Muslims, women and men, spoke and how they listened to other speakers. To be heard in this context, Shakir and other Muslim authorities had to communicate in a way that echoed the new American Muslim common sense of justice, which now included a sense of gender justice. Therefore, it is not surprising that his language also included an emphasis on harmony, which was so pronounced in Wadud's 1994 and 2005 sermons. The "harmony" in Shakir's statement, however, was likely an indirect echo of Wadud. Because of this, it was even more significant: it echoed Wadud's language because her articulations shaped the language of her audiences, who, in turn, influenced the speech of wider circles of American Muslims, including those who would eventually speak in opposition to her 2005 prayer.

Another, likely more direct, example of Wadud's influence in the United States was a document titled "Women Friendly Mosques and Community Centers: Working Together to Reclaim Our Heritage," which shortly after Wadud's 2005 prayer became adopted by ISNA as a blueprint for more equitable inclusion of women in mosques and other Muslim institutions. It was endorsed and promoted by several other major organizations, such as the Council on American-Islamic Relations (CAIR), the ICNA, and the Muslim Alliance of North America. This document's development was spearheaded by Aisha Al-Adawiyya, the founder of Women in Islam, Inc., a New York City–based organization whose mission and work paralleled the Malaysian Sisters in Islam.

In 2005 none of the organizations that endorsed the "Women Friendly Mosques" document supported Wadud's prayer. In private conversations some of those involved in preparing this document, and others who later supported it, shared with me their disagreement with Wadud's serving as a leader of a mixed-gender Friday congregational prayer. Many of them agreed in general with Wadud's exegesis, as she presented it in *Qur'an and Woman*. Some recalled that until 2005 they promoted that book and recommended it to Muslim and non-Muslim audiences. But, like Shakir, they thought that Wadud's precedent of reconfiguring Muslim ritual life was a step too far. Therefore, "Women Friendly Mosques" did not acknowledge in any way the influence of Wadud's scholarship and activism, which was undoubtedly central in American Muslim discourses since the early 1990s. Moreover, al-Adawiyya and her colleagues had been working on this document long before Wadud's prayer. For them it was important that the statement would not be perceived as a direct response to the controversy of the female-led prayer. Yet, the timing of this document's publication, a few months after Wadud's sermon, indicated that Wadud's action created a stir that had to be addressed by major American Muslim organizations. Her prayer made gender justice the issue of the day.

Beyond politics, however, more important was the striking similarity between Wadud's articulations and the language of "Women Friendly Mosques." Consider, for instance, the following excerpt from the introduction to the document. It echoed Wadud's Qur'anic reminders, particularly the notion of human equality before God and, like Wadud's oral and written exegesis, advanced its argument as based on Qur'an 30:21:

> Muslims are answerable to Allah in every sphere of their life, including their personal and public relations. Human relations and gender relations in Islam are an *amanah,* a sacred trust that we must guard and make manifest in our interpersonal interactions and institutional arrangements. Islam demands that women and men be spiritual equals. It defines relations between women and men as mutually complementary, and indeed, this mutuality is itself a sign of the Divine (Qur'an 30:21). Both women and men have been entrusted with the charge of preserving the social order and establishing a just and moral society. Both have been given the guidance to inspire goodness in each other, and thereby, the goodness in all society. The respect, compassion, and mutuality that Allah has placed between women and men must be visible in not only your family life, but also in how Muslims conduct public transactions. Women and men, girls and boys should have equal access to and must feel equally welcome to participate in schools, the *masajid* (mosques), and other civic and cultural institutions.[39]

The language of this document speaks to Wadud's impact on broader American Muslim discourses, particularly her insistence on gender justice as an undeniable and centrally important Muslim principle.

···VIII···

Wadud's preaching highlighted the unique power of speech to crystalize, through sound, a multitude of meanings in one single word or phrase. Indeed, Wadud utilized this feature of oral communication in her 2005 sermon, where she kept referring to God as "He," "She," and "It." By doing so, she provided a contemporary exegetical and theological correction to the routine depiction of God as a "He." In her view this practice, which most people carry out instinctually, preconditioned the Qur'an's readers and listeners to think, speak, and act in male-centered ways. Her phrasing was shocking for many of her listeners and, subsequently, readers, who knew that the Qur'an uses the pronoun "he" when it speaks of God. Yet, this unsettling effect was precisely what Wadud attempted to cultivate. Like the Qur'an itself, she taught her audiences through reminders. Through this striking articulation, she reminded them about the scriptural principle of the essential human equality before God. The effectiveness of this reminder depended on a deeper, more organic, and engrained notion in the collective memory of Muslims: the idea that God cannot be confined within human descriptions, including gendered ones.

Wadud's contrapuntal articulation of God was at once Muslim and feminist, or, as she would put it, "pro-feminist."[40] It was also American, because it embodied the legacy of African American struggles for justice. Her notion of God as "He/She/It" was, in a sense, a rendition of the African American Christian slogan "God is Black!," which had its roots in the rhetoric of Henry McNeal Turner (1834–1915), a towering intellectual in African American Christian life of the late nineteenth and early twentieth centuries. Like Wadud's father, Turner was a Methodist preacher. His original phrase was "God is a Negro!"[41] And it was meant to be shocking. Its power originated in Turner's art of preaching. In this one phrase he expressed the theologically complex notion of God's affinity with human beings, in all of their complex situations, and made it viscerally resonant with his listeners and readers. This phrase spoke to the centrality of lived experience in African American theological thought. In the face of the unspeakable horror of slavery and its aftermaths, God for Turner could not be anything but a "Negro"—otherwise, on whose side would God be? Various renditions of Turner's slogan became central in the discourses of black nationalism and black liberation theology in the twentieth century, including their Muslim iterations.[42] Some African American Muslims, like members of the Nation of Islam, developed this expression in somewhat literal fashions. Most others never used this trope explicitly, while still utilizing the cultural logic of liberation embedded in it. Perhaps this is what Wadud meant when several years after her 2005 sermon she explained, "I am my father's daughter"?[43]

In the same sermon, Wadud carried out another telling wordplay, which distilled and synthesized meanings and, because of that, crystalized in one moment how the Qur'an is being constantly translated into an American sacred text—how, through dialogue with its American faithful, it takes on and then transforms their thinkables. This was her spoken rendition of one characteristically Christian word, "atonement." The fact that she, an American Muslim, used a Christian word is not unusual. Zaid Shakir, for instance, did something similar in his statement when he wrote, "we live for our Lord."

Indeed, "lord" is a direct translation of the Arabic word *rabb*. But Arabic does not have capital letters, and Shakir's capitalized "Lord" was an iteration of an American English and Christian expression. What he and Wadud did followed a much wider trend: non-Christian religious people in the United States often take on Christian terminology and make it their own. They do so because some Christian words and concepts are also the terms of the broader culture. The first Buddhist temple in New York City, for example, was established in 1938 and is still, as of 2017, called the New York Buddhist Church. Also, think about all the Buddhist, Hindu, Jewish, Muslim, and Native American chaplains who now work in the American armed forces, hospitals, prisons, and universities. They use the title "chaplain," which was originally Christian. But, because of who they are, they make it Buddhist, Hindu, Jewish, Muslim, and Native American.[44] Likewise, Wadud's rendering of the word "atonement" took on a word from American colloquial language, influenced as it was by Christianity, and transformed it into a Qur'anic and Muslim term: in her voice, it became "at-one-ment." In this rendition, it all of a sudden came to embody the Muslim notion of *tawhid*, the Oneness of God, and *taqwa*, the believers' potential to attain a degree of affinity with God through their engaged surrender to the divine—if only for one moment.

Most of us, those who did not hear Wadud pronounce this word in her sermon, would be well served to try and say it out loud: "at-one-ment." Without sound the meaning of this word is flat: it comes across as what a printed dictionary would tell us it is, a Christian word of English origin, which later became Jewish as well. With sound, however, it comes alive and acquires additional meanings, which fluctuate depending on who pronounces it, as well as how and when it is pronounced. Wadud's "at-one-ment" highlights the poetic quality of her spoken exegesis. Like poetry, preaching exists through vocalization of words. Like poets, preachers synthesize new resonances, sounds and meanings from what has been said before. Without such *re-soundings* cultural translation of texts is at best incomplete.

Chapter Three

REDEMPTION

What good is knowledge if you can't hear it? The Bible says blessed is he that has an ear to hear. So what good is the body of knowledge we call religion if nobody can hear it?

Warith Deen Mohammed, *As the Light Shineth*, 67

I was freed by the revelation.

Anonymous, interview with author, August 11, 2009

···|···

When does the Qur'an emerge as an American sacred text? When it strikes the chords of local Muslim collective memory. One such moment occurred during a lecture by an African American Muslim speaker, Imam Warith Deen Mohammed, which he delivered in Cleveland, Ohio, in November 1987 in front of some two hundred African American Muslim men. Much of it he spent retelling the Qur'anic (and biblical) story of Joseph. Somewhere in the middle of that retelling, after a joke, he suddenly stopped, waited for the hearty laughter of his audience to subside, and delivered his sermon's key rhetorical punch: "Remember," he told his listeners—some of whom, like many other black men, had been incarcerated—that Joseph had been thrown into jail for "wanting what the big man wanted."

Behind the pops and cracks of the audio recording, there came a barely audible response: some of the men groaned.[1] In that moment and for that audience, the story of the Qur'anic prophet was no longer a tale from a far-away past, depicted in a foreign language of an old and exotic scripture, or in a seemingly neutral translation by a foreign Muslim authority in a printed book that rested somewhere on the top shelf in their homes and houses of worship. The sound of their response signaled a deep, felt-in-the-bones connection between the Qur'an and who they were. It embodied the resonance between their collective memory and their Qur'an.

Of course, the phrase "big man" is not Qur'anic. It is an African American expression, whose cultural roots reach back to slavery. It is a polyvocal term, whose meanings include a slave owner, a slave driver, or a prison guard. In either sense, it is a figure of authority, who in no time at all can inflict unspeakable pain on a black human being because of a suspicion of wrongdoing, or just to maintain the status quo of the American racial hierarchy by inflicting terror on a random black body that would serve as an example for other black men, women, and children. It is a phrase that connotes the history of humiliation and dehumanization. It is likely that Mohammed's abrupt reminder resurrected in his listeners' bodies the physical memory of lynching, which was a close memory for many black people of that generation (his father witnessed a lynching when he was a child). In the Qur'an, Joseph was incarcerated because he was accused of lusting after his master's wife. And the people who listened to the Cleveland sermon knew very well what had happened to men like them when they were suspected of glancing improperly at a white woman. Their collective groan was the sound of black bodies remembering the whippings and crucifixions of slavery and Jim Crow.[2] It was an American sound of the Qur'an.

···II···

This chapter explores the Qur'an-based language of African American Muslims by examining the oral *tafsir* of Imam W. D. Mohammed, with a particular focus on the speeches and sermons he gave from the mid-1980s and until his passing in 2008. During this period, approximately half of African American Muslims affiliated themselves with his leadership, which amounted to as much as 20 percent of the overall Muslim population in the United States.[3]

Wallace D. Muhammad was born in 1933 in Hamtramck, Michigan, near Detroit, in the family of Elijah and Clara Pool, African American migrants from Georgia. Two years before his birth, his father had encountered a mysterious stranger, who presented himself to Detroit's African Americans as a messenger of Islam. The stranger explained that Islam was the original religion of the black people, which they had forgotten after being enslaved in America. What he said was not unique: the idea of Islam as a viable and, for some, more authentic religion was relatively widespread among African Americans in the urban North after World War I. While present among groups that identified themselves as Muslim, such as the Moorish Science Temple, it was also part of the broader discourse. The largest black nationalist movement of the time, the Universal Negro Improvement Association of Marcus Garvey, included Muslims. Even non-Muslim affiliates of this movement often talked of Islam as an authentic African American religion.[4] Elijah Pool's teacher spoke of it as the only way toward the liberation of black Americans, through which they would be able to restore their status as the original human beings and true masters of God's creation. The stranger used a variety of names and titles: Professor Ford, Mr. Farrad Mohammad, F. Mohammad Ali, Mr. Wali Farrad, and W. D. Fard. Later, he would be most often remembered as Fard Muhammad. (People who affiliate themselves with this history pronounce the first name as "Farad" while spelling it as "Fard.")

Elijah Pool converted to the new religion and assumed a new name: first, Elijah Kareem, and later, Elijah Muhammad.

Within a couple of years, Elijah Muhammad became Fard Muhammad's chief representative. In 1934 his teacher disappeared, and the disciple became the leader of the organization, which came to be known as the Nation of Islam. Over the next several decades, it became the largest black nationalist movement in U.S. history. At the height of its influence from the 1950s to the mid-1970s, it had a mosque in every major American city, owned a newspaper that boasted the largest distribution of any African American publication, and operated countless businesses, including banks, farms, restaurants, and food-distribution companies. Malcolm X was the Nation's most famous representative. Martin Luther King, Jr., used the Nation of Islam as a sort of a scarecrow: he spoke of it as a terrible alternative that awaited America if it did not move away from its racist practices.[5] Muslims, African American and immigrant, who did not affiliate with the Nation, repudiated its teachings. Particularly troublesome to them was its denial of the doctrine of the afterlife and its belief that Fard Muhammad was a God and that Elijah Muhammad was the messenger of that God. Along with such tenets came the Nation's theological notions of the collective divinity of black and other non-Caucasian human beings, which was contrasted with the notion that whites were by nature devils. Yet, in its rhetoric—which resonated in many ways with the language of Christian and other black nationalists, such as Henry M. Turner—there was a powerful message of racial uplift, which the Nation translated into its theology and practice. The broader influence of this message was evident in the Black Power movement.

In 1975 Elijah Muhammad died and his son, Wallace Muhammad, took the reins of the Nation of Islam. His authority rested partly on the story of his birth: according to the lore of the Nation's members, Fard Muhammad had assigned a special status to this child of his favorite student. Of course, there were complications. Elijah Muhammad excommunicated his son Wallace from the movement on several occasions. The first time it happened was in 1957. Influenced by his interactions with other African American and immigrant Muslims, Wallace Muhammad came to disagree with the Nation's theological tenets. Authentic and orthodox Islam for him was Sunni Islam. And so, while serving as a minister at the Nation's mosque in Philadelphia, he taught its members Sunni Muslim doctrines and practices. Another problem he ran into was related to his role as a confidant and advisor to Malcolm X during Malcolm's all-too-public and scandalous break with the Nation in 1964. Yet, throughout this time he remained close to the movement. Each excommunication was followed by reunion. The final reconciliation between Wallace Muhammad and his father took place in 1974, shortly before Elijah Muhammad's death.

This paved the way to Wallace Muhammad's crowning as the Supreme Minister of the Nation of Islam. After taking control of the organization, he led the effort to gradually convert its members to Sunni Islam. By the early 1980s the transformation was complete. Most members of the Nation followed Elijah's son—who in the late 1970s adopted the name Warith Deen Muhammad (later to be changed to Warith Deen Mohammed)—and embraced the Sunni Muslim identity. Some split from Imam Mohammed's group and formed new versions of the Nation. The most famous of them was the reconstituted Nation of Islam of Minister Louis Farrakhan (b. 1933).

···III···

What I just presented is the story of Mohammed's life as it has been usually told. When he died on September 9, 2008, numerous newspapers issued obituaries about the man who turned the "fiery" Nation of Islam into a mainstream movement.[6] Most academic reflections have followed a similar outline, focusing primarily on the late 1970s and early 1980s. The classic work that set this trend was C. Eric Lincoln's *The Black Muslims in America*. There have been, of course, several academic works that went further and deeper. Mattias Gardell's *In the Name of Elijah Muhammad* is a superb ethnography of Louis Farrakhan's Nation of Islam, which includes nuanced analysis of its relationship with W. D. Mohammed's movement. *Islam in Black America* by Edward E. Curtis IV offers an outstanding overview of the history of the Nation of Islam and its successors. Both Curtis and Gardell provide excellent analysis of African American Muslim discourses. In Gardell's book, however, Mohammed and his group are side characters, and Curtis's analysis of his rhetoric stops with the 1980s.

Journalists and academics have a good reason to pay particular attention to the Nation's transition into a Sunni movement. In the 1960s and 1970s, it was the largest African American Muslim community, which happened to be very different from the Muslim groups that are usually called "orthodox." Mohammed's accomplishment of converting most of its members was monumental. No less a charismatic figure than Malcolm X had tried his hand at this task and failed: faced with the overwhelmingly negative reaction from his former coreligionists, he bitterly exclaimed, "I had known . . . that Negroes would not rush to follow me into the orthodox Islam."[7] Mohammed accomplished this undertaking through an ingenious strategy of gradual reinterpretation of the Nation's beliefs and practices. As he later explained, it was a strategy of change through preaching: "What I have done is simply talk on the double meaning of Elijah Muhammad's teaching."[8]

Preaching is an art of rhetoric, and rhetoric is an art of persuasion. One of the characteristics of Mohammed's rhetoric from the period of his reform was his use of the Book of Revelation from the New Testament, which had

72

been an important source for his father's interpretations of both the Qur'an and the Bible.[9] Throughout the late 1970s, Mohammed presented his reformation as the culmination of the process initiated by his father and Fard Muhammad. The period of their leadership, he proposed, was akin to the "First Coming of Christ." It was the "First Resurrection" of African Americans to Islam, their natural and original faith. His reform was the "Second Resurrection": "In the First Resurrection," Mohammed explained, "God began to raise us out of the graves by beginning to unveil the Truth. In the Second Resurrection the Truth is not just unveiled in a sense of scriptural interpretation, but we come to a kind of a natural interpretation. . . . We have been taught many things in the teachings of the Great Master W. F. Muhammad [Fard Muhammad] and the Honorable Elijah Muhammad that prepared us for this time."[10]

What happened after this "Second Resurrection?" Nothing dramatic—if we are to believe the common version of the story, reflected in the *New York Times* obituary: "Imam Mohammed moved decisively toward the religious mainstream. In 1992, he became the first Muslim to deliver the invocation for the United States Senate. He led prayers at both inaugurals of President Bill Clinton. He addressed a conference of Muslims and Reform Jews in 1995, and participated in several major interfaith dialogues with Roman Catholic cardinals. He met with the pope in 1996 and 1999."[11]

Indeed, this record of his activities is impressive. But it reads like a depiction of the life of a former statesperson whose most important achievements were in the past. The problem with such a presentation is that it creates an impression of a leader who had spent the last twenty-eight years of his life in semiretirement.

For the people from his community, nothing could be further from reality. For them, he was an authentic voice of the Qur'an, which emerged most clearly after the "Second Resurrection." The three decades after the mid-1980s were crucial precisely because they were relatively free from the ordeals of the period of reform. During this time, he was continuously developing an African American way of understanding the Qur'an, which he taught in countless sermons. These were the decades when he preached what his audiences would later come to call "the *tafsir* of Imam W. Deen Mohammed."[12]

··· I V ···

In the 1980s, 1990s, and 2000s, Mohammed and his community organized countless gatherings where he would teach and preach. Central among those were annual Ramadan sessions. On one such occasion in 2003, a young woman in the audience stood up and asked him, "When will you translate the Qur'an?" He answered, "I am doing it all alone but I hope to one day call together a team at least to meet once a month. And I'm working on it all of the time so that we can actually start collecting my commentary. . . . We can do it, *in sha' allah,* one day soon. But I think it is Allah's, *subhanahu wa ta'ala* ['may He be glorified and exalted,' a Muslim equivalent of 'Praise be to God'], will that I just do it as I work with you. And you are taking notes and we can pull it together one day soon, *in sha' allah.*"[13]

The young woman made a technical mistake: Imam Mohammed never produced a formal translation of the Qur'an. He was not a translator in the technical sense like Muhammad Pickthall, Yusuf Ali, or Thomas Irving. In his response, however, he glided right over this point—maybe because, as a skilled teacher, he was careful not to sidetrack his audience with an unnecessary correction. He talked instead about his commentary on the Qur'an. In this one instance, he summarized the nature of his *tafsir.* It was not what academics would call a *tafsir*—it was not a book. Rather, it was his lifelong effort of preaching and interpreting the Qur'an for the benefit of his and other communities. From this standpoint, there was perhaps a deeper reason why Imam Mohammed skipped over his student's technical slipup. On a deeper level, she was absolutely right: his *tafsir* was indeed a form of translation—not technical, but cultural.

Another possible reason for his response was that, at this exact time, he was in fact discussing with some of his colleagues a project of translating the Qur'an. This effort came to be spearheaded in 2006 by two of his close associates, Imam Darnell Karim and Imam Vernon Fareed. Within the next three years, they published five sets of CDs under the title *Tafseer of Imam W. Deen Mohammed.* These CDs contained recordings of Arabic recitations by Imam Karim, readings of their English translation by Imam Fareed, and interviews with Imam Mohammed. During the interviews, Fareed asked Mohammed to comment on specific Qur'anic verses, expressions, and ideas.[14] That was the exegetical part of the CDs. The translation part was not a made-from-scratch original. Rather, it was a modification of Yusuf Ali's translation of the Qur'an, which Fareed customized to be more in tune with contemporary American spoken English and resonant with his community's tradition of reading the Qur'an.

The choice of Yusuf Ali's translation reflected the history of the Qur'an in Imam Mohammed's movement, as well as among wider circles of African American Muslims. One of the first initiatives he undertook when he became the leader of the Nation of Islam was to shift his community to the use of Ali's translation. Before then, Elijah Muhammad and other authorities of the Nation worked with the translation by Muhammad Ali (not Muhammad Ali the boxer; the boxer was named after Muhammad Ali the translator). That translation came to the Nation of Islam via Ahmadi Muslim missionaries from India, who had been active in African American neighborhoods in the 1920s and 1930s.[15] The consequent shift to Yusuf Ali's translation was part of the transition away from Elijah Muhammad's interpretations of the

Qur'an. For example, Elijah Muhammad used Muhammad Ali's translation of Qur'an 20:102—"On that day [of resurrection] when the trumpet shall be blown, and We will gather the guilty, blue-eyed, on that day"—as the scriptural proof of his theological claim about the devilish nature of the white people. In his reading, the whites were the "blue-eyed devils" of the Qur'an.[16] W. D. Mohammed's shift to Yusuf Ali's translation was also fitting because it established a shared textual basis between his and other Muslim communities. This translation was widely distributed by immigrant and international Muslim groups, most notably by the Muslim World League. At the same time, while promoting and largely relying on Yusuf Ali's translation, Mohammed emphasized the need for indigenous African American engagement with the Arabic Qur'an and its independent translation. His sermons and lectures were the rhetorical spaces where he performed, in front of his audiences, his cultural translation of the Qur'an. On such occasions he taught them how to translate the scripture into their lives. His hope was that, perhaps, a technical translation would follow at some point in the future. The priority, however, was the Qur'an's ongoing cultural translation.

Fareed's modifications of Yusuf Ali's translation presented some of his teacher's key exegetical insights. Most notable among them was Imam Mohammed's rendition of the *basmala,* a Qur'anic invocation, which Muslims repeat at the beginning of every important action. Yusuf Ali translated this Arabic phrase—*bi-smi llah al-rahman al-rahim*—as "in the name of Allah, the Beneficent, the Merciful." This became a common phrase in the American Muslim vernacular. Its wide usage was an indication of the influence of Yusuf Ali's translation, and the institutions that fostered it. Mohammed's version was different: "With G-d's Name, The Merciful Benefactor, the Merciful Redeemer."

Two details are important about Mohammed's basmala. First, it demonstrated his engagement with the printed Qur'an; and second, it reflected his lifelong work of translating the Arabic scripture into the African American Muslim vernacular. On the immediate level, he translated the Arabic word *"allah"* into an English word, which was pronounced as "God," but printed as "G-d." The pronunciation established an obvious shared ground between the cultural background of his audience, overwhelmingly former Christians, and the language of their Christian families, neighbors, and friends. By urging his audiences to use this word, he prompted them to speak in a way that resonated with the broader American and African American way of speaking. (After 9/11 many immigrant Muslims started emphasizing the use of "God" instead of "Allah" for a similar reason.) The printed version of "G-d" was likely borrowed from a parallel Jewish convention. It was likely a result of Mohammed's extensive interfaith work, which had begun in the mid-1980s. At the same time there was another, uniquely Muslim logic behind this move. On a more subtle level, the spelling of "G-d," which omits the vowel "o," is reminiscent of the Arabic writing and print. Arabic words are based on their consonants. In Arabic, consonants are written and printed, but short vowels, like the second "a" in *"allah,"* are often omitted. Instead, they are typically filled through oral pronunciation. Therefore, it is likely that, by printing "G-d," Mohammed provided a visual bridge between the printed English of his audiences and the Qur'anic Arabic.

More important, however, was yet another feature of his *basmala:* his translation referred to God as the "Redeemer." Redemption was the essential theme in his engagement with the Qur'an. His articulations of redemption as a Qur'anic idea remained key throughout his career. Of course, his use of this theme shifted over time because his sermons and lectures always related the Qur'an to changing practical concerns. As concrete issues changed, so did his interpretative emphases. In the 1970s and early 1980s, his task was to transform his father's movement into a Sunni group. Later on and until his passing in 2008, his mission was more substantial: he endeavored to provide the tools that would help his community and other African American Muslims to live as confident—independent but not isolated—participants in American life. In this respect, his oral exegesis was vital. Through preaching, he continuously transformed the Qur'an into a spoken sacred text. He spoke from the Qur'an and by doing so taught others how to speak as American Muslims. The fact that his community's language was based on the Qur'an made it Muslim. The fact that it was distinctly African American made it American.

Two of the words I just used are likely to be problematic for some of my readers. For some people in Imam Mohammed's community, it would be the word "preacher." For some other Muslims that word would be "redemption." Mohammed used both words but, of course, in ways that were specific to him. Quite often in his speeches, for example, he would refer to something another "preacher said." Typically, he would mention that on his way to a venue where he was delivering his talk he was listening to the radio and heard a "preacher say" something resonant with what he was about to teach. What he never said was that a station and preacher he was listening to was Christian. It was obvious because his community never used this word for Muslim speakers such as W. D. Mohammed. They reserved "preacher" for Christians. At the same time, the fact that their teacher listened to Christian preachers was for most of them neither unusual nor alarming. They were, after all, a part of the African American world. Their neighbors and many of their family members were Christian, and Imam Mohammed often spoke in front of Christian audiences. Yes, his community was Muslim; but they came from the culture of the black church, and their Islamic tradition belonged to what some academics call "Black Religion."[17] From this perspective the word "preacher" is inescapable: for those not accustomed to the vocabulary of Imam Mohammed's community, like most of this book's readers, it conveys his role and his work more readily. Besides, if what he did was not preaching, why would he compare what and how he taught with what he was hearing from other preachers?

Mohammed's other word, "redemption," might come across as strange for some other Muslims because it is characteristically African American. Indeed, "redemption" stems from the Christian vocabulary, where it is tied to the concept of original sin. In most Muslim interpretations, the Qur'anic view of human history does not include this notion, at least not substantively so (although there are some parallel, but distinct, articulations in the Shi'i tradition).[18] Fazlur Rahman, for example, stated emphatically in his *Major Themes* that "for Islam, there is no particular [idea of] 'salvation': there is only success *[falah]* or failure *[khusran]* in the task of building the world."[19] Tellingly, Rahman wrote this passage as a commentary on what he perceived as a dominant trend in the interreligious dialogue between Muslims and Christians, where Muslims and other non-Christians are often compelled to communicate through Christian-sounding terms. Without such an engagement with Christians, at least for Rahman, there was no reason to look in the Qur'an for the idea of "salvation" or redemption. This subject of conversation became thinkable for him only through interreligious exchanges with Christians. For African American Muslims, however, the very sense of who they are includes their Christian cultural heritage and the Bible-based language of their broader community.

In African American religious discourses, the language of redemption is inescapable. Since the nineteenth century African American preachers and writers have developed a tradition of biblical interpretation that articulates redemption as the vital answer to the large-scale suffering of their people. James H. Cone, a famous Christian theologian, reflected on this tradition when he stated that African American exegesis conceived suffering as the "badge of true discipleship." This pairing of suffering and discipleship enabled African American exegetes, most often preachers and their listeners, to make sense of their collective suffering. They did so by retelling the stories of the biblical Israelites, particularly the story of Exodus, and by speaking of Jesus as a suffering servant. Crucial here was that they identified African Americans—as a collective, a people—with Jesus and the Israelites: like Jesus, they suffered; like the Israelites, they were chosen because of their collective suffering. The redemption they preached was collective as well—the redemption of African Americans as a people.[20] Another unique feature of this tradition is the stress on redemption as a "this world" concept, a process that has been unfolding through African American collective history.

Mohammed's Qur'an-based message of redemption was grounded in this cultural legacy. It was also a development of the tradition of preaching of the Nation of Islam, where the theme of redemption was central. Elijah

Muhammad spoke of it when he taught that "Islam is our salvation" and stressed that the salvation of the black people was taking place in this world, during the lifetime of his followers. This was the theological basis for his rejection of the Christian and Muslim notions of the afterlife. His son disagreed and taught that his father's dismissal of the afterlife was profoundly un-Islamic. Yet, even after his movement had become Sunni, he continued to speak about redemption. What he borrowed from his father—and from the broader African American religious discourse—was the articulation of the redemption of black people in terms of their concrete realities. For him, redemption was about an uplift of the African American people in this world, which included social, economic, and spiritual aspects of their lives. And the promise of such redemption, for him, was in the Qur'an. As he declared in a speech from the late 1980s, it was "Allah's will . . . that this religion of al-Islam and the Book of Qur'an are destined to be our Savior."[21]

··· V ···

From the very first speech Mohammed gave upon inheriting his father's office, at the age of forty-one in 1975, he presented himself as an agent of a Qur'an-based transformation. On that occasion, he declared that his father had "unlocked the Bible and by unlocking the Bible he made us unlock our minds." He explained that, before Elijah Muhammad, they "only read the scripture in print." But reading a printed scripture, he said, was not enough because "the scripture says, blessed is he who hears the word!"[22] The new stage in the movement's history, he indicated, would be based on *hearing* the Qur'an.

From that moment on, Mohammed inextricably linked his authority to the Qur'an. He relied on this connection, for example, in the early 1980s, when he was introducing a notion of an African American methodology *(madhhab)* of Islamic jurisprudence. At that point, in a speech at Masjid Malcolm Shabazz in Harlem, a mosque named after Malcolm X, he offered his own interpretation of Qur'an 5:51. Yusuf Ali translated that passage as "O ye who believe! take not the Jews and the Christians for your friends and protectors: they are but friends and protectors to each other." Mohammed interpreted it as not speaking about some eternal categories of people, "Christians" or "Jews," but about specific Jewish and Christian communities in Arabia at the time of the Prophet Muhammad, who were politically antagonistic to the nascent Muslim polity. Based on this observation, he argued that his community and other African American Muslims must be wary of taking as "friends and protectors" specifically those who opposed the independent growth of African American Muslims. He explained that, at that particular time, such people included some foreign Muslim authorities and some immigrant and African American Muslims who "represent[ed] foreign concerns."[23] Through this exegesis, he responded to a two-pronged opposition his movement was facing at that particular period of its history—from those who criticized him as not being sufficiently "orthodox," like Brooklyn's famous African American Sunni leader and former member of the Nation of Islam, Imam Siraj Wahhaj (b. 1950), and also from those, like Farrakhan, who charged W. D. Mohammed with betraying the legacy of Elijah Muhammad. Imam Mohammed did not spell this out, but it is quite possible that by "foreign concerns" he meant Wahhaj's close affinity with international Muslim authorities, such as the Muslim World League, and Farrakhan's partnership with the Libyan government of Muammar Gaddafi. His broader argument prompted his community to keep developing an independent orientation in religious and social life.

Mohammed's exegesis of Qur'an 5:51 at Masjid Malcolm Shabazz reflected a rhetorical move that was typical throughout his career. Like Muhammad Ali—the boxer, not the translator of the Qur'an—he used his challengers' strengths by utilizing the energy of their attacks and ultimately turning it onto themselves. (He and his community often talked about Muhammad Ali.) Of course, his art was rhetorical. He was not a boxer, although he had boxed in his youth. His preaching, however, resonated with the skills he had learned as a boxer. His preferred method of public speaking was through the Qur'an, which was the prime weapon of his rhetorical defense and attack. How he used it to buttress his authority is reflected in a statement he made in another mid-1980s speech: "There are those who want to charge me with something because they don't want to follow the Qur'an. They don't want to be real Muslims. It isn't me. None of those people have anything against me personally."[24] This was a martial-arts type of rhetoric: under attack by his critics, who used the Qur'an as a key source of their oratorical strength, he avoided their punches and simultaneously responded with a Qur'an-based retort of his own. His phrasing, however, was about more than sparring with his critics. It was his way of communicating an intimate relationship he cultivated with the Qur'an. For his community, those who heard him, this was the foundation of their teacher's authority. He assured them of it constantly, as he did in one of the last speeches he gave right before his passing in 2008. "When I am talking," he reminded his audience, "I am speaking from Scripture. Don't think that I am giving you my words; I don't have any words. All of my words come from Scripture or from somewhere else."[25]

How did Imam Mohammed speak from the Qur'an? How did he make its words his own? And how did he teach it? As he retold the scripture's stories, recited its verses in Arabic and interpreted its "signs" in the colloquial English of his African American audiences, he presented his oral exegesis of the Qur'an. But there was more to his preaching than content. His sermons demonstrated to his community how to speak the scripture. From such efforts, there emerged a particular tradition of African American exegesis of the Qur'an. It was unique to his movement. Yet, it also reflected the language of the broader African American Muslim community.

Mohammed's oral *tafsir* belonged to an African American tradition of Qur'an-based speaking. To understand it, it must be heard, because "what good is knowledge if you can't hear it?" The best way to hear it is by listening to how it came to be developed, through constant rearticulations, by Mohammed himself and by the people who learned how to speak Qur'anically by listening to his sermons. Therefore, what follows is my experiment in comparative hearing. My first example is a lecture Mohammed gave at Masjid Bilal in Cleveland, Ohio, in November 1987 during an annual gathering of local leaders within his movement, the National Imams' Meeting. (This chapter's opening vignette is based on that sermon.) To provide a broader contextual reading, or hearing, of his rhetoric, I will juxtapose it with some of his other speeches, from the 1980s, 1990s, and 2000s. My second key sample is a 2009 sermon by one of his students, Imam Faheem Shuaibe. I was not among the original audience who listened to Mohammed's Cleveland address: I found a CD recording of it, titled "National Imams Meeting: Yusuf Analogy," while conducting research for this book. I was, however, at As-Salaam Islamic Center of Raleigh on Friday, May 22, 2009, when Shuaibe delivered his *khutba,* which he titled "Fear Not For Allah Is With Us." My analysis of both speeches is informed by conversations with people in the community.

Preachers' exegeses are inseparable from their immediate contexts. In this sense these two sermons were distinct. In the 1980s, for instance, the idea of an African American President of the United States was thinkable—Jesse Jackson (and W. D. Mohammed) worked toward it—but it was still a dream. In 2009, when Shuaibe spoke to his audience, it was a reality. Yet, despite this temporal distance, these sermons had much in common, primarily because their language was at once African American and Qur'anic. They were additionally resonant because they were delivered at times of crisis. Mohammed spoke in 1987, when his organization lost a protracted legal case over his fathers' estate, which had begun in 1979. As he recalled sixteen years later, in 2003, this was a serious financial blow to his community's institutional life, which resulted, for instance, in the closing of many of its private schools, including one in Raleigh.[26] Shuaibe addressed the North Carolina community less than a year after the passing of Imam Mohammed and during an immense economic crisis, which, as happens too often, hit African Americans the hardest. On both occasions, as different as they were, these two preachers taught the redemptive message of the Qur'an.

··· VI ···

Mohammed's 1987 speech at Masjid Bilal was connected to a series of events that revolved around the mosque's Tenth Annual Awards Dinner.

These dinners were a local tradition, which the Cleveland community used to highlight their contributions to their city's life: they typically included as guests and honorees representatives of local government, business, and nonprofit sectors. The 1987 dinner was organized to coincide with a National Meeting of imams of Mohammed's movement. His lecture addressed that specific audience. Its excerpts were later published in his organization's newspaper, *Muslim Journal.* In the late 2000s its complete recording was distributed by his office as a part of its "History Speaks" series of audio and video records.[27]

In terms of style this speech was fairly typical. Mohammed spoke from a rough outline and mostly improvised. In this way he followed the rhetorical tradition of Elijah Muhammad, who also tended to improvise: both of them were more "spiritual," rather than "manuscript," types of preachers.[28] Mohammed himself acknowledged his father's influence on his style of preaching. In one respect it shored up his authority. It also signaled that he shared his listeners' cultural location—or, as he would put it, "home"—as African Americans and former members of the Nation of Islam. Even his demeanor reminded them of his father, who taught them, "Don't act proud. Be humble and yet commanding."[29] This was certainly his son's public persona.

Content-wise, this lecture was representative of how Mohammed spoke in the posttransformation period of his career. By 1987 he no longer argued against his father's theological formulations. By that point all who had wanted to leave his movement had already left. For those who chose to stay, their new, post–Nation of Islam identity was a given. And so, unlike in his speeches from the late 1970s and early 1980s, he engaged in these later talks with the memory of his father and with the time of transition not as an explicit ground for rhetorical contestation but rather as a shared story whose outcome was established and whose experience united him with his audience.

Structurally, the sermon revolved around two Qur'anic passages. Its first half was a commentary on the Qur'an 3:110, which lasted over an hour. Yusuf Ali translated this verse as "Ye are the best of peoples, evolved for mankind, enjoining what is right, forbidding what is wrong, and believing in Allah. If only the People of the Book had faith it were best for them; among them are some who have faith, but most of them are perverted transgressors." The second half of the lecture, which was also over an hour long, was his commentary on sura Yusuf (Qur'an 12). Mohammed referred to this Qur'anic and biblical figure as both "Yusuf" and "Joseph," thus providing a bridge between the Arabic scripture and his English-speaking audience. For the rest of this chapter, I will follow this practice as well.

The first half of Qur'an 3:110 is among the Qur'an's most frequently quoted passages. If there is such a phenomenon as Muslim collective memory, then the phrase "you are the best community" is certainly central in it.

In sermons it often serves as praise directed at an audience: it wins them over and then prepares them to hear what comes next, which is typically a corrective message. In fact, this verse reflects one of the peculiar features of the Qur'anic text itself: like many of its other passages, it presents a conditional status of being Muslim, a person or community who professes submission to the divine will. It affirms that belonging to this community is indeed a high status, but it also states that it needs to be continuously reasserted through action, by "enjoining what is right" and "forbidding what is wrong." This rhetorical move is characteristic of the Qur'an as a text of didactic discourse: during the time of the Prophet Muhammad, and through his recitations, it communicated with his often apprehensive audiences to persuade them to change their lives. W. D. Mohammed took a cue from his scripture's rhetorical style and used this passage pedagogically as well, to highlight how it was speaking directly to his African American listeners.

He began his lecture by reciting Qur'an 3:110 in Arabic, then made an important digression, and returned to this verse some twenty minutes later. During that detour he reminded his listeners about an observation he had made repeatedly in many of his other speeches after 1976, when, during his movement's annual gathering, the Savior's Day, he had lifted the American flag and announced that from now on they would work to become fully incorporated into American civic life. In 1976, only a year after he had become the head of the Nation of Islam, this declaration came as a shock to many within and outside the organization. The Savior's Day was the Nation's central recurring event, during which Elijah Muhammad would preach his message of black separatism, segregation from the "devilish" American society, which included a policy of officially abstaining from participation in American politics.[30] W. D. Mohammed used this symbolic occasion to announce a radically new direction in the public stance of his movement. He did this by proposing an inherent correspondence between the Qur'an and the U.S. Constitution. By 1987 this declaration became a staple in his speeches.[31] In Cleveland he gestured toward it as he was preparing the ground for his exegesis of Qur'an 3:110. He reminded his listeners that "our religion gives the concept of our personal and community life," which, he further explained, was reflected in the Qur'anic phrase "one community": "One community under God, isn't that what we are? *Ummatun wahidatun* under God, responsible to Allah. Ah? You've heard that same language, haven't you—one nation under God. Now, that language from the Constitution of the United States, or its introduction, or preamble to the constitution of the United States—one nation under God—is not new. Fourteen hundred years ago, that's more than 1000 years before that language was formed—same language: one community, responsible to Allah. And we may say 'one nation under God,' because '*umma*' can be translated as 'nation' sometimes.

Ah? *Ummatan wahida*—one united people, responsible to Allah, responsible to God."[32]

Most Qur'anic passages that speak about "one community" use this phrase as a lament: they state that the humanity had once been one *umma*, one community of believers, but as time passed, most people forgot that the purpose of their creation was to serve God and thus became dispersed into many groups.[33] This note of scriptural lamentation was important to Imam Mohammed. He would often say, with sadness in his voice, that most people—African Americans, Muslims, and others—had led themselves astray and become disconnected from God-consciousness. But for him this Qur'anic phrase also promised that human beings could once again unite, in all their diversity, to work toward the establishment of a better society. This promise, he never tired of reiterating, had come true in human history repeatedly. The most recent such example for him was the success of the civil rights movement. In that case—and, as he emphasized, in the Qur'anic telling of human history as well—success was not attained by a majority but rather by select human beings who retained and cultivated their awareness of God. Thus, in another late 1980s speech, he challenged his audience: "Do you think people are saved by a majority? Study history. Societies are always saved by a minority, a select few."[34] In a 2003 speech he repeated the same idea, all along echoing the Qur'anic lamentation and promise of redemption. And as was typical of his overall rhetoric, he used these notes to interweave his understanding of the Qur'anic pattern of history with the African American collective experience: "I'm convinced also that leaders in the history of African-American people who are Christian, and that is a great majority, they got help from God and God has been in that work and God has been with us as long as we were with God and until we went after the dollar. . . . He is still with us. Few of us. And that's too bad. But don't feel discouraged because never in the history of a people there were many leading them. Always a few. Always a few."[35]

In the 1987 sermon W. D. Mohammed's civic message was likely an elaboration on Qur'an 21:92 or 23:52, which celebrated the community of the people who followed the Prophet Muhammad as "one community." He echoed this note of celebration when, some twenty minutes into the speech, he began interpreting Qur'an 3:110. He stressed that the correspondence between the Qur'anic *"ummatun wahidatun"* and the American "one nation under God" was not coincidental. This was how "God identified us," he explained; it was a divine hint that indicated African Americans' unique place in history: "[God] also said that you're a community. That 'you're the best community brought out'— *'ukhrijat.' 'Ukhrijat'* means 'brought out,' *ukhrijat.* 'Exodus' means brought out. So no wonder that Muslims recognize that we also have Exodus. In order to join the Muslim life, the Muslim community, you also have to come out. Come out of Egypt! Come out of the world, to enter the community of al-Islam. The best community brought out. 'For what?,' God asks us—for the good of all people. For the good of all people."[36]

A written rendition of this statement loses some of its key aural characteristics and therefore its sound and meaning. Mohammed's transition from his commentary on "one community" to the celebration of "the best community" and to the idea of Exodus was seamless: there was no pause before "Exodus." By speaking live, he conflated the Qur'anic word *"ukhrijat"* with "Exodus" as though their correspondence was natural and commonsense. For him, in the Qur'an there was an indication of the idea of Exodus that resonated with African American interpretations of the biblical Exodus, which drew vital parallels between the collective suffering of the black people and the suffering of the biblical Hebrews. Had he been speaking to a more general audience, which included Muslims from outside his community, he might have explained that the Qur'anic *"ukhrijat"* was a linguistic sign for the concept of Exodus, and that the Exodus of the Israelites was but one example of the God-ordained process of bringing a community out of slavery, literal or otherwise. But, speaking to imams in his movement, he did not need to spell this out. By preaching, speaking live, and alluding to the meanings embedded in their vernacular, he made them hear his point.

Mohammed's exegesis of *"ukhrijat"* was ingenious. The only other prominent interpreter who also commented on this Qur'anic word was Sayyid Qutb.[37] A degree of similarity between Mohammed and Qutb may not be coincidental. Both exegetes engaged in a particular modern form of *tafsir,* which emphasized Qur'anic themes. And they both found in the Qur'anic *"ukhrijat"* the theme of God-ordained societal movement towards God-consciousness. For Qutb this particular word and passage presented an occasion to comment on the political message of the Qur'an and its relevance for contemporary Muslim activism. In this case he was following the logic of Mawdudi, who had influenced both him and Mohammed. Yet, Mohammed's weaving together of *"ukhrijat"* and the African American concept of Exodus was unique. It was also typical of his preaching throughout his life. In speech after speech, particularly since the early 1980s, he repeatedly drew parallels between the Qur'anic stories of Moses and the Israelites and the African American experience. In one early 1980s speech, for example, he declared, "We're like Israelites. . . . [And, like African-Americans in the United States,] Moses was like an adopted son in the house of the Pharaoh."[38]

In the Cleveland sermon, Mohammed used the word *"ukhrijat"* to draw contemporary lessons from the story—or, rather, the concept—of Exodus. He explained that the real meaning of Exodus was not about departing from a place but about moving toward a condition promised by God. This, he said, African Americans had not yet done: they had not yet "accepted that we are a legitimate part of this country entitled to a share of it like everyone else." And he illustrated his point by reminding his listeners of their shared history: "After I became a leader, I lifted the flag in respect, the American flag. And my picture was taken. [But the reaction was,] 'Hey, there is a crazy man!' Most of my own people didn't like it. I hadn't had a single political leader or church leader come and say we're proud of what you did. Why? Because most of them feel like they are on the outside too!"[39]

As he offered this recollection, his audience responded with murmurs of approval, which became particularly pronounced when he said, "most of them feel like they are on the outside." Riding this wave, he expanded upon his Qur'an-inspired interpretation of the role that African Americans and Muslims had to play in American life: "We're a minority in this country with a double job of establishing ourselves. . . . As a minority in America we have to start with a double concern: . . . one to establish ourselves, and one to complement America, to be a beautifying addition, a healthy addition . . . in this plural society we call America."[40]

Mohammed's reference to all American Muslims, and not just African Americans, was characteristic of his overall rhetoric. He presented his community's experiences as valuable for their immigrant and other coreligionists. In the 1980s it was one of the major themes of his speeches. In 1982, two years before Jesse Jackson's first presidential campaign, he openly mused that he might one day run for the office of the president of the United States. In a 1988 radio interview, which was meant for the general audience, he reminisced about that unofficial musing and reflected on deeper motivations behind it: "Our religion promotes democratic process. . . . In fact, our religion is a democracy. . . . Maybe I'll never be a president of the United States, but I don't think the country should overlook the fact that we have some unique kinds of mentality and personality and sensitivities in people here in America who used to be cut off from the American privileges, but now have grown with this country and have now become sensitive to the needs of the American people—and we are also Muslims."[41]

In later years he developed his interpretation of the *"ukhrijat"* further. In one of his last speeches, he translated this word not as "brought out" but as "evolved." This new iteration emphasized the organic connotation of this word: "evolved," he explained, "means [that] He [God] raised it up naturally. . . . He brought you out of nature. You are evolved upon the excellence of your nature."[42] In this later rendition of his exegesis, he again connected *"ukhrijat"* with "one community." While continuing to urge participation in public life, he also stressed broader implications of this concept. Public life, he taught in a 2007 address to students of the Sister Clara Muhammad School in Washington, D.C., developed in accordance with the pattern of human movement through life. To him it was based on the logic of nature, exemplified by the

Qur'an's depictions of the collectively harmonious life of animals, such as the bees in sura 16. Just as there was a God-ordained logic in the movement of nature, he explained, there was also a parallel logic in "the movement of Scripture": "Eventually, there is the public life. Streets to connect the smaller communities and businesses form great transportation and transportation systems. All of this evolves from human life. The needs that God has clocked into human life produce all that we see in man's life. If you lose those sacred bonds, you give yourself into slavery. We have come now to the unity of the family of man: that we all are the same creation. In science, if you want to study the human species, you have to accept, firstly, that the human species is one life or one creation."[43]

In the 2007 speech Mohammed was commenting on, without directly quoting, another Qur'anic verse that talks about community, Qur'an 16:120: *"inna ibrahima kana ummatan qanitan li-l-lahi hanifan,"* which Yusuf Ali translated as "Abraham was indeed a model devoutly obedient to Allah, (and) true in faith." Ali's translation skipped over the difficult phrase *"ibrahima kana ummatan,"* which literally means, "Ibrahim was a community." Mohammed revisited its literal meaning and found in it a message that spoke to African Americans as a people. For him, Ibrahim was indeed a community: like all scriptural characters, he was not a model for individuals only but for the people who strove to be faithful to the revelation and their divinely created nature.

···VII···

Like many preachers, Imam Mohammed did not just summarize or quote scriptural stories but retold and often reenacted them. In the second half of his 1987 speech, he acted out whole scenes from the Qur'anic story of Yusuf in sura 12. His voice became tender when he spoke about the anguish of Joseph's father, whose son was tricked by his devious brothers and left abandoned in a well, to be eventually sold into slavery. At another point his audience responded with roars of laughter when he mimicked the voices of maidens enamored with Yusuf—he was, after all, a man of unsurpassed natural beauty. It was at this moment, as he relaxed the senses of his listeners through a hearty joke, that he stopped, waited for them to quiet down, and then reminded them that Joseph, a prisoner and slave, stood accused of the crime of "wanting what the big man wanted"—that he was accused of a sexual transgression against his master's wife. Before this moment of comic relief—which Mohammed immediately followed by a rhetorical strike to the solar plexus of the African American collective memory—he had set up his retelling of Yusuf's story: he recited in Arabic, and then translated the Qur'an's insistence that Joseph and his brothers were signs for those who seek answers (Qur'an 12:6). He explained that he was relating this story and interpreting its signs "for the interest of the leadership . . . and the future of Muslims in America."[44]

The serious purpose of the sermon's humorous features was to relax and therefore open and prepare his listeners to hear his central message—that, through the story of Yusuf, the Qur'an was speaking to them about their "true nature" and redemption. After all, as he explained in a 2008 speech, "one of the meanings of redeem is 'to get back'" to one's true nature.[45] Mohammed's style of disarming his audience with a joke and then delivering a serious punch was characteristic of his art of preaching. In speech after speech, he used this move to shape the Qur'an-based language of African American Muslims. Its effectiveness was subtle but powerful. He did not explain what was too difficult to explain. Rather, through a joke and a poke, he made it possible for his listeners to become open to hearing the Qur'an.

Another key instant in his retelling of Joseph's story occurred when he once again highlighted the redemptive quality of the Arabic Qur'an. He did so by interpreting the word *"ghayaba"* in the first part of Qur'an 12:15, which depicts the moment when Yusuf's brothers threw him into the well:

> But before his imprisonment in Egypt, they had put him in the hole. Right? And according to the words of God, the hole was without water. And empty. And they put him in the lowest depths of the hole. And the term that's used in the Qur'an is *"ghayabati-l-jubb,"* *"ghayabati-l-jubb."* And the word *"ghayaba"* is from also *"ghaib,"* which means "unseen"—unseen, not manifest, not existing presently. So they put him in something that wasn't seen. They put him to a test, when he could not see what was there. Uhm? What was there was absence: the bottomless pit. The bottomless pit. Now, if you ain't got no bottom, you can't see no bottom, you can't see the foundation. Ah? So they put him in the hole, and the depth to which they put him is called *"ghayaba,"* *"ghayaba,"* *"ghayaba"*—meaning, where, that it was at that point, where things are so mystified, things are so indefinite that nothing can be visualized, nothing can be defined. Nothing is really present. The foundation is in the future. Ah?[46]

Once again, a transcription of an oral uttering fails to convey the sounds that infuse it with meaning. What does not come across in the printed iteration of Imam Mohammed's exegesis is significant. He pronounced the Arabic phrase *"ghayabati al-jubb"* with the emphasis on the double "b" at the end. In this way he followed the standard rules of Arabic pronunciation. But then in a way that provided an acoustic correlation between Arabic and English sounds, he pronounced his translation—"the bottomless pit"—with a playful double "t." In his rendition, Joseph was thrown not into a "pit" but into a "piᴛᴛ!" Sound was an important dimension of meaning in his cultural translation of the Qur'an. It was a vital element of his spoken Qur'an. What a transcription can imitate, however, is how he kept interjecting his sentences with "Right?" and "Uhm?" and "Ah?" He peppered all his speeches with such interjections. They emphasized his key points. Embodied in this function, however, was yet another and deeper purpose: through his "ahs" and "uhms" and "rights," he continuously called on his listeners to engage in a dialogical call-and-response with the Qur'an and with him as its speaker.

In the rest of the sermon, Mohammed built on his definition of the word "*ghayaba.*" By bringing up the image of the bottomless pit, he articulated the Qur'an as a scripture that addressed the collective memory of his audience, as the people who had been denied freedom. And, as he continued to retell sura 12, he connected the Qur'anic sign of "the bottomless pit" with Qur'an 12:21, which he quoted in Arabic, translated into English, and then commented upon. Again, sound was important here. Or rather, in this particular uttering, crucial were his pauses and intonations, which I note in brackets and italics: "And also God says of him [Joseph], he says, '*wa li-nu'allimahu min ta'wil al-ahadith*'—'and that We may teach him' *[long pause]* the mystery *[long pause]*, 'the mysterious interpretation of some of the great reports, *ahadith*' [plural form of the word *hadith*]. Praise be to Allah *[quick pause].* Now, I was talking on the interpretation of the Qur'an once and some of my, eh, learned elder, he said, 'you're reading the Qur'an wrong, brother imam: "no one knows the *ta'wil* except Allah"' *[long pause].* Well *[short pause]*, God says that He taught Yusuf *[short pause]* some of the '*ta'wil al-ahadith*'! *[long pause filled with the listeners' laughter].* We know that only Allah knows it but He doesn't keep it to Himself, He gives it to whomsoever He wills."[47]

Perhaps the most significant pauses in this passage were before and after the word "mystery," which Mohammed pronounced mysteriously. The sound of his silence conjured a sense of the transformative realm of the God-ordained unknown, the "*ghayaba,*" or "the bottomless piᴛᴛ." This was the place where his lecture's two major themes, redemption and nature, intertwined. These were the ideas behind his presentation of Joseph as a scriptural sign for the African American people, which he made explicit within the next few minutes. African American collective suffering, he insisted, had a parallel in the Qur'an. Like Joseph, he said, they were once "cast off, considered to be worthless." And just as God lifted up Joseph, God was looking out for African Americans as well. What connected their stories was suffering. But suffering alone was not enough. To be redemptive, it had to be endured purposefully, which, in Imam Mohammed's *tafsir,* meant staying true to one's nature. "And [Joseph] was tested, wasn't he?" he asked. "But they couldn't take him away from his home. They couldn't take Joseph away from his home."[48] Joseph's home, he explained, was his God-created human nature. It was a spiritual, rather than a physical, home. As his audience surely remembered, people could be stolen away from their families and sold into slavery, or thrown in jail. But as long as they remained conscious of God and truthful to their nature, they would be ultimately saved.

There was another lesson in Mohammed's retelling of Yusuf's story. One can hear it in the hypothetical but surely based-on-experience exchange between him and his "learned elder." Of course, before saying, "learned elder," he paused briefly, filling the moment not with silence, but with an "eh." And then, as he often did while preparing a serious punch, he made his listeners laugh. All of a sudden, while retelling another Muslim authority's words, he began to speak with a heavy Egyptian accent: "you're reading the Qur'an wrong, brother imam: 'no one knows the *ta'wil* except Allah.'" Through this light-sounding note, Mohammed addressed two serious matters, both of which had to do with *ta'wil*, a term for a mystical type of interpretation of divine signs, which Joseph, the Qur'an says, was naturally able to perform.

No one can imitate an accent without extended exposure to its sounds. Mohammed's ability to reproduce a particular Arabic accent—and not some generic, Hollywood-style simulation—reflected the fact that he knew and was friends with many Arabic-speaking Muslims in the United States and abroad (Muhammad Abdul Rauf, whom I mentioned in chapter 1, was among his close personal friends). The Egyptian "elder" who corrected Mohammed was also likely a friend: he called him a "brother." The appraisal this "brother" offered—"you're reading the Qur'an wrong"—was fairly typical among Imam Mohammed's immigrant and foreign observers. Most of them pronounced it with the best intentions, as brotherly advice. Yet, it was a strike to the very core of this African American leader's authority, which was based on his ability to interpret the Qur'an for his people.

What made Mohammed's response to this challenge particularly delicate was that he himself, through sermons and personal example, encouraged his community to learn from other Muslim authorities. Many of his students followed this suggestion. Islam, after all, is a transnational religion and its preeminent centers of learning, such as the Egyptian al-Azhar Seminary, are located abroad. This reality, however, often produces a perception, shared by many in the American Muslim community, that foreign authorities are somehow more authentic and their voices more central. Because of the delicate nature of this dynamic, Mohammed delivered his response informally. He did not spell out what I just explained. Rather, through a joke, he relegated the foreign critic to the margins of his community's religious discourses. In this sermon and for that particular audience, it was Imam Mohammed who came to occupy the center of the learned Muslim dialogical space—because he spoke the Qur'an fluently, in their language, while his Egyptian "brother," with his heavy accent, appeared out of place.

There was, however, yet another and deeper connotation in his reply. In this humorous interjection, he delved into one of the Qur'an's most difficult passages, Qur'an 3:7, which, in Yusuf Ali's translation, states, "He it is Who has sent down to thee the Book: in it are verses basic or fundamental (of established meaning); they are the foundation of the Book: others are not of well-established meaning. But those in whose hearts is perversity follow the part thereof that is not of well-established meaning. Seeking discord, and searching for its interpretation, but no one knows its true meanings except Allah, and those who are firmly grounded in knowledge say: 'We believe in it; the whole of it is from our Lord; and none will grasp the Message except men of understanding.'"

Throughout the centuries this verse has fueled numerous arguments, which boil down to the question about the limits of the human understanding of God's revelation. For the Qur'an's interpreters, key in this passage have been two words and a pause. The words are *"muhkamat,"* which Ali translated as "basic or fundamental," and *"mutashabihat,"* which he rendered as "not of well-established meaning." Both of them are understood as describing two categories of the Qur'an's phrases: *"muhkamat"* designates expressions whose meanings are easily accessible; *"mutashabihat"* is a word that stands for the scripture's mysterious signs. And here lies the central dilemma of the Qur'an or any other divine revelation: who can access its mysteries and how can they do it? What, for example, is the meaning of "God is the light" in Qur'an 24:35? Yet, before answering this question, exegetes have had to deal with a more immediate problem: where do the phrases in Qur'an 3:7 begin, and where do they end? Without this important detail, any uttering, divine or human, is not clear. This is why the question of the pause in this verse is crucial. The written Arabic text of the Qur'an, however, does not answer it: it has no commas or periods. By itself it does not signal whether or not there is a pause between "no one knows its true meaning except Allah" and "and those who are firmly grounded in knowledge."

This conundrum stems from the fact that the Qur'an was—and is—a re-cited, oral text. The breaks between its phrases were—and still are—determined by various traditions of recitation. Its earliest manuscripts had no marks guiding its pronunciation; later manuscripts and printed editions have used elocutionary symbols derived from different schools of recitation. In modern printed English translations, interpreters who think that there is a stop between "except Allah" and "and those" designate it with a period. This definitive punctuation means, as the Imam Mohammed's Egyptian "elder" and many other Muslim authorities maintain, that "no one knows the *ta'wil* except Allah." Period. End of discussion. But other Muslim interpreters have heard the Qur'an differently. Their traditions of recitation do not have a pause between "except Allah" and "and those." Such traditions of reciting and hearing the Qur'an, which conflate the two phrases into a single uttering, authorize *ta'wil*, the mystical type of interpretation.

Yusuf Ali, of course, marked this contested space with a comma, a tentative pause. In this way, he elegantly and subtly walked between two opposing camps of the Qur'an's interpreters. Had he used a period, he would have sided with one camp. Had he used no punctuation mark at all, he would have signaled his belonging to another. His comma was a compromise: it allowed both sides of the exegetical conflict to see in his printed translation a representation of their view. At the same time it was also likely an understated expression of his exegetical opinion. By using a comma and not a period, he avoided limiting the naturally polyvocal quality of this passage and thus hinted that mystical exegesis was indeed possible—for select people, those "who are firmly grounded in knowledge." Punctuation, with its commas and periods, is a distinct tool of the modern technology of print. And Ali, it seems, was using the tools at his disposal to perform a delicate, almost surgical, exegetical move.

Mohammed's interpretation was just as elegant. Because he delivered it as live speech, an informal-sounding dialogue with his students, he was able to utilize the power of spoken language, which, if it is shared, enables its participants to complete each other's phrases. As a preacher, he made use of allusions. His spoken exegesis resonated with his audience because he spoke their language and because many of them learned how to decipher his connotations by hearing him speak and discussing his speeches year after year. Like Yusuf Ali's, his exegesis was subtle. He chose to engage with the central controversy of the Qur'anic exegesis by telling a humorous anecdote. Yet, for those who were meant to hear it, his lesson was powerfully direct. Through Joseph's example he answered the centuries-old Muslim debate about the possibility of mystical interpretations. His answer was simple: *ta'wil*, the inspired type of exegesis, was real in the Qur'anic narrative of Yusuf. His obvious allusion, which he did not need to spell out, was that it was also a historical fact. Based on everything else he had said in this and other sermons, at least some of his listeners, perhaps a select few, were prepared to hear what he was implying. They knew that God's intervention was real. Their collective memory, embodied in their and their preacher's language, told them that African Americans were uniquely chosen participants in the divinely guided human history. Otherwise, their experience of slavery and their trials in postslavery America would be inexplicable. Their perseverance of suffering made them, as a people, unique; it gave them distinct sensibilities. They heard Imam Mohammed telling them that they were like Joseph. They felt that the Qur'an was speaking to them through Yusuf. And some of them must have also heard a particularly controversial element of their teacher's message, which he made sure not to say in a way that could be quoted and therefore misunderstood: do not be surprised if a black man, whom many "cast off" and dismiss, is inspired to understand God's mysterious signs.

Allusion is a powerful preaching tool, which Mohammed used often. Recurring in his sermons were allusions to his ability to understand the Qur'an and the Bible. Echoing his interpretation of Joseph's story, he often implied that this ability was at once unique and natural. The word through which he signaled this correlation was "innocence." In his oral *tafsir* the words "innocence" and "innocent" were often related to the state of being uncorrupted by the oppressive environment and remaining connected to one's *fitra*, to the natural human disposition toward following the divine path.[49] In the 1987 sermon he spoke about the innocence of Joseph, which was to him Yusuf's truly unique quality. The preservation and cultivation of that innocence was Joseph's strength. Despite being thrown into the "bottomless pit," sold into slavery, and imprisoned, he survived and retained the ability to understand God's signs.

In another speech, at Harlem's Apollo Theater in 2003, Mohammed explained that such natural innocence was also the force behind his own ability to understand the scripture. On that occasion, addressing an audience of Christian and Muslim African Americans, he offered a prolonged biblical exegesis, which he tied to his interpretation of the Qur'an. Then, using a peculiar trait of oral communication that is prominent in the Qur'an, he referred to himself in the third person and said:

> Don't forget that this man is an excellent student of the Bible *[audience reacts: applause from some Christians and Muslims, and "allahu akbar," a Muslim equivalent of applause, from some Muslims]* and in the discussion of the Bible and its wisdom, et cetera, are bar none *[laughter, applause]*. I am not intimidated by the Pope of Rome, or the President or the Bishop of the Baptist Conference, or what you call it?—the Baptist National Convention. None of them make me feel uncomfortable. In fact, I can go to sleep and they wake me up and I will continue the conversation *[laughter]*. Yeh. Not bragging! Not bragging! But I've studied diligently and for a long many years and I thank God—God preserved my innocence, my truthfulness. And I was not selfish. I was not reading the Bible to prove something for myself or to disprove something against somebody else. I read it just to know. I didn't have any prejudices or anything. And God has blessed me with more than most Christian leaders have. I assure you of that. And why shouldn't He bless me? I do believe in divine intervention! And Mister Fard was divine intervention. Elijah Muhammad, his able spokesperson, divine intervention. Malcolm X—my old friend and the father of this wonderful girl over there *[one of Malcolm X's daughters was in the audience]*—divine intervention.

Yes. The Civil Rights Movement, Rosa Parks, Dr. King taking up the cause—divine intervention. So I believe in divine intervention. Yes. Wallace D. Mohammed, breaking the lifeline of the Honorable Elijah Muhammad and Mister Fard, cutting you off, cutting the umbilical cord so that you can live again *[applause]*—divine intervention! Yes! So I believe in the divine intervention. So why shouldn't God then— if I believe that Wallace Deen Mohammed is the divine intervention and He has prepared me to teach you Islam, the Qur'an and the way of our Prophet, prayers and peace be upon him: I live in a pre-dominantly Christian society, my neighbors are Christian and it's a Christian public listening, or they will hear it later. And whatever we do in this society, we do it amidst the Christians, on their block, in their neighborhood. So you think God wouldn't prepare me to also understand and speak with Christians and help you to live better with your Christian neighbors? Yes. So God had to educate me both in Christianity and Islam in order for me to serve His cause here in America *[applause]*. And I will never be big headed! If I come swollen-headed, if I get an ego, it's a curse of God on me. It ain't my nature. Ain't nothing in me want that. Nothing in me wanna be big shot. Nothing in me wants to be seen. I don't want to be seen. I want you to see what you need to see to help your life! Not me as a person. Not me. I'm happy not to be seen! . . . And because of that, I think that's why God has made me the leader of these people that's going to change the world *[applause and a pause]*. I shouldn't have said "finish changing the world." Because from the moment that they picked us up and singled us out for abuses, I think we were already being an influence for changing the world. Yes, for changing all the world![50]

In introducing Mohammed's 1987 speech, I mentioned that it took place at a time of crisis, the negative conclusion of a major legal proceeding. At the end of the sermon, after he had delineated his interpretive authority and commented on Joseph's God-inspired *ta'wil,* he delivered his concluding remarks. Mindful that his listeners had a shared concern, he made sure to answer their question preemptively: how should they deal with their current predicament? His message, as always, came from the Qur'an. He reminded them that their scripture communicated the story of Joseph for a specific group of people, for those who "seek answers." Joseph's story, then, was a model for his community who, like Joseph, were facing trials and tribulations. And so he preached on:

> Now, looking at Joseph's situation God says He "taught him the mysterious interpretation of some of the great reports." And God, behind

that, He says that God takes charge over His command. He will not leave His orders and commands to others! What does He mean by that? God will not leave the circumstances and commands that He himself has charge over, has given Himself to, he Has pledged Himself to. He has pledged Himself to looking over those things. He will not leave those things to men of the world [*brief pause, then proceeding in a rapid tempo*]: That's telling the wile, that's telling the imperialist, that's telling dictators, that's telling the world powers that God will not accept that you suppress the urges that He put in His creature, to put him in his full life and his full existence. Those that are inclined to be in accord with God's will, He himself will look after them. And if you try to imprison them, He will break that situation. If you try to imprison their mind, He will break that situation. If you try to deceive their instincts, He will break that situation! No matter how much knowledge you get of science and the manipulation of human life, the science and psychology—no you can't come up with nothing that God has not already devised a scheme that will overcome it. Yeh, that's what Allah is telling!

This was the high note of the sermon, which Imam Mohammed ended abruptly with yet another reminder. He returned once again to Qur'an 3:110, which he recited in Arabic and then translated: "you are the best community brought out for the good of all people, commanding by the highest standards and prohibiting all that is offensive and believing in God."[51]

···VIII···

Mohammed's rendition of the Qur'anic story of Yusuf made it African American. His preaching belonged to the tradition of African American religious rhetoric. Like other black preachers, he wove the collective memory of his people into the scriptural narratives he spoke. His Christian counterparts developed the tradition of the African American spoken Bible. In conversation with his listeners and many other American Muslims, he participated in the ongoing process of the shaping of an American spoken Qur'an.

One of the best collections of African American Christian sermons is Cleophus A. LaRue's *The Heart of Black Preaching*. Among its many samples, which parallel Imam Mohammed's technique of enabling scriptural stories to speak in the African American vernacular, is an early 1990s sermon by Reverend Jeremiah A. Wright Jr., a contemporary of Mohammed, who became famous in the late 2000s as Barak Obama's Chicago-based pastor. That sermon, which Wright entitled "What Makes You So Strong?," sounded similar to Mohammed's retelling of the Qur'anic story of Yusuf: it was a rendition of the biblical story of Samson. Wright presented Samson as a biblical personality, whose qualities were a sign for African Americans. Samson's strength, like the strength of the black people, was inspired by God. It was shaped through suffering. But it was not suffering per se that made Samson strong. It was his perseverance and endurance of suffering. In Wright's articulation, divinely guided endurance was a badge of African American discipleship and the path toward their redemption.[52]

Mohammed's Cleveland sermon carried out a parallel retelling and drew analogous conclusions. Yet, what it did was also distinct. An important feature of his oral *tafsir* was his style of engaging with the Arabic Qur'an, which made use of its polysemy. After all, as I have implied, what makes a preacher effective is her or his ability to bring up different shades of scriptural meanings, which resonate with their listeners in particular moments of their lives. For the community of Imam Mohammed, what resonated was his ability to make the Qur'an speak to African Americans as a people. That was the reason why he stressed that Yusuf was a sign for African American hearers of the Qur'an. And that is why he emphasized that Ibrahim was indeed an *umma*. By speaking the Qur'an with African American emphases and intonations, he made it come alive for those who heard him. He did what the Qur'an itself calls on its listeners to do: he responded to its invitation to engage in a dialogic communication with the revelation. Of course, such dialogue is possible only when humans and their communities speak from their own memory and their own, ever-changing, and very specific circumstances.

The strength of Mohammed's preaching is evident in the responses of his audiences, and the extent to which, through several decades, many of them held on to his unique message. The following analysis of a particular example highlights the perseverance and unique characteristics of W. D. Mohammed's tradition of speaking Qur'an.

···IX···

Friday, May 22, 2009, was unusual. The ordinarily quiet parking lot in front of the As-Salaam Islamic Center in Raleigh transformed into a mini-bazaar. The typical Friday gathering of some forty people swelled to almost a hundred. The reason for the change was a visiting *khatib*, Imam Faheem Shuaibe. The congregation's leader, Imam Oliver Muhammad, introduced Shuaibe to his community as a "person who needs no introduction." He later told me that Shuaibe was known as one of the "first-row students of Imam Warith Deen Mohammed." In May 2009 Shuaibe was on a speaking tour of the United States. The mosques, such as the one in Raleigh, invited him to speak at a critical juncture in the history of their movement: their leader had passed away less than a year before, and the community throughout the country was struggling with questions of authority, including their interpretive authority. There was, of course, an additional element of crisis: it was also the time of an economic depression, and many people in this middle-class congregation were losing, or afraid of losing, their jobs and homes. Over the festive atmosphere of their Friday gathering—which included a "Fry-day" cookout with the best fried catfish I ever tasted—hovered a cloud of distress.

Shuaibe's mission during the tour was related to his status as a "first-row" student of Imam Mohammed. For at least thirty years, he had served as one of the premier exponents of his leader's teachings. For example, in the 1990s he published a series of brochures that defended Mohammed's interpretations of the Qur'an from attacks by some African American, immigrant, and foreign-based critics, whom Shuaibe described as "Salafi."[53] I heard about these brochures in my research in North Carolina and in California's Bay Area, where I interviewed students of Hamza Yusuf and Zaid Shakir, some of whom spoke highly of Shuaibe as a prominent local leader. In the late 2000s his presence was prolific on the websites affiliated with W. D. Mohammed's leadership, such as www.newafricaradio.com. His base was in Oakland, California, where he served as the imam of Masjid Waritheen and director of the Mohammed Schools of Oakland.

At least two other details distinguished Imam Shuaibe. The first—and, as my conversation partners in W. D. Mohammed's community often stressed, minor detail—was that his predecessor at the Oakland mosque was a person known as "Mr. Muhammad Abdullah." Many, including Shuaibe, believed that Mr. Abdullah was none other than Fard Muhammad, the founder of the Nation of Islam. Apparently W. D. Mohammed never confirmed Mr. Abdullah's identity publicly. Shuaibe recalled in one of our conversations that Imam Mohammed had introduced this man once in the 1990s to a large gathering in Los Angeles. While speaking from a stage, he invited Mr. Abdullah to come next to him and said, "This man is not that man."[54] Shuaibe's take on this phrase was indicative of the discipline of interpretation Imam Mohammed had instilled in his listeners. For Imam Shuaibe, it meant that his teacher did not deny the "material reality" of Mr. Abdullah being the same person as Fard Muhammad. Yet, he emphasized that the mind of "this man" was different from the mind of "that man," of Fard Muhammad in the early years of the Nation—because, like most members of the movement, Mr. Abdullah/Professor Fard changed through the teachings of W. D. Mohammed.

The second detail is more important. People inside and outside of W. D. Mohammed's community, those who knew about Shuaibe and spoke highly of him, emphasized to me his reputation as a Muslim scholar actively involved in dialogue with Muslim authorities outside the movement.[55] During his *khutba* at the Raleigh mosque, he relied on this reputation. This came across in the friendly explanations that several people in the audience offered to me as we milled around in the mosque's lobby and its parking lot after the prayer: "He is one of our scholars," "He teaches well," and "If you want to learn about Imam Mohammed, listen to Imam Shuaibe." Some also added that the future of the movement was ensured by the work of people like Shuaibe, who "carry on the tradition." One key aspect in the continuation of this tradition was in how its adherents negotiated their unique religious articulations within the dialogical space they shared with competing American and international Muslim discourses. Here, of paramount importance was their connection to the Qur'an and their distinctive discipline of its interpretation.

Shuaibe began his *khutba* with a Qur'anic passage, verse 40 from sura 9 (*"al-tawba,"* or "Repentance"). His sermon was a meditation on this verse, which he presented as speaking directly to African Americans in any situation, including the time after the passing of their teacher. His choice of sura *al-Tawba* was significant. Many Muslim exegetes regard it as the last revealed sura of the Qur'an. In addition, his selection of verse 40 was particularly relevant in the context of his sermon, because in it the Qur'an addressed the memory of its first community of listeners: it spoke directly to the companions of the Prophet Muhammad and reminded them about an episode from their short history—the story of the Prophet and one of his close followers, Abu Bakr, fleeing from Mecca toward Medina to escape the persecution of their Meccan foes. At one point in their journey, the two fugitives were about to be caught by a Meccan posse, which included experienced trackers, who were hunting after the runaways by tracing their footprints. The fugitives hid in a cave. By a miracle of God, the pursuers did not enter that sanctuary, and the Prophet and his companion were saved.

By choosing to speak from this passage, Shuaibe attempted to interweave this Qur'anic memory—as the Qur'an had once told it to its first associates—with the memory of the "associates of Imam W. D. Mohammed." He recited Qur'an 9:40 in Arabic and then provided his own translation. Or rather, in the style of Imam Mohammed, his translation was an interpretative rendering of Yusuf Ali's translation.[56] He continued,

> Just a general translation: "If you don't help, surely Allah helped him when he was driven out by the unbelievers being one among the two, being the second of two, when the two were in the cave, when he said to his companion, 'don't fear'—or actually—'don't grieve, surely Allah is with us.' And Allah sent down upon him tranquility and security and strengthened him by forces you did not see. And Allah made the word of those who reject *as-sufla'*—"He humbled it," "He lowered it."[57]

Shuaibe's "or actually" was his corrective interjection into a foreign authority's interpretation of the Qur'an. It set the tone for the rest of his sermon. He used Ali's translation as a basis for his message. It was a convenient choice: his audience, following W. D. Mohammed's instructions, had been reading Ali's text since the late 1970s. But Shuaibe, like his teacher, immediately signaled that he was speaking directly from the Arabic Qur'an. The Qur'an emerged here as a text of his community, whose interpretation had to be done by them.

To underscore this point, Shuaibe immediately confirmed that this verse was part of the ritual and speaking practice of the congregation he was addressing. "You can make this connection right away," he told them, repeating in Arabic a phrase from another Qur'anic sura, "*thumma raddadnahu asfala safilin'*—diminished it, right?" Through this move, without translation, he connected his interpretation of the word *"as-sufla"* in Qur'an 9:40 to Qur'an 95:5, which Yusuf Ali translated as, "Then do We abase him (to be) the lowest of the low."

Sura 95 is one of the Qur'an's shortest chapters. Because it is short, it is often recited in prayer and meditation. Therefore, for the audience at the Raleigh mosque, as for most practicing Muslims, Shuaibe's Qur'anic quote required no translation. His act of skipping translation had a didactic purpose: it prompted his listeners to begin engaging directly with his exegesis of the Arabic Qur'an, based on their own Qur'anic memory. His allusion to Qur'an 95 was additionally pertinent because this particular sura had been central in the oral *tafsir* of his and his listeners' teacher. Imam Mohammed's preferred way of interpreting the Qur'an was by the Qur'an itself, and Qur'an 95 featured prominently in his interpretations of other Qur'anic passages.[58]

Subtler still was Shuaibe's attempt to follow W. D. Mohammed's technique of relating the sound of the Arabic Qur'an to the everyday words and experiences of his African American audience. In Mohammed's 1987 sermon it came across in his rendering of the phrase "bottomless pit" as a "bottomless pɪᴛᴛ!," which sounded like the Arabic *"jubb."* In the Raleigh *khutba*, Shuaibe did something similar right after he had offered his translation of the phrase in 9:40 that contains the word *"as-sufla."* His technical translation of this passage, which in Arabic reads, *"wa ja'ala kalimata alladhina kafaru as-sufla,"* was, "And Allah made the word of those who reject *as-sufla.*" Then he added an explanation: "He [God] humbled it, He lowered it." To provide a cultural translation, however, he brought up an example from the run-of-the-mill experience of his listeners, especially, he said, "the sisters." (About 60 percent of the people in his audience that day were women.) "Do you hear?" he asked, "What does the word '*sufla*' sound like?—Soufflé!"

Through this acoustic resonance between similar-sounding but unrelated words, Shuaibe made the first subtle move toward the exegetical lesson of his sermon, which had to do with fear. What does it mean that God made the "the word of those who reject [the revelation] *as-sufla*"? This means, he explained, that it had become like a soufflé. And, "when you prepare soufflé, what is one thing you fear? Falling! One breath—puff, it's gone!" Later in the sermon he would remind his listeners about what the Qur'an and W. D. Mohammed had said: "Adam was made from sounding clay. It wasn't just clay; it was sounding clay. Meaning that part of the nature of Adam is how he relates to sound. Ah?"[59]

Shuaibe's technique of conveying scriptural meanings through sound followed an African American tradition of preaching.[60] In the Raleigh sermon, as in many of his other speeches, he added to it an interpretation through etymology of words. In this respect he was also moving along the trajectory charted by other figures who shared the legacy of the Nation of Islam. In the Nation a classic example of a similar rhetorical practice, which went beyond scripture, was Malcolm X's explanation of the word "negro," which he deciphered as being derived from the Greek word *"nekros"* or "a dead body."[61] The Nation's religious teachings, he stipulated, were meant to resurrect the "dead body" of the African American people for a new life. W. D. Mohammed also used the word "negro" in a way that was similar to Malcolm X's explanation. In the 1987 sermon this word connoted a black person who had not yet discovered his or her true nature. That true nature was *muslim*—as in any person who submits to God and not necessarily "Muslim" as an identity marker. Another example, which some of my conversation partners in W. D. Mohamed's community brought up, was his play with the sound of the name of the Qur'anic Adam. What does "Adam" sound like? Mohammed answered that it sounds like "atom" and taught that, in nature, the atom is the basic building block for everything else, which contains the potential for everything else. In his *tafsir*, the Qur'anic Adam was the symbol for the human potential inherent in every human being.[62]

Shuaibe structured his Raleigh *khutba* as a dialogical progression toward its rhetorical peak. He climbed the mount of his sermon together with his audience and used the Qur'an to mark their path. Each step he took, each of the sermon's transitional points, was demarcated by yet another Qur'anic signpost. And as he spoke, he intertwined the Qur'an with references—more often implicit than obvious—to the collective memory of his listeners. Central here was the story of the Prophet Muhammad and Abu Bakr's miraculous escape from the Meccan posse.

After reciting and translating Qur'an 9:40, he acknowledged, "you all surely know this story," and explained that, while preparing the sermon, he had consulted some sources: *The Life of Muhammad* by the Egyptian writer Muhammad Husayn Haykal, Mawdudi's *tafsir*, and the classic biography of the Prophet Muhammad by Muhammad ibn Ishaq, an eighth-century Iraqi scholar. He said that these and many other sources depicted the moment of the Prophet and Abu Bakr's miraculous salvation in the cave as "the turning point, the key moment" in the history of Muslims. Had the Prophet and Abu

Bakr been captured and killed, the history would certainly be different. "Of course," Shuaibe immediately affirmed, "Allah wouldn't allow this." But, at the moment when the two runaways were hiding in their cave, the danger they faced looked very real. To underscore this peril, Shuaibe reminded his listeners that the Meccan trackers, who were pursuing Muhammad and Abu Bakr, were "professionals—these guys don't miss!" And so they tracked the trail, left by the Messenger of God and the person who would become the first caliph, to the entrance of the cave where the two were hiding.

This, Shuaibe remarked, was where Yusuf Ali's translation failed. The Arabic Qur'an records the words of assurance, which the Prophet had offered to Abu Bakr, as *"la tahzan."* Ali interpreted this phrase as "don't fear." Shuaibe, however, stressed that this Qur'anic phrase must be translated in the way closest to its plain Arabic meaning: "don't grieve." This interpretation was informed by a contextual approach to the Qur'an. Shuaibe explained this by reminding his audience that the situation the Prophet and Abu Bakr had been facing was so dire that Abu Bakr "was like 'it's over now!'" He continued, "It wasn't just like fear. It was like—'oh, man, it's over now!' What the Qur'anic word means is that, in Abu Bakr's mind, the situation was already resolved—they were already caught, there was no way for them to be rescued. And [that is] when the Prophet said, *'la tahzan inna allaha ma'ana!'*— don't grieve surely Allah is with us!"

Of course, this Shuaibe's audience knew the outcome of this narrative well: God had protected the two refugees by inspiring a bird to build a nest at the entrance to the cave and a spider to weave a web over it. The trackers thought that surely such things could not happen overnight and decided not to enter the cavern. For his listeners, at that particular time in their lives, Shuaibe brought up an additional meaning of this story. Alluding to the crisis in the movement and explicitly commenting on the economic crisis in the country, which threatened many African Americans in Raleigh, he preached in a loud staccato: "That has to become your regular equipment in life! Whenever you think, 'oh, it's over now! They're gonna take away my house!'—*la tahzan!* Don't fear! Surely God is with you!" But then he paused, waited to hear his community's quiet attention, and said in a low voice, "Now, you gotta be innocent now."

By preaching the concept of innocence, Shuaibe engaged a powerful trope from W. D. Mohammed's rhetoric, which time and again reminded his people that, through the revelation, God spoke directly to them and that, no matter how difficult their circumstances, they would be saved as long as they were with God. Shuaibe continued to speak in this tradition as he went on with his sermon. He preached that, if people in his community wanted to remain true to God, they should strive to heed the words of the Qur'an and the Prophet Muhammad: "don't grieve, surely Allah is with us." Like Abu Bakr, they should neither grieve nor fear—even when their teacher had just passed away and even as agents of predatory banks were about to enter their homes and take away their families' places of refuge.[63] "If you're in Allah's plan," he reminded them, "you're in Allah's hands."

But how would the hearers of the Qur'an at the Raleigh mosque know that they were in God's hands? Shuaibe formulated his answer through yet another Qur'anic citation, aided, once again, by Yusuf Ali's translation:

> Allah has a project, an assignment for us—*wa-l-takun minkum ummatun*—Let there arise out of you a band of people inviting to all that is good. . . .[64] Our job is to build an *umma* and a *jumu'a* [a Friday congregation] is not an *umma*. . . . Until you look like the Chinese or Koreans look in Chinatown or Korea town, until you look like the Hispanics look in their location, until we, as Muslims, look like they look, we don't have *umma*. Ah? Until I walk out of my house and I don't have to go to no other school but my school, and when I leave school, when I go into a corporation, I go into a business, I go into a business with the support of my community. Ah? When I go to get my clothes clean, I hear the person at the register say '*as-salamu 'alaykum*.' *[The audience reacts with* 'allahu akbar!'*]* When I go to the gas station, when I go to the theater, the movies that I see, when I go to a bookstore, the books that I open up, when I hear the songs on my radio station, and I see the programs on my television station—Now we're talking *umma!* Until then, we're just renters in this situation. . . . But that's Allah's project, Allah wants Muslims to have that. He don't need that. We need that! "*wa-l-takun minkum ummatun*" [literally, "and let there be among them a community"]—you and I be an *umma!*

My, or any, transcription of this passage fails to convey the rises and quells in the volume and tempo of the preacher's delivery. This passage was one of the high moments in the sermon, which became audible when his phrasing became rapid and his voice, projected from a classroom-style podium, rose and swept across the men sitting on the floor in the front of the prayer space and women sitting on chairs behind them. Shuaibe punctuated his sequences of high-volume and elongated sentences through meaningful pauses. He stopped for a second before his quietly interrogative "ahs." Immediately after the second "ah," he almost shouted: "Now we are talking *umma!*" His pauses highlighted the words "*umma*" and "community." What gave strength to the sound, style and substance of his speaking was the long tradition of African American Christian and Muslim preaching, with its characteristic stress on community uplift. After this passage, quite suddenly and to give yet another acoustic sign of transition, he paused once again, looked around the room, and then proceeded to teach in a low voice, in a manner that was distinctly slow and methodical.

Shuaibe's rhythm of preaching reflected his training in W. D. Mohammed's school of rhetoric. His teacher would do something very similar in many of his speeches. He would typically start his lectures by speaking slowly, in a low voice. He would raise the tempo of his delivery several times in a sermon, with each high note marking a key point in his commentary on the revelation and African American life. Then, abruptly, he would make sure to slow down again. And he would always conclude on a quiet, contemplative note. Both preachers' styles were undoubtedly influenced by the African American Christian tradition of preaching. It was also in line with the oratorical legacy of the Nation of Islam. Elijah Muhammad and W. D. Mohammed spoke more like teachers than preachers. Through this distinction their preaching rhetorically enacted the message of Professor Fard Muhammad. The fiery style of preaching was too Christian for the people who had converted out of Christianity. Their mode of public speaking was deliberately lecture-like; it was their way of speaking as Muslims.

In the Raleigh sermon, Shuaibe followed this trajectory of his community's tradition. And although for a few moments he sounded like a fiery preacher, he made sure to quickly slow down and begin to speak, once again, like a teacher and not a preacher. What made this transition visible was that, after the pause, he opened his copy of the Qur'an and adjusted it on the shelf of his podium. He took another moment to lean down and search for something in the briefcase stored underneath his lectern. From there he took out another book, which he then placed next to his Qur'an. After this professorial-looking maneuver, he opened up the Qur'an and began to read it out loud. Acoustically and visually, his busy pause was the quietest point in the sermon. It was the precursor to its punch line.

Shuaibe resumed his progress toward his *khutba*'s climax by returning again to Qur'an 9:40. In a low-key and methodical manner, he recited in Arabic the opening line of the verse: *"illa tansurahu faqad nasarahu allahu idh akhrajahu alladhina kafaru thania ithnayn idh huma fi-l-ghari—*when the two of them were in *al-ghari."* That was how he spoke this passage—most of it in Arabic. Of course, he had interpreted it already, at the beginning of his sermon. Here, he translated a part of it—"when the two of them were in"—to remind his listeners about what they had already heard and to highlight the next Qur'anic word, which he made sure not to translate: *"al-ghar."* Then he made yet another pause, looked over his audience to see that they were paying attention, and continued to speak slowly: "Now, that's the key word here, for this subject. It's translated [by Yusuf Ali] as 'cave.' That's how you translate it. It's translated as 'cave.' But you know the name of the sura, sura 18? You know the name of that sura? *Al-Kahf. Al-Kahf.* Translated as 'cave.'

Well, this is God speaking. So how come [in 9:40] He didn't say they were both in the *kahf? [pause].* Let's see."

At this point, Shuaibe opened his other book. He half-lifted it up and explained, "It's a dictionary of the Qur'an." Before using it, however, he reminded his listeners that in their community the preferred method of interpreting the Qur'an was by the Qur'an itself: "Of course, the Qur'an is the best dictionary. But this is very good. It's recommended by the Imam [W. D. Mohammed], *rahim allahu ʿalayhi* ['mercy of God be upon him,' a Muslim equivalent of 'God rest his soul']. Maybe that will help you."[65] He explained that he merely wanted to see what the dictionary said about the word *"ghar"*: "This *ghar.* I just want to look at, look at." And then he stopped in midsentence, paused again, and sighed: "Ah. Imam Mohammed, *rahim allahu ʿalayhi,* he *[pause].* There is *[pause].* Well, I'm not capable of measuring of what he's done for us *[pause].* Because what he's done for us hasn't come to the end yet. So how do you measure? You can't measure. Don't think that his life ended with his physical life on this earth. That was Allah's mercy to him and to us *[long pause].* Because we aren't easy people to hang around too long *[surge of laughter].*"

Through this humorous, self-deprecating, and almost familial note Shuaibe gestured toward all the memories he had shared with his listeners— all the moments of their complex experiences as members of W. D. Mohammed's community, including those they viscerally remembered as instances of their human failings. In close groups, as in families, people often speak in comparable modes. Through hints, jokes, and half-sentences, they share memories that must not be explicitly voiced. Such memories are too intimate to be openly displayed, even among closest associates. Allusions to such delicate recollections are among the most effective ways of making rhetorical connections. They recall shared and intimate bonds among those who "get it." Because of this, skillful preachers often use such allusions, often phrased as jokes, when they attempt to establish an affinity with their audiences. In the Raleigh sermon this moment of intimate connection was a part of Shuaibe's teaching moment. Through a wave of spirited laughter, his listeners let him know that they heard what he was saying. And like any effective preacher, he was not going to waste this opportunity by saying something superfluous. What followed was his critique of who his people were as Muslims, of how they engaged with the Qur'an and their realities. This correction would become his way of guiding his audience toward a Qur'anic response to their current trials.

"You see," he explained, ordinarily the word *"ghar"* was "translated as a 'cave.'" But the dictionary recommended by W. D. Mohammed indicated that such a translation was incorrect. Most translators, he said, misinterpreted this word.[66] They did not notice that the actual root of *"ghar"* consisted of three Arabic consonants: *ghayr*, *ya*, and *ra*. This root, he explained, indicated a condition of and a potential for change. From it, he taught, came the Arabic nouns for "change" and "transformation" and their corresponding verbs.

After this technical intervention, he paused once again, and said in a quiet and intimate voice:

> Now why is it important? It's important. That is so important because, as I introduced this idea, I mentioned Imam Mohammed. And I say that because *[pause]*—the fact that Imam Mohammed, what he brought us, has not been thoroughly appreciated, because we haven't yet learned how to read the Qur'an in the original language. That's really, that's a large part of why you don't get this proximity of energy and language and life between [the Qur'an and] most of the community associated with Imam Mohammed. And, if I'm wrong I stand to be corrected, but *[another pause]*—we are not yet readers of the Qur'an, and understanding it in the original language, and therefore unable to make a connection between the thought that Imam Mohammed has given us, which is borne out of the Qur'an, and the Qur'an itself.

Shuaibe's critique was weighty. No wonder he worked so hard to establish a sense of intimacy with his listeners. It enabled him to deliver his harsh lesson without so much as a murmur of apprehension from his audience. Besides, he was already known for offering such critique on many occasions. His reputation in W. D. Mohammed's community was that of a leading Muslim scholar. In this capacity he participated in the effort to educate the young people in the movement. His role as the head of a K-12 Muslim school in Oakland was a part of this reputation. In addition and very significantly, he had spearheaded the effort to facilitate the training of his community's young adults at Muslim educational centers abroad. On his visit to Raleigh, he was accompanied by a young man who had recently returned from studying in Syria.

But there was more to Shuaibe's ability to deliver his critique than his skill as a preacher and his reputation as his community's religious authority. His sermon was yet another reminder about the intimate connection between W. D. Mohammed and the Qur'an. Mohammed's authority rested on this relationship. And Shuaibe preached that the future of those who called themselves "associates of Imam W. D. Mohammed" depended on their ability to read and understand the scripture. The obvious implication, which he did not need to explicate, was that they needed to overcome their reliance on immigrant and foreign intermediaries. That was the reason behind his working through Yusuf Ali's translation. His critique was a reiteration of a message that W. D. Mohammed had constantly and variously repeated: now that the former members of the Nation of Islam had embraced a Sunni Muslim identity, they had to cultivate their own way of being members of the global *umma*. Shuaibe told the Raleigh community, echoing Mohammed, that the key to this complex balancing act—of being independent and yet not disconnected from other Muslims—was in their hands, that they needed to "read the Qur'an on [their] own." He explained that they needed to tread toward this goal by following the "methodology of Imam Mohammed" and that "[although] Imam Mohammed didn't live long enough to tell us everything that we need to understand about the Qur'an, he worked hard, *al-hamdu li-llah*, and long to give us insights, tools that you can have in your own little tool belt. Ah?"

How could the people in the community read and understand the Qur'an on their own, after their teacher's death and without excessive dependency on foreign authorities? Following "the methodology of Imam Mohammed," Shuaibe pointed to a Qur'anic sign that illuminated the path his listeners had to walk. That sign was the Qur'anic *"ghar."* He explained that, in the Qur'an, it was a polyvocal sign. Its quality of conveying a multitude of meanings reflected God's way of speaking to different communities and that African American hearers of the Qur'an would find in it their unique connotations: "So if Allah, *subhanahu wa ta'ala*, chose to use this word, *'ghar'* as opposed to *'kahf,'* it means something! Allah don't talk like us *[listeners' laughter; preacher's pause]*. Allah means exactly, precisely, scientifically what He meant to say. And when you look deeper you find a broader connection. So what's the connection, brother?"

Like his teacher, Shuaibe formulated his answer by reading the Qur'an by the Qur'an; he discovered the answer in another Qur'anic passage. Likely by the habit cultivated over his three decades of preaching, he located the prooftext for his interpretation in a verse that many Muslim preachers all over the world recite and interpret routinely, Qur'an 8:53. Muslims who attend Friday prayers hear it often. Therefore, he recited it quickly, from memory and without searching for it in his still-open copy of the Qur'an. He trusted that his community knew its meaning and provided only a partial translation: "*'dhalika bi-anna allaha lam yaku mughayyiran ni'matan an'amaha 'ala qawmin hatta yughayyiru ma bi-anfusihim'*—Allah will never change the condition of the people until they change it themselves with their own, with what's going on in their own self."[67]

Leaning upon the shared memory of an often-repeated Qur'anic phrase, he then made another step towards his sermon's apex. The importance of this step was audible in the increasingly rapid tempo of his delivery and the elevated volume of his voice, which he suddenly slowed down and lowered in the middle of the utterance after an expressive pause:

So the same thing that you get change from, same word, the same three radicals give us that word 'cave.' So Abu Bakr and Muhammad, they were in the middle of the biggest transition ever! The biggest change that was about to take place in the history of man! What was going on in that moment in that cave?! The whole world was about to change! The whole world was about to change! *[He pauses and switches to a lower octave.]* And it all hinged upon whether the Meccans listened to the trackers. Ah? Or whether Abu Bakr was going to say, "I give up!" Ah? He wasn't gonna do that. But he was grieving. So that was an important *ghar*. That was an important moment of transition. That was an important situation. That was an important change. That was a change that had the tendency to provoke fear and grief.

Here, Shuaibe made yet another preacherly pause. He gave a long glance over his audience. For a second he looked directly at me. He did not know who I was. The community's leader, Imam Oliver Muhammad, would introduce me to him after that Friday prayer. From what I could tell, I was the only non–African American Muslim in that gathering, and probably the only person not affiliated with the larger W. D. Mohammed community. It seemed that Shuaibe noticed my out-of-placeness. Then he sighed, paused again, and continued to speak:

Listen associates of Imam Warith Deen Mohammed—forgive me if I'm being too parochial for some of you, but I'm here now and I'm gonna have to talk to folks *[pause, and then a sudden outburst of volume]*—YOU ARE IN THE CAVE! You're in an important moment of transition. You're going through changes. You have doubts. You don't know who to listen to. You don't know who's right, who's wrong. They're coming at us this way, they're coming at us that way: "Oh look at so and so!—they're doing that!" Well it says, *"la tahzan inna allaha ma'ana!"* Don't grieve! Allah was in charge before, Allah is in charge now and Allah is always in charge! You have nothing to fear if you're in touch with the plan and the project of Allah *[pause]*. Now, if you're not sure if you're in Allah's plans, I understand *[quiet laughter]*. But, those who are in the plan, you know what I'm saying.

This was the sermon's crescendo, whose energy Shuaibe used to expound the message of his exegesis. He emphasized that God had helped the Prophet and his companion exactly when they needed a miracle most, at the moment of their historical change. When things seemed to hang by a thread, "that's when Allah helped them." And here he reminded his listeners of what the Qur'an says in its depiction of that crucial moment—that God had "sent down *sakina* [tranquility and calmness]" upon the Prophet and his associate. To accentuate it, he repeated it one more time: "Allah sent down the *sakina.*"

Shuaibe spent the rest of his seventy-two-minute sermon tracking down from this rhetorical summit. He spoke more about salvation at times of tribulation. And he reiterated that deliverance was in the hands of the believers: that they had to persevere and strive to be "in Allah's plan." After he had completed his *khutba,* he led the community in their collective Friday prayer. As he and we prayed, he recited a long passage from sura *al-Tawba,* which included "don't grieve."

··· X ···

Shuaibe's sermon is an example of the profound influence of W. D. Mohammed's oral *tafsir* on his movement's speakers. To be effective, a preacher must speak in the language of his or her listeners, connect with their memories and be in sync with their sensitivities. A sound sermon, therefore, is a dynamic reflection of the community to which it belongs. Like speech itself, sermons are always collective. Some of their most telling meanings are not even, technically speaking, linguistic: they are embodied in the listeners' responses, audible in their laughter, silences, or groans, which signal that they know what the preacher is saying. It is on this level—the level of sensibilities—that W.D. Mohammed translated the Qur'an into an African American sacred text. How did he do it? By constantly preaching and speaking the scripture.

I mentioned earlier that many academic and journalistic depictions of W. D. Mohammed and his community tend to focus on the reform of the Nation of Islam and overlook the subsequent decades of their lives. This tendency is understandable: many journalists and academics, particularly historians, examine their subjects with the help of dates that mark dramatic transformations. From this perspective, the period after "Imam Mohammed moved decisively toward the religious mainstream" may appear uneventful, perhaps even boring, and therefore uninteresting to explore. After the reform, there were no big dates to their history. Most of the time, after this period, Mohammed devoted to preaching. And preaching, by its nature, is very repetitive. The change it cultivates is difficult to demarcate.

In the 1980s, 1990s, and 2000s, Imam Mohammed repeated himself a lot. In speech after speech, until his passing in 2008, he returned to the same key ideas: nature, history, community life, and, most of all, redemption. Time after time, he used the same, or similar, phrases and made the same, or similar, points. He did it because he taught his community the Qur'an. And scriptures are not like other books—they are not textbooks or novels, which can be read once or twice, and then comfortably forgotten. People hold on to their scriptures because they want them to inform their lives. They want their Qur'an, or any other sacred text, to keep on speaking.

In one conversation I asked Imam Shuaibe what he thought about the repetitive nature of his teacher's preaching. "Of course," he told me, Imam Mohammed repeated the same notes: "he was like a trumpet"—trumpets have three plungers, and the music flows from it based on which plungers are held down or up—"and that's how he played his tune to the world."[68] I liked his comeback because it resonated with my own hearing of his teacher's unique sound. To me, Warith Deen Mohammed sounded like Thelonious Sphere Monk (1917–1982). Light listeners of jazz might know Monk's name, they may even give him a listen, but then they tend to cast him off, because, to an unaccustomed ear, his sound is jarring. Yet, for those who take time to hear it, his music eventually emerges, like Yusuf from "the bottomless pitt," as a creation of unparalleled beauty.

To translate this into an academic vernacular, Shuaibe's explanation is akin to Walter Ong's description of the art of authors/speakers of oral texts: they "rhapsodize"; they stitch "songs together." W. D. Mohammed's preaching contained in it volumes upon volumes of oral *tafsir*, where he stitched together the stories and sounds of the Qur'an and the collective memory, the "songs," of his people. His text was oral and oral texts are distinct. As Ong explained, they live through repetitive "voicings."[69] (On a different note, those who do not give time to the Qur'an often complain that it is too repetitive and, therefore, confusing and perhaps even boring.)[70]

Indeed, Mohammed's work over the last three decades of his life involved incessant repetitions of scriptural signs. Yet, in each moment, his Qur'anic renditions were also different, because each time he spoke, he addressed an audience facing a different trial: he spoke to people moving through life. And because of this movement of life, he constantly repeated that his listeners needed to keep themselves attuned to what he called "the movement of Scripture." What he meant by it was the Qur'an's polyvocality, which allows its diverse communities of hearers to hear it differently, at different times. Therefore, he kept moving and speaking. Each year, he traversed the country dozens of times to speak in front of live audiences. All along, he spoke "from Scripture" and "from somewhere else"—the collective experiences and memories of his people.

During my research, many people in Mohammed's community reminded me about a slogan he had coined in the late 1970s: "Words make people." To them the words he taught throughout his life were Qur'anic. And in a way he wanted them to live their lives as a Qur'anic people as well—not as some strange new creatures, who would suddenly forget their own memories, but as people who would be at once fully Muslim and African American. In his last public speech, which he delivered two days before his passing, he said,

"When I'm talking to an audience, I'm really concerned for my students. I want them to be present and take notes, because I've always given information to my students at the same time as speaking to a public audience."[71] Through this comment he summarized his lifelong endeavor, which was to engage his listeners in the discipline of hearing the Qur'an. What they heard was him speaking a Qur'an-based language, which he fashioned through his own hearing of the revelation. In the Qur'an he heard redemption. He spoke what he heard.

This chapter's two opening quotations are a call-and-response from Mohammed and one of his hearers. Mohammed's quote—"What good is knowledge if you can't hear it?"—is from a speech he gave in the late 1970s. The respondent, who chose to be anonymous, was one of my mentors, an elder in the community who helped me learn its language. One of our tutoring sessions took place on the front porch of his house, on a hot late afternoon in the summer of 2009. We spent a couple of hours together, mostly consumed by his recollections. After a while, our conversation came to a long pause: he was tired and I ran out of questions. But we still had time. So we sat looking over his neighborhood's quietly beautiful tree-lined street, with some kids riding bikes at a distance. We shared a silence. And then he said, "You know, I was freed by the revelation."

I think I heard him. From what I know, he was not speaking of an exact dramatic moment, an earth-shaking event to which a historian might be able to assign a date. He was not freed in a second, or a week, or a year. Rather, he transformed himself as he was hearing, time after time and for at least four decades, the oral *tafsir* of his teacher. His freedom was not a date but a process—because, as Imam Mohammed taught, freedom is a way of living, which must be ceaselessly nurtured. A redemptive scripture must be perpetually remembered. What Mohammed taught was a language of the Qur'an. For him and his community, it was the language of their collective salvation. After all, as he once said, "human beings are formed by language." And, "if you can create a new language environment for a people, you can give that people a new lease on life."[72]

In some technical respects his *tafsir* was not unusual. His declared method of interpreting the Qur'an by the Qur'an, for example, was not exclusive to him. The fact that he spoke about it reflected his engagement with other Muslim authorities. The *tafsir* of his community, therefore, was not out of sync with international Muslim currents. At the same time, while speaking as members of the global Muslim family, this community has had a unique sound. They have been speaking the Qur'an with a distinctly African American conceptual accent. An example of it is Imam Shuaibe's exegetical pursuit of redemption in the Qur'anic *"ghar,"* which reprised his teacher's search for salvation in Joseph's *"ghayaba."* Such echoing communicated their belonging to a particular tradition of African American engagement with the revelation. A sign of this tradition is the quest for redemption in the Arabic Qur'an.

What a sacred text says depends on how humans voice it. An African American spoken Qur'an cannot but speak the language of redemption. And "surely God is a hearer."[73]

Chapter Four

POLITICS

Memory . . . is like a crossroads. What we see at this juncture depends on
the direction in which we are traveling.

Patrick H. Hutton, *History as an Art of Memory,* 26

··· | ···

A key political address of Shaykh Hamza Yusuf's career, "Give and Take
For God's Sake," opened on a jarring note, which no one seemed to notice. In the second minute of the speech, he began reciting a reminder from
the third verse of the Qur'an's second chapter: "For those who believe, Allah,
subhanahu wa ta'ala, reminds them immediately in the Qur'an: *'alladhina
amanu.'*" Then he paused, reflected for a second, and continued to speak:
"*'bi-l-ghayb'*—those who believe in the unseen— *'wa mimma razaqnahum
yunfiqun'*—and from what We have given them, they give out."[1]

Yusuf's misstep was minute. Speaking live, he rendered this Qur'anic
passage in a way that was grammatically plausible and fluent in terms of
its meaning. His translation, therefore, needed no alteration. Yet, for those
who knew how to recite the Qur'an—and paid attention—his Arabic phrasing must have sounded off key, because his recitation was incorrect. Yusuf's
hesitation likely indicated that he suspected it as well: he had changed the
canonical *"yu'minuna"* ("those who believe") into an *"amanu."*

This speech was the shaykh's keynote address to the Fortieth Annual
Convention of ISNA, held in Chicago in August 2003.[2] In the 1990s and
2000s, ISNA conventions were the largest gatherings of Muslims in the
United States, typically bringing together twenty to forty thousand people.
Yusuf preached two years after 9/11 during the opening stages of the Second
Iraq War (2003–2011). It was a time of heightened anti-Muslim sentiments,
which many of his listeners were experiencing firsthand and saw reflected in
their country's domestic and foreign policies.[3] In this context Yusuf's sermon
was fitting: it instructed his audience how to be involved in public life, a message many of them had already supported.[4]

But Yusuf was also the same preacher who before 9/11 had a different
sound. Until this watershed event he had consistently instructed his audiences to cultivate an attitude of separation from secular life, including American politics. Moreover, for his followers, he was not just another authority

but a "traditional shaykh." Many of them shared a common contemporary sense of tradition as something essentially unchanging. Therefore, for some of them, what was immediately jarring was not his misrecitation but the reorientation of his message. "What the heck happened to Hamza Yusuf," some wondered in online forums; it "seems like he's a different person."[5]

Throughout the mid-1990s and 2000s, Yusuf was an immensely popular preacher. The overwhelming majority of his listeners were young, American, and Muslim. He was also well known among Muslims in Canada, the United Kingdom, and the Scandinavian countries, where English served as a Muslim tongue.[6] He traveled incessantly, and wherever he went, he would "pack the house."[7] By the late 1990s he acquired a virtually uncontested status as the most listened-to online English-speaking Muslim preacher.[8]

What happened to him and his listeners was 9/11. This tragedy and the subsequent changes in American domestic and foreign policies transformed American Muslims into their country's new problematic minority. Politics became an inescapable and often menacing presence in their lives. In response they became more involved in public life. And Yusuf began to speak to their new realities and preach about Islam as an American public religion. This change was both timely and resonant: while some of his occasional listeners were puzzled, and some of them turned to other authorities, he had gained tens of thousands additional listeners. His renewed appeal was based on what he had developed before: an ability to speak to his audiences' experiences and common senses, which changed after 9/11.

This chapter's immediate subject is Yusuf's political rhetoric, but its significance is broader, because language is collective and preachers' sermons, although they appear as monologues, are dialogical. Yusuf's speeches echoed and intervened in the discourses of his audiences, and listening to him presents an opportunity to hear how many young American Muslims made sense of themselves before and after 9/11. Here, therefore, I consider their reflections before proceeding to an analysis of two of his speeches: "Making Sense of Our Past," which he delivered on January 12, 2001, just nine months before 9/11, in Toronto, Canada, and "Give and Take for God's Sake."

For a book that explores American vocalizations of the Qur'an, Toronto is an inconvenient location. "Making Sense," however, was at once Canadian and American. Its preacher was American. His audience, while mostly Canadian, included many Americans. What and how he preached on that occasion was remarkably similar to his other pre-9/11 speeches, such as his "On Muslim Youth" address to the Muslim Youth of North America (MYNA) workshop at ISNA's 2000 convention, where there were many Canadians as well.[9] "Making Sense" was also one of Yusuf's all-time online hits. And it was on the Internet where his American listeners heard him most often.[10]

On the surface the two lectures could not be more different. "Give and Take" was obviously political, while "Making Sense" had an either anti- or apolitical tone. Yet, at a deeper level, these speeches had much in common. Before and after 9/11 Yusuf spoke as a religious authority. His message was directed not at the ordinary understanding of politics, as electoral campaigns or contestations between nation-states, but dealt with the cultural politics of being religious in the contemporary world. From this perspective there was an additional continuity in his rhetoric: it belonged to a long tradition of American religious critiques of some American values.

This matters because one of the most insidious charges that American Muslims faced after 9/11 did not address their politics per se but their religious values and, hence, their cultural politics. A wide array of public figures, such as the politicians mentioned in the introduction, perceived American Muslims' religious values as somehow fundamentally un-American. Such assessment was echoed by some academics as well. For example, Peter Skerry, a political scientist at the Brookings Institution, wrote about the younger generation of American Muslims, who were Yusuf's core constituency, and proposed that their "drama involves . . . adapting to a society whose values are sharply at odds with their religious heritage." He supported this hypothesis by quoting the 2007 and 2011 Pew polls of American Muslim opinions, which revealed that some 40 percent of the younger respondents, those between the ages of eighteen and twenty-nine, indicated that they perceived "a natural conflict between being a devout Muslim and living in a modern society." For Skerry it meant that they were defining "themselves not only in opposition to the government but to American society and culture." And the people responsible for it, he claimed, were "Muslim-American leaders."[11]

What such critics typically forget is that the same logic has been applied to other American religious communities as well: until very recently American Catholics, for example, were regularly described as America's "problem." Reinhold Niebuhr, a preeminent Protestant theologian, expressed this notion in the 1950s, when he stated that "the inflexible authoritarianism of the Catholic religion" was directly at odds with "the presuppositions of a free society." Or, as one sociologist explained, Catholics were "a thing apart in the heart of American body politic" because of their religious values.[12] Proponents of this anti-Catholic common sense, among them many politicians, including presidents, pointed to the rhetoric of American and foreign Catholic authorities, including popes, who before World War II often spoke about their religion as being "completely opposed" to modernity and, based on this dichotomy, criticized American culture and politics, which they perceived as too secular.[13]

Similar formulations can be easily found in Yusuf's rhetoric, and its analysis sheds light on what so many young American Muslims, among whom he was the most listened-to preacher, meant when they answered "yes" to a pollster's loaded question. This observation points to the deeper subject of this chapter. Through Yusuf's preaching—and specifically his articulations of the Qur'an—it explores the language of American Muslim cultural politics. The implications of this investigation are pertinent to most Americans, especially those who struggle to be religious and American.

Yet, why did I begin this chapter with the preacher's slipup? I did so because what makes the Qur'an an American text is how its American believers speak it and, through speaking, bring it into conversation with their dilemmas. Yusuf's mispronunciation of the Qur'anic *"yu'minuna"* is a tangible illustration of a straightforward fact: preachers are not reciters. This observation is so commonsensical that its effects can easily go unnoticed. The most consequential of them is that spoken renditions of the Qur'an are distinct from the canonical Qur'an. The canonical Qur'an is the recited Qur'an. Reciters are its primary guardians and transmitters. Of course, preachers and reciters work with the same officially unchangeable text. But they perform it differently, and their audiences listen to them differently as well. Reciters' authority rests on how well they articulate the canonical text, which limits what they can actually do with it. They cannot, for example, recount one passage from one sura and then immediately connect it with a phrase from another Qur'anic place. Preachers, however, do this routinely.

The art of preaching is inherently versatile. A case in point is the common contemporary tendency of preaching in an improvisational style, which Yusuf had practiced throughout his career.[14] Preaching "off-the-cuff" is an acquired skill, which many preachers cultivate because it allows them to connect with their listeners on a more immediate level (and to compete with other speakers, such as radio personalities).[15] Such real-time preaching also enables them to translate more fluently the texts of the pasts into their audiences' presents. Their listeners are used to this technique: they expect their preachers to interweave scriptural stories with their experiences. And preachers respond by incessantly infusing resonant samples of divine discourses into their contextually specific sermons.

What emerges in this process are spoken renditions of sacred texts, be they based on the Qur'an, the Bible, or the Sutras. These are the texts that preachers and their audiences most often utter. They appear when people speak and make sense of their experiences by remembering their scriptures. Spoken scriptures are human dialogues that engage and sometimes embody sacred texts. To emphasize the difference between canonical and spoken scriptures, however, is to invite the impression that what preachers do is somehow unorthodox. And few, if any, preachers would say what I just wrote—although W. D. Mohammed hinted at this dynamic when he said that his words came "from Scripture or from somewhere else." Preaching is a precarious art. It belongs in the field of rhetoric, and rhetoric, as an art of persuasion, entails twisting and mixing words. (This may be a reason why preachers, like lawyers, have a reputation of speaking with forked tongues: just Google "preacher"—or, better yet, "Muslim preacher"—and see what comes up.) Yet preaching is a risk worth taking. It reinfuses sacred texts into human languages and senses more fluently than other genres of scriptural communication, because preachers persistently and inconspicuously remember what officially can never be changed.

Here, consider one caveat. When reciters of the Qur'an make a mistake, they are expected to notice it, stop, and repeat from the beginning the phrase they just misquoted. But when Yusuf slipped, he paused but did not turn back and repeat his uttering. In addition, if a reciter does not notice his or her mistake, those in their audience who do hear it are expected to politely interject with a canonical correction. This is a basic element of the etiquette of listening to the recited Qur'an. Yet, from what I could tell, no one corrected the shaykh—not a single person at the ISNA convention and no one among the additional tens of thousands of Muslims who heard him on the Internet.[16]

Yusuf's listeners had a sound reason for letting his mistake go into one ear and out the other. Had he been a reciter, he and many of them would have certainly noticed it. But he was a preacher, and preachers re-member the Qur'an more fluently. Besides, it is likely that, in this fleeting moment of speaking, he was not even sure that he had made this mistake: had he been confident of it, he would have been obligated to stop and repeat the canonical quote from the beginning. Within a split second he had to perform a preacherly type of give-and-take: he had to decide whether to interrupt his speech because of a nagging feeling that he might have made a mistake, or whether to continue building the momentum of his Qur'anic reminder. The choice he appeared to make prioritized the genre of preaching, upon which depended how fluently his listeners would hear what the Qur'an, through its speaker, had to say about their current travails. Surely, it was a crucial crossroads.

···II···

At the peak of his fame, in the first decade after 9/11, Yusuf—or "Shaykh Hamza," as his followers called him—was known to hundreds of thousands of American Muslims. Many of them spoke about him as though he was a member of an exclusive circle of globally recognized American Muslim celebrities, such as Malcolm X, Muhammad Ali, Kareem Abdul-Jabbar, or Mos Def. Like most such figures, he was a convert, and his life was a story of transformation. Unlike them, he was a preacher, and white. Before his time there had been many other famous American Muslim preachers, such as W. D. Mohammed and Siraj Wahhaj. His message, however, was distinct. In the 1990s he was among the first American preachers to stress an allegiance to what he called "traditional Islam." Within a decade, this emphasis became an American Muslim common sense.

Mark Hanson, the person who would become Shaykh Hamza, was born in 1960 in Walla Walla, Washington. His father was Catholic and a university professor. His mother was Greek Orthodox. He grew up close to Berkeley, California, and was raised in his mother's faith. As he later recalled, in his childhood and youth he had been "a serious Orthodox."[17] He was educated, however, in Catholic schools. At the age of seventeen, after a near-fatal car accident, he converted to Islam in Santa Barbara, California.[18] Soon after he traveled in the pursuit of knowledge. First he moved to the United Kingdom and then went on to study for close to a decade in the Middle East and North Africa. In his subsequent recollections, he particularly highlighted the time he had spent with Islamic teachers in Mauritania.[19] One of his teachers there was Shaykh Abdallah bin Mahfudh ibn Bayyah (b. 1935), a former vice president of the country, as well as a member of the European Council for Fatwa and Research.

Yusuf returned to California in 1988. In the early 1990s he served as an imam at the Muslim Community Association (MCA), a mosque in Santa Clara, California. At the same time he completed a nursing degree, worked at a local hospital, and graduated with a B.A. in religious studies from San Jose State University. In the mid-1990s his career took a dramatic turn when he cofounded Zaytuna Institute. Under his leadership and thanks in part to his growing fame, Zaytuna soon became the leading American center for the propagation of traditional Muslim education. He named it after the legendary Tunisian Jami'a al-Zaytuna, one of the oldest Muslim centers of learning. This name connected it with the premodern heritage of Islamic learning and thus projected an aura of traditional stability. Its American location, however, necessitated adaptability. And Zaytuna's subsequent development reflected that the Islamic traditionalism Yusuf taught was flexible. In its first few years, its organizers presented it as a madrasa that trained local *ulama*. By the late 1990s they refashioned it into a "seminary," a word that signaled its belonging within the American landscape of religious education.[20] In 2009 it became Zaytuna College and was advertised, somewhat erroneously, as "America's first Muslim college."[21] Its leadership, which now included Zaid Shakir, spoke of it as continuing the tradition of American Catholic and Jewish colleges. Consistent through all these transitions was its overall mission of translating traditional Islam into an American reality.

What was this traditional Islam? Yusuf's understanding of tradition mirrored the definition of this concept by Daniel W. Brown, an academic specialist in Islamic Studies (who happened to be a student of Fazlur Rahman): "a tradition in an old-fashioned sense," as "a deposit of knowledge or truth, originating with a past authority, and handed down within a religious community."[22] This sense of tradition was reflected in the deeper allusion behind Zaytuna's name. For Yusuf's regular listeners, it was obvious: it highlighted the legacy of Shaykh Ahmad Zarruq (1442–1493), one of the Tunisian Zaytuna's most famous teachers, whom Yusuf often remembered as a model for what it meant to be properly traditional, because he was known for emphasizing a natural balance between Islam's legal tradition and Sufism.[23]

Yusuf has preached this tradition by constantly remembering his teachers. Typical is a story he told at ISNA's 2000 convention about his Mauritanian Sufi shaykh, Murabit al-Hajj bin Fahfu. Shaykh Murabit al-Hajj, he reminisced on that occasion, "[rises] four hours before *fajr* [morning prayer] and recites *tahajjud* [voluntary night prayer] . . . and as he reads the Qur'an he weeps from the fear of Allah, *subhanahu wa ta'ala*"; then he walks to the mosque—"he's 92 years old and he walks like a young man!"—and he "teaches from *fajr* to *dhuhr* [midday prayer] . . . and keeps teaching in between prayers . . . And this has been his life for over 70 years and thousands of Muslims have studied with him from all over North Africa and West Africa."[24]

Crucial in this recollection was Yusuf's message about religious—as opposed to secular—sense of time. His teacher's day was an example of a distinct mode of living, which made him a "true embodiment of the spirit of Islam."[25] Clearly, most of his listeners did not spend their days like Shaykh Murabit al-Hajj: like most contemporary human beings, they organized their lives around secular schedules. And while they were busying themselves with their everyday tasks, Yusuf implied, his shaykh remembered God. Through this dichotomy he urged them to remember what it meant to be religious, to remember the Qur'an and in the process re-member themselves.

This story illustrates how Yusuf has presented the Islamic tradition as something persistent and continuous, as a stream of practiced knowledge that was never interrupted by modernity and its secular common senses. What he taught was not entirely new. Many American Muslim intellectuals before him, like Faruqi, were critical of the secular aspects of modernity. What was novel was Yusuf's insistence on the authority of the *ulama* such as Zarruq and bin Bayyah. Until the mid-1990s the soundscape of American Muslim preaching was saturated with reiterations of the arguments by Qutb and Mawdudi, who were technically not *ulama*, in part because they did not graduate from Muslim seminaries. As Shaykh Abdullah bin Hamid Ali, a teacher at Zaytuna and an avid listener of Yusuf's recorded speeches in the 1990s, explained in one of our conversations, the central "accomplishment of Shaykh Hamza . . . [was that] he was able to communicate to [American] Muslims the position and status of a Muslim scholar."[26]

The group of American Muslim authorities and institutions that promoted such deference to the ʿulama was expanding throughout Yusuf's career. In the 2000s the closest to Zaytuna in its vision was the Chicago-based Nawawi Foundation, directed by Umar Faruq Abd-Allah (who also was a student of Fazlur Rahman). In my conversations with Yusuf's audiences, other names that frequently came up were Zaid Shakir, Abdul Hakim Murad, Khalid Yahya Blankinship, Abd al-Hakim (Sherman) Jackson, Nuh Ha Mim Keller, and Suhaib Webb. These individuals happened to be converts (and many of them university professors). Their audiences and students, however, were mostly second-generation Muslims, like bin Hamid Ali, who came from an African American Muslim family, and Noura Shamma, an Egyptian American scholar, who studied at Zaytuna in California and with Nuh Ha Mim Keller in Jordan. In the late 2000s Shamma taught at SunniPath, a popular online academy and an important node in the network of American Muslim traditionalism. Like Yusuf, she had a "unique story-telling style of teaching," which brought "the past alive" and connected "it with the present."[27]

As bin Hamid Ali explained in a personal interview, what unified this cohort of Western scholars was their effort to overcome the global trend of "Protestantization of Islam," which began with the European colonization of most Muslim countries in the nineteenth century. His explanation echoed what I heard from many other traditionalists, who similarly noted that the modern changes in Muslim societies led to a decline of ordinary Muslims' respect toward the ʿulama. Among the people responsible for it, I often heard, were Muslim "modernists" and "Islamists." In the twentieth century these camps were typically in conflict with each other. Yet they shared two important traits: while interpreting Muslim foundational texts, they typically bypassed premodern exegetical traditions, and they dismissed or deemphasized Sufism. By doing so, both "Islamists" and "modernists," in the view of the people who called themselves "traditional," "turned Islam into an ideology."[28]

To counter this trend, Yusuf has frequently reminded his listeners about the hadith that tells of an occasion when the angel Gabriel publically quizzed the Prophet Muhammad about the religion of the revelation. He asked three questions. The first was about the meaning of *islam* (literally, "submission"), the second about the nature of *iman* (faith), and the third about the value of *ihsan* (beauty). What came from this exchange was that Islam, as a religion, was more than a set of rituals and beliefs; it was a mode of God-conscious living. The key element in it was *ihsan*, which meant, as the Prophet explained it, that "you should worship God as if you see God, and if you do not see God, God sees you."[29] Following a centuries-old convention, Yusuf has often clarified that beauty/*ihsan* was Islam's spirituality and that Muslims had traditionally cultivated it through the disciplines of Sufism. Therefore, to dismiss Sufism, he argued, was to reject "one third of Islam."[30]

Yusuf's traditionalism is best illustrated by how he has interpreted the Qur'an. Of course, he is a preacher, and his exegesis is oral and informal. Yet it has consistently adhered to a classical Sunni consensus, whose roots go back to the scholarship of Muhammad Ibn Idris al-Shafi'i (d. 820). From the point of view of this consensus, the Qur'an and Hadith have the same status: they are two indivisible currents of the same revelation, and not separate bodies of literature. The key difference between them is that the Qur'an is *wahy matlu*, a "recited revelation"—a scripture preserved verbatim—while the Hadith is a revelation *ghayr matlu*, "not recited," which means that it had been transmitted through paraphrasing until it was eventually canonized. Indeed, many modern exegetes, including Rahman, Qutb, Mawdudi, and Wadud, tended to elevate the status of the Qur'an over the Hadith; and for many—perhaps most—contemporary Muslims this hierarchy has been commonsense. Yusuf's response to this trend came across in a lecture he gave in 2007 at Zaytuna, where he provided an extensive commentary on sura 49, *al-hujurat* ("The Chambers"). His audience on that occasion consisted mostly of Zaytuna's students. Yet, in his introduction, he made sure to remind them that "the Sunna is the Qur'an—they are not separate; [it] is the practical application of the Qur'an in the world. And that's how you learn how to interpret the Qur'an by following the actions of the Prophet, *salla-llahu 'alayhi wa sallam* [peace and blessings of God be upon him]."[31]

Yusuf's fame is partly based on how well he embodies the traditionalist transformation he teaches. Its marker is his near-native command of the Arabic language. For many of his listeners, it has made his authority distinct. This impression is conveyed in a story from one of his early followers and close friends. The first time he heard Yusuf was in 1992, when "Shaykh Hamza" was an imam in Santa Clara and my interviewee—a young Afghan immigrant raised partly "back home" and partly in the United States—was "mosque-hopping" in search of a community and a teacher. He heard about Yusuf from his cousin, who asked, "Have you heard this white man? His name is Hamza Yusuf. You have to check him out. You've got to listen to him!" And so, he went to the MCA for a Friday prayer, expecting to hear a "white man." Instead, "we had this Arabic guy come in, in his turban and the Arabic *thawb* [a robe-like attire] . . . and he used so many Arabic words" that the young man could barely understand him. The follower-to-be was disappointed: he had come "to see an American guy named Hamza Yusuf and instead heard an Arabic guy using Arabic words." A few days later, his cousin asked him what he thought about the shaykh. "I have no opinion," he responded, "the guy wasn't there." The cousin laughed: "That was him! That was Hamza Yusuf!"[32]

By the middle of the 1990s, most young and devout American Muslims would know the name of this convert, who had transformed himself into a traditional Muslim. But that was not the end of Yusuf's transformational story. His second metamorphosis occurred after 9/11. This was the time when journalists began to pay more attention to American Muslims and noticed their popular preacher. To convey his fame, they called him a "Muslim rock star" or "the Elvis Presley" of American Islam.[33] In a sense, this moniker was astute: like Elvis, Yusuf was able to perform in different modes and cross markets. After 9/11 his Muslim audiences expanded, and he began to preach to non-Muslims as well. In this transformation he relied on the preacherly skills he had developed before. His rhetorical dexterity is exemplified by a phrase he coined on October 11, 2001, when he joined a group of Christian and Jewish leaders for a meeting with President George W. Bush: on the lawn outside the White House, he declared, "Islam was hijacked on that September 11, 2001, on that plane as an innocent victim."[34]

"Islam was hijacked" soon became an American trope. It was repeated myriad times—by Muslims and other Americans, who opposed the excesses of the so-called War on Terror, and by some politicians, who used the same meme to explain post-9/11 realities. One such political figure is Karen Hughes, a former member of the Bush administration, who in 2010 wrote an opinion piece about Park51, a Muslim community center near the site of the World Trade Center. No longer technically a politician, Hughes wrote from the position of "common sense," which, in her estimation, linked all Muslims to the 9/11 terrorists—while forgetting that common senses do not arise out of nowhere; that they are influenced by politicians and pundits, such as herself. She conveyed this "common sense" through a classic minority-bashing move: it was "a Muslim American friend" who told her, "As much as I hate it, those hijackers called themselves Muslim." Hughes acknowledged that this association was unfortunate and recalled that she had "met many Muslims around the world who feel that, along with airplanes, the terrorists hijacked their religion." And then she requested that the Muslims behind Park51 "respect" her opinion and "locate their mosque elsewhere."[35] Hughes's appropriation of Yusuf's line was innovative: I doubt he meant for it to serve as a prelude to an expulsion of Muslims from the grounds of American public life, including New York's Ground Zero. Tropes, of course, can be twisted every which way. Understanding preachers takes time, which is why it is worthwhile to examine those who invested significant portions of their lives to hearing Yusuf correctly.

···III···

Sadaf Khan had arrived at Zaytuna before Yusuf became an "Elvis." When she was nineteen, she asked her parents' permission to leave her home in Pennsylvania and move to California. "That was in 1999," she recalled. A year before, she went on hajj and realized that she "wanted to study Islam." At first, she planned to go abroad. But her father, "of course, would not allow that." He did, however, approve her plan B: to study at Zaytuna, while also attending a local college. "Of course," she said, "the reason for choosing Zaytuna was because of Shaykh Hamza." "Why Shaykh Hamza?" I asked. "Well," she explained, "he resonated with me. He made Islam make sense, especially to me as an American teenager."[36]

I interviewed Sadaf in the summer of 2008 at Zaytuna's library, in an unremarkable office building in Berkeley. Shortly before my visit, Zaytuna had moved there from its original home in Hayward, California. I was in the area to listen to Yusuf's listeners, people from the local Muslim community and Zaytuna's students, staff, volunteers, and faculty. Sadaf was the coordinator of its Minara Program, which conducted educational workshops in the United States, Canada, and the United Kingdom.

For Sadaf the need for making sense arrived in the mid-1990s. "Well, I remember," she explained, "when I first heard Shaykh Hamza, I was fifteen or sixteen years old." To understand his impact, she said, "you have to also understand" her situation. She was born and raised in the United States. Her parents were South Asian immigrants. "You see," she said, "we were cultural Muslims, kind of like everyday Muslims": they celebrated Muslim holidays; her father went to mosque on Fridays; and her parents had taught her "how to read the Qur'an . . . but that's it." She did not remember having a deeper connection with her religion. Things changed after her parents divorced. She stayed with her mother, who all of a sudden "found out that her Pakistani so-called close friends didn't want to have anything to do with her because she was a divorced woman." Instead of her ethnic community, Sadaf's mother found support in Muslim circles: "She became very active. Every weekend we traveled to a [Muslim] conference or event in New York, Philadelphia, or D.C.—anywhere where she could experience community."

During one such trip, Sadaf first heard about Yusuf. In the 1990s his reputation spread by word of mouth, with one listener conscripting another into an emerging community of hearers. Sadaf's mother heard about him from a friend, who insisted, "Hear this man. He is amazing!" She then related this advice to her daughter. Their first chance to listen to him came in 1995 at an ICNA conference in Bloomsburg, Pennsylvania. But like many teenagers, Sadaf was a bit stubborn: she decided to skip Yusuf's lecture and "hang out at a bazaar or something like that." Her mother, however, attended the talk and was very impressed: "my mom was just like—'this man tells it like it is! And he makes sense!'" This testimony convinced Sadaf to give the shaykh a listen, which she did at the next ICNA conference in Valley Forge, Pennsylvania, in 1996:

And I had heard him and he was just like—he was the first scholar
that I had heard that I wanted to listen to, you know? I didn't want
to leave, or I wasn't daydreaming. I was actually listening to what

he had to say. And what he said made sense to me. Because here he is and he's not just talking about what the Prophet, *salla-llahu ʿalayhi wa sallam*, said and what's in the Qur'an. Like, you know, most speakers, when you hear them, they are just rattling off ayas in the Qur'an to you and, you know, you have no clue what they are saying. But he's bringing it home to you. He's telling you what Malcolm X said. He's quoting Thoreau. He is, you know, he is talking about Shakespeare and he's talking about things that you yourself—that I myself, growing up in America, am more familiar with. You know, I grew up reading Shakespeare in high school, so I know, I understand where he's coming from. He's coming from a very Western idea. Not from back home. And so it made sense to me, you know? . . . It resonated with me. So that's just what I remember: here is the first Islamic scholar that I'd heard that doesn't bore me to death!

After this, Sadaf said, her path led her "naturally to Zaytuna." She began listening to his recordings, "bought all of his tapes," and became "obviously a big supporter and . . . a long-distance student." "How did he resonate?" I asked. "I'll tell you exactly what I mean. Growing up, Islam was about rules—pray, fast, girls don't wear shorts after they get their period, and I can't have a boyfriend, and things I can't do, and all about rules. To me, that's what Islam was! But what Shaykh Hamza did, he didn't make it sound like rules, you know. He made it sound like—this is a beautiful tradition. We have such a beautiful tradition. We should be proud of our tradition. He made it beautiful, whereas our parents made it something that, I don't want to say ugly, but they didn't make it beautiful."

Sadaf's explanation resonated with what I heard from many of Yusuf's listeners. In the 1990s his audiences consisted mostly of high school or college students, many of whom, perhaps two thirds, were children of immigrants who grew up in this country. Being American for them was a given, while being Muslim required cultural translation, which Yusuf provided with a little Shakespeare and a lot of the Qur'an.

One could hear the Qur'an in Sadaf's speech. She said that Yusuf made Islam sound "beautiful," the word echoing the advice that the Qur'an gives to its communicators: invite people to the way of the Lord "with wisdom and beautiful preaching."[37] What the Qur'an urges is the practice of harmonious dialogues between preachers and listeners. Such dialogues are initiated by listeners, who search for preachers whose articulations resonate with their sense of beauty. To a significant degree the effectiveness of their listening depends on their willingness to submit to the authority of the preacher.[38] Yet preaching is dialogical, and to be effective, preachers must also continuously listen—and therefore submit—to their listeners.

This is the dynamic highlighted by Sadaf's story. Yusuf was not the first preacher she heard. But he was the first she "wanted to listen to," because his lectures—which, in the 1990s, were typically over two hours long—did not make her want to leave to visit a "bazaar or something like that." Certainly, it was Sadaf's mother who compelled her to listen to this "amazing man." Yet it was entirely in Sadaf's power to pretend that she was listening and daydream instead. Her not tuning him out was her initial "give" in the dialogical give-and-take of preaching. Yusuf's contribution was in how he spoke. To her, his preaching "made sense" and was "beautiful" because it resonated with her sense of beauty, which is always contextual. For years, she continued to invest in hearing him, in sincerely trying to understand and follow his teachings. And time after time, he continued "bringing it home." She stayed tuned in to his preaching because, to her, it remained "natural"—because he kept striving to stay resonant. As times changed, she changed as well, but so did his sound and the language they shared.

Sadaf "first heard Shaykh Hamza" before 9/11. The challenges she confronted at the time were mostly personal. Another of my conversation partners, a student at Zaytuna who would later become an imam, became Yusuf's regular listener in a different era, while searching for a different sense. Like Yusuf, he was a convert. He became Muslim in 1995, at the age of twenty, and "began hearing about Shaykh Hamza since about 1996." But he "did not pay attention." His mentors at the time were older South Asian immigrants, "uncles and aunts" at a mosque he attended. But then 9/11 struck, and he encountered a deep dissonance between what was sound to him and what he was hearing from his advisors. He was searching for deep answers but often heard "conspiracy theories" and "nonsense." It was then that he "started to pay more attention" to Yusuf and found in his speeches the needed "common sense." Before this juncture, he recalled, he had been willing to listen to "black and white" explanations that presented a clear "dichotomy between those who believe and don't believe." Yet, in Yusuf's preaching he discovered depictions of "the world that is more Technicolor than anything else." He explained, "Shaykh Hamza was the first person I've heard addressing this reality: that we live in time when things are vague, the world as I see it, not as I hear about—black and white. . . . And he had a Qur'anic reference for what I was hearing! That's the example of when things kind of lined up."[39]

Like Sadaf's story, the account of my anonymous interviewee, who happened to be Sadaf's friend, speaks to the reciprocal nature of preaching. It also highlights the importance of timing, for the senses that preachers and their listeners make are inseparable from their contexts. Sadaf and her friend became immersed in Yusuf's language in two different eras. When Sadaf decided to listen to Yusuf, his speeches sounded like "Making Sense" and focused mostly on his listeners' personal struggles. Her friend "started to pay more attention" during the time of "Give and Take," which addressed their public dilemmas.

Most of Yusuf's listeners have been ordinary people who desired to be devout—or "lukewarm Muslims," as one of his close observers told me in an informal conversation, by which he meant people who were not—or not yet—studying to become *ulama.* For them, Yusuf preaches in an accessible way. He does not dwell on Sufism but stresses spirituality. And he does not spell out the relationship between *wahy matlu* and *ghayr matlu* but always links the Qur'an with the Hadith.

Like most public speakers, he has connected with his listeners through allusions to the memories he shared with them, such as evocations of Thoreau or Malcolm X. When it comes to the Qur'an, his employment of allusions is exceptionally deft. While it is quite apparent that many of his listeners do not know every scriptural phrase or story he has told, he has often preached as though they did. He has routinely omitted or half-completed translations of canonical phrases and then filled such gaps with his own interpretations. His habit of seemingly overestimating his listeners' knowledge has had a didactic effect—inconspicuously prodding them to continue listening and discovering what they, as sound Muslims, are meant to remember. Simultaneously, his interpretations demonstrate how to remember correctly. This is his way of teaching an alternative mode of speaking, which infuses the scripture into his listeners' language, collective memories, and common senses.

Another significant element of his style has come across in how he constructs his arguments. Most of his speeches have been dialectical: he will begin with a common ground (typically scriptural), then create a series of outwardly insurmountable contradictions (often between "us" and "them"), and then merge such dichotomies in a dramatic fashion. His sermons' lessons crystalize in such moments of syntheses. This style of speaking has likely been a reflection of his Muslim and Catholic education—Muslims and Catholics inherited their dialectical logics from the ancient Greeks.[40] Of course, how he has applied this and other methods of "bringing it home" has depended on the contexts in which he has preached.

···IV···

One of the telltale signs of Yusuf's pre-9/11 rhetoric was his practice of addressing his listeners as "Muslims in the West." He did it consistently in the United States, Canada, and the United Kingdom. Why did he not call them Americans, Canadians, or Brits? It was not because he did not know to whom he was speaking. He was always careful to tailor his speeches to specific audiences: when he spoke to predominantly South Asian audiences, for instance, he often referenced the poetry of Iqbal. Rather, this peculiar expression—which many Muslim speakers, particularly immigrants, used at the time—was due to the composition of his audiences and the institutional realities of organizations that invited him to speak. From the mid-1960s and until 2001, ISNA, ICNA, and several other immigrant groups were structurally North American, and "Muslims in the West" was a common way of addressing their transnational constituents.

From this perspective, the Toronto event, where Yusuf delivered his "Making Sense of Our Past" and addressed Canadian and American Muslims, was typical. What made it distinct was that it was a precursor to the series of annual conferences, "Reviving The Islamic Spirit" (RIS), which would officially commence in 2003.[41] The explicit agenda of these gatherings, before and after their transformation into a perennial event, were to disseminate the message of "traditional Islam," which on the surface was apolitical and which resonated with the deeper political reason behind Yusuf's "Muslims in the West" routine. At this particular juncture in his and his listeners' lives, he glossed over the distinctions between his American and Canadian audiences, instead emphasizing what they shared: their "Western" location. The "West" in his pre-9/11 rhetoric stood for the global economic, political, and cultural system of secular materialism.[42] In the language of the 1990s, when the Cold War had ended and the United States was the world's sole superpower, he described the world of his listeners as the "Pax Americana."

"Making Sense" was representative of Yusuf's pre-9/11 preaching. It was ninety-seven minutes long and focused on remembrance. He opened it with a characteristically humble reflection:

> I was thinking on the way to the airport actually that I really, in a sense, don't have anything to add to this discourse that's original, because this condition which we find ourselves in, which is in a sense exacerbated in the present times for a number of reasons, is nonetheless a condition that this *umma* has been in for quite some time. And some, who are more scholarly and more intelligent people than myself or others, have looked at it and considered it quite deeply. . . . And yet, the process goes on and continues and, as I was thinking that, an *aya* [verse] in the Qur'an came to me . . . *"wa dhakkir fa-inna al-dhikra tanfaʻu al-muʼminin"*—remind people, because it reminds the people of the *iman*.[43] And so, in a sense, we have nothing to offer anymore, in terms of discourse of people speaking in this age, other than reminders, in a hope that ourselves and the others will heed the reminders. And it's the purpose of *dhikr* [remembrance]—that we remember.[44]

Yusuf's note of humility elevated the authority of the people and texts on whose behalf he appeared to speak. It also invited his listeners to become humble as well, so that they could hear his message, which from the start he grounded in the Qur'an. His next uttering was Qur'anic as well.

"Allah," he reminded them, "says in the Qur'an, *'qad ja'tkum maw'izatun min rabbikum'*—this Qur'an has come as a *maw'izatun*, an exhortation. . . . and it's a *shifa'*—it's a healing. . . . *li-ma fi-s-sudur*, for what's in the breast of diseases and illnesses."[45] "And so the language of medicine," he said, "is the language of the Qur'an and the prophets." But, it was not "the medicine" as it was understood in the West, he explained, and through this explanation constructed his lecture's first dichotomy: "This culture is brilliant at articulating signs and symptoms, and yet they have not a clue as to the cause, the underlying diseases that are affecting humanity, that are afflicting humanity in any time and place. They have no understanding whatsoever because they know the outward of this world: *'ya'alamuna zahiran min al-hayati wa hum 'an al-akhirati hum ghafilun'*—they know the outer of this world, they can elicit the signs, but they do not know the inward. They don't know the cause . . . and they are the furthest from knowing that Allah, *subhanahu wa ta'ala*, is ultimately the only cause, that everything else in fact is means."[46]

This was Yusuf's introduction to his lecture's key didactic dichotomy, which, at this moment, appeared rigid. The two opposing categories were "us" and "them," "Muslims," and "the West." What distinguished the two was the Qur'an: Muslims had it, and non-Muslim Westerners did not, which is why "they" knew only "the outer of this world." Yet, right after this commendation of "us," he shared with his audience what he kept hearing from them: "that Muslims are in trouble now because of technology." This common complaint, he then pointed out, reflected a deeper problem with Muslims, because it addressed "the condition" of Muslims through the language of Western materialism.

And then he reminded his Western Muslim listeners about the Satan. Echoing Qur'an 2:34, he noted that the Satan's "fundamental disease is envy." This, he observed, was a sign of what was happening presently: the world, he preached, was experiencing a pandemic envy. "This is important," he emphasized, "in understanding the present condition of Muslims." The condition they faced, he proposed, was being surrounded by the all-consuming culture of Western materialism, which, he diagnosed, represented a culture of *kufr*, or denial of God. He supported this interpretation by remembering a Prophetic statement: "*'kufr millatun wahidatun'*—*kufr* is one system." And, drawing with his hand an imaginary circle, he translated this hadith into his listeners' reality: "All *kufr* is one millah: you have the Marxists, the atheists, the communists, the socialists, the national socialists, international socialists, the capitalists, the free-market capitalists, the American anti-NAFTA . . . —all ultimately one phenomenon called *kufr*. It's all *kufr*! It goes under the rubric of *kufr*. But it has different permutations. And you can see syphilis—very interesting disease, because syphilis is called the great mimicker. Syphilis can look like a lot of different diseases. And this is a syphilitic culture, right?"

Yusuf's "right?" was a rhetorical question. It summoned his listeners to reflect on the symptoms they already knew. To develop resistance to "this syphilitic culture," he urged them to remember the Qur'an, "because much of the Qur'an is in the explaining of *kufr*—so we understand it." This is where his cultural translation appeared indispensable. He, like his listeners, was from "this culture." And the modern *kufr* they inhabited, he explained, "is very different from other *kufr*." It was because "their religion," Christianity, "was tainted from very early on." Almost from the start, "they had partial truths mixed with a lot of pseudo truths, things that appear to be truth." Westerners' real fall from grace, he lectured, occurred when they attempted to appropriate Islamic rational sciences, such as algebra, philosophy, and medicine: "They took this teaching, which was the intellectual and natural sciences of the Muslims, and it began to go diametrically in opposition to their own religion." Because of their originally incorrect understanding of God's communication, he lectured, they could not properly absorb what Muslims had developed and went into the direction of "complete materialism." "And that," he summated, "is the crisis of the modern world."[47] To buttress this verdict, he offered a litany of symptoms that described the modern Western permutations of the perennial *kufr*. The deadliest of them was the "bitter fruit of their abandonment of their religion," which made the spiritual "center [not] hold in this society anymore." He continued, "And this is where you got the leveling of their nihilistic tendencies. It has become a world of the most base aspects of the human nature. The bestial nature is exalted, the angelic nature is denied . . . greed is good; get what you can; stab them in the back before they stab you."

Yusuf's principal examples of "this culture" were American. He noted that something was deeply wrong with this country when one of its best-selling books was Harvey Mackay's *Swim with the Sharks without Being Eaten Alive*. What that book taught, he said, was, "in other words, how to become a shark . . . . [how to] market oneself, the human being, as a commodity. This is the game of this culture. And this is a type of *kufr*." To illustrate this game, he recalled a magazine article that in 1997 complimented Hillary Clinton for "glamorously turning fifty" and interpreted this phrase as a sign of the very nature of American politics, where politicians turned themselves into political products and struggled to appear youthful to appeal to their consumers. "They work very hard at it," he added quietly, with a mischievous snicker. His listeners heard him and responded with a wave of clued-in giggles.

This jejune humor, which Yusuf would drop after 9/11, had a somber purpose: the "we" who were chuckling at "them" were about to discover that the joke was really on them. Once the giggles subsided, he reminded them that they too were exposed to this virus of *kufr*. He noted that Muslims all over the world were now speaking as though their religion was some kind of a nationalist ideology. This tendency, he explained, was a Western colonial import and that all Muslims were unconscious carriers of the languages and common senses instilled into them by modern nation-states. As a result, he said, "we no longer see ourselves as within the fold of Islam, the brotherhood that Allah, *subhanahu wa ta'ala*, has given us. . . . We now see ourselves—I am an American Muslim, he's a Pakistani Muslim . . . and on and on and on—false designations that Islam rejects completely." This, he preached, was a symptom of the "condition we find ourselves in." And one of its causes was that "Muslims have become deeply envious of the West," including its technology.

At this critical point, which highlighted his listeners' vulnerability, the shaykh introduced his lecture's pivotal story, the Qur'anic parable of Qarun, whose biblical name is Korah. For many Muslims, Qarun is a peripheral scriptural character. His tale appears in Qur'an 28:76–82. Elsewhere, the Qur'an mentions him only twice. Yet, Yusuf preached as though the story was at the tip of his listeners' tongues: he merely reminded them that this ancient Egyptian Israelite was a contemporary of Moses, that God had tested him with titanic wealth, and that he became arrogant and met his end when God made him sink into the very soil upon which he happened to stand. To make this fable relatable, he inserted a quick note: "Bill Gates—modern Qarun, right?"

While a reciter's performance of the Qur'an's six verses about Qarun would take about a minute, Yusuf's retelling of them stretched to over ten. He took some time to quote and translate the Qur'an, but most of it he devoted to filling the gaps of memory and time that separated his listeners from the revelation. The crucial moment came when he reached the first uttering of verse 78, which quotes Qarun's retort to those who dared to remind him that his wealth was from God. "But what did he say?" the shaykh urged his listeners to recollect. "He says, '*qala inna-ma 'utituhu 'ala 'ilmin 'indi*' - No! This wealth is from me! I have a knowledge, I have a PhD from Harvard! That's how I got this wealth. I'm more clever than you are. Really! I've invented this machine, and I got the patent. That's how I got it. Allah didn't give it to me—That's what they think!"

The Qur'anic quote in Yusuf's rendition was short. His technical translation, which he performed by puffing his chest, was equally brief: "No! This wealth is from me! I have a knowledge." Had he aimed to let the Qur'an speak for itself, he would have stopped there. But he did not. He continued speaking, while extending the words and the time that the scripture had allocated to Qarun and bringing its message into his listeners' present. In his performance, Qarun kept speaking, bragging about his "PhD from Harvard," his "machine," and "patent"—all obviously extra-scriptural concepts.

This is how Yusuf interpreted, and spoke, the Qur'an. The fluidity of his preaching made his exegesis inconspicuous. Neither he nor his audiences characterized what he did as *tafsir*. They reserved this term for technically proper exegeses. Yet his preaching was unmistakably exegetical. It was embodied in how he intertwined his own and Qur'anic phrases and how he produced his interpretations from this mix. This methodology was in a sense traditional. His premodern antecessors also translated the Qur'an across time and inserted into it their words and ideas. Some of them, for example, described Qarun as an alchemist.[48] And their "alchemy" was as much an extra-Qur'anic concept as Yusuf's modern "patent" and "machine." Yusuf's oral *tafsir* had all the elusive benefits of speaking. It was powerful because it was immediately resonant. And it was resonant because he was merely speaking and not delivering a formal exegesis. By merely speaking, he injected some of the Qur'an's linguistic medicine into the language of those who heard him. This intervention was potent precisely because he administered it live, by simultaneously speaking like his listeners and the Qur'an.

His contemporary American insertions into the Qur'anic text illustrate the American character of his cultural translations, which he carried out by evoking American memes, or cultural symbols, such as "Bill Gates" and "Harvard." For his listeners these words were clear allusions to their commonsense concepts. His "Bill Gates" was a meme, not a name, whose meaning was so palpable that it needed no explanation. And "Harvard" was not a university but a caricature of an arrogant elite institution populated by those who puff their chests and inspire envy. Yusuf's allusions made the Qur'an speak the language of an American collective memory. That it crossed an international border was not a problem: at the time of his speech, American symbols had a global reach, especially in places like Toronto.

While Yusuf's up-to-date cultural references were effective, more important was the conversational style of his preaching. Consider, for example, that the Qur'anic Qarun never said, "Allah didn't give it to me," and God never responded in the Qur'an with "That's what they think!" These were Yusuf's additions. They were not foreign to the Qur'an as a text: it is saturated with conversations between its characters, and their dialogues are typically punctuated with didactic summations. Both the Qur'an and Yusuf's renditions of it highlight that any communication is dialogical. We engage with other people or texts by repeating their words and injecting our own. Speaking a text faithfully does not mean its exact recitation. And that is what Yusuf did: by imitating the Qur'anic style, he remained faithful to it, but to "bring it home" into his listeners' realities, he infused it with their words and memes. This was a powerful move. It transformed the canonical Qur'an, a fixed text with ancient fables, into a living presence. This reanimation, however, depended entirely on the evanescent nature of human speech.

Yusuf's reenactment of this one scriptural story reflects how he spoke the Qur'an with an American conceptual accent, which is always time-specific. (In the 2000s, for example, when Bill Gates would become the world's leading philanthropist, Yusuf's equation of Qarun with Bill Gates would have sounded off-key.) His listeners, however, noticed neither his accent nor the time-bound nature of his Qur'anic rendition. To them, his sound was natural because he spoke with their accent and in their time. They did not listen to him as I did, to hear the Qur'an's American sounds. They directed their efforts toward hearing what the Qur'an had to say about them. And their teacher reciprocated with an explicit lesson, which was a didactic synthesis: "So here's Qarun," he pointed out, "a man from *bani isra'il* [the people of Israel]—and *bani isra'il* were Muslims of that time, let us not forget."

This reminder was the lecture's central teaching moment, where the message embedded in Yusuf's initial dichotomy of "us versus them" became clear. It was based on his Qur'anic diagnosis of his listeners' condition. He taught that "they" used to be "us" and stressed that now "we have many, many Qaruns in the Muslim world—many of them." Worse yet, most ordinary Muslims had become infected with the disease of envy. Like Qarun's contemporaries, he said, they kept saying, "Oh, if only we had what Qarun had!"[49] "See," he gestured, "this is the disease. . . . They want what others have, the Muslims want what America has, they want what Europe has . . . and they are getting it: they are getting the corruption, the television, the destruction of the families. It's all happening. Now, not only do they have social corruption, they also have corruption within the family itself."

Yusuf's merger of "us" and "them" was dramatic. It highlighted just how insecure it was to be religious in the modern world, and prompted his listeners to grasp for something enduring, such as the Qur'an and its tradition. He capitalized on their sense of deep vulnerability, which opened them up to hearing his message, to create yet another and more profound dichotomy: between his listeners—the ordinary, "lukewarm" Muslims—and the Qur'an's true believers. To be truly *muslim*, he preached, was not to have a mere identity. It was not something set and inherited, like the contemporary notions of citizenship and ethnicity. Rather, it was a lifelong struggle of remembering God in the midst of the modern culture of forgetting.

Those who paid attention to his lecture, which lasted longer than an average movie, must have realized the magnitude of their teacher's challenge. Therefore, he made sure to conclude it on an inspiring note. In the last minute, he promised that their battle would result in a new "intellectual renaissance" of Muslims. They would succeed, he assured them, if they removed from their "heart . . . the love of the *dunya* [the material world]." This was possible, he promised, because "Islam is powerful," the Qur'an "is transformative, and it can transform every single one of us—if we are open to it." And, "at an individual level," he said at the end, "all of us have to make an absolute commitment to studying our *deen* [religion] . . . in its most comprehensive and broad-based orthopraxic tradition."

···V···

What was political about "Making Sense"? Throughout his career Yusuf has preached the message of Muslims' traditional reorientation, which was a political move. To broaden the influence of the traditionalist camp, he took on the contemporary—and, in the 1990s, more widespread—Muslim discourses and reshaped them.[50] Some of the people he competed with were modernists. Others were the authorities who presented themselves as also, in a sense, traditional. Among those particularly audible were Muslim preachers with Salafi orientations, who promoted a return to the scriptures that bypassed much of the premodern Muslim scholarship, the very tradition that Yusuf and his colleagues perceived as indispensible. This is why, in speech after speech, he referenced "more scholarly . . . people" like his teachers and their antecessors, such as Ahmad Zarruq and Ibn ʿAtaʾillah al-Iskandari (d. 1309). He did it regularly but not excessively, so as not to overburden the "lukewarm" Muslims used to modern modes of preaching.

Perhaps the most obviously political aspect of his intervention was in how he re-membered the concept of jihad, or struggle. Echoing Salafi preachers, he used the trope of "Islam versus the West." But he reiterated that, traditionally speaking, the spiritual jihad—the jihad of the self—had a higher esteem than the military jihad. In the 1990s this intervention was timely because many American Muslim preachers, such as Siraj Wahhaj, still often spoke as though the 1980s had never ended. Some of them kept talking about jihad as though they were still raising funds for the Afghan mujahideen—literally "jihadists" and America's allies in the final conflict of the Cold War, whose cause many American Muslim organizations supported with endorsement from U.S. politicians such as President Reagan, who translated the term *"mujahidin"* into "freedom fighters."[51]

One of the preachers Yusuf competed with at that time, though never mentioned by name, was Bilal Phillips (b. 1949), a Canadian Muslim of Jamaican heritage. Like Yusuf, he was a prolific Internet preacher and often spoke about a dichotomy between "Islam" and "the West." Unlike Yusuf, he translated this trope into explicit endorsements of military jihad in such places as Afghanistan and Bosnia. He was also known, unlike Yusuf, for repeatedly castigating those coreligionists who did not conform to his view of orthodoxy, especially the Shiʿi Muslims.

What Phillips never preached, but Yusuf did routinely, was dialectics. Phillips's logic was circular: it began and ended with a clash with the "other." Yet, when Yusuf preached about "their" diseases, he was leading his listeners to realize that "the other" were, in fact, themselves. And those who listened to him faithfully understood their jihad differently. Phillips's jihad was entrenched in the flow of secular politics, such as the Cold War struggle of America and its Muslim allies, Saudi Arabia and Pakistan, against the Soviet

Union. Yusuf's "Making Sense," however, was not about secular politics but about the cultural politics of being religious in the contemporary world.

To borrow from Susan Harding, an anthropologist who studied the language of American fundamentalist Christians, Yusuf's rhetoric was "political in a broad sense of rearranging cultural power relations."[52] His caricatures of American official politics, for example, highlighted its temporal and fickle nature. He contrasted it with the image of the Islamic tradition that had been preserved by the "scholarly people," the *'ulama*. He preached that his listeners needed to remember this continuous tradition and translate it into their lives in order to remain religious, even in the midst of "this culture." This tradition's premodern roots, he taught, were vital because they enabled modern Muslims to live in a counter-modern mode. What Yusuf preached, therefore, was an alternative cultural politics. His speeches incorporated and then destabilized and reshaped, with help from the Qur'an, the conceptual vocabulary and grammar, the invisible cultural logics, of his modern listeners.

Yet politics and language are always collective. And from this perspective, the conclusion of "Making Sense" was paradoxical. For ninety-six minutes Yusuf urged his listeners to rearrange their "cultural power relations" and spoke about them as a collective. His final message, however, was distinctly individualistic: at the end he rushed his listeners to retreat into their private spaces and study. It was as though, when the time came to be practical, this teacher of a counter-modern culture slipped up and spoke from a very modern common sense of religion, where it is supposed to be a private affair and the church—or mosque—must quarantine itself from secular politics and public life.[53] So, what was political, and therefore collective and public, about his preaching? To explain this I need to clarify what I mean by the word "public" and introduce its correlate, "counterpublic."

In the academic literature, the term "public," as well as its cognates "public sphere" and "public life," are often associated with the works of the German philosopher Jürgen Habermas. In the words of Nancy Fraser, another philosopher, Habermas's notion of the public sphere "designates a theater in modern societies in which political [participants] . . . deliberate about their common affairs." It is "an institutionalized arena of discursive interaction," which means that institutions of public life—such as educational, judicial, and other more obviously political structures—shape what can be said, or even be thinkable, in public settings, as well as how it can be said. Yet, Fraser noted, this is a description of the *official* public sphere. It is not the only way of being public. Its alternatives are counterpublics.[54]

This matters for religious people because the common senses and languages of official public spheres restrict how they express themselves publicly. To enter official politics, they must translate their ways of speaking into the terms of official public discourses, which are overwhelmingly secular.[55] In the United States this secularity is demarcated by the notion of the separation of church and state, which has been a blessing for many religious minorities, such as Catholics and Jews, who used it to secure their places at the table of American life. But to arrive there, they had to learn how to communicate publicly with American secular accents.[56] It did not happen overnight. Parts of such journeys were often counterpublic.

As Michael Warner, another theorist, noted, "a public subaltern is only a counterpublic when its participants are addressed in a counterpublic way."[57] This means that counterpublic groups challenge official public realities by incorporating and reformulating within their discourses the languages of official public spheres. Fraser added to this that counterpublic communities typically develop in two phases: on the basic level they serve as "spaces of withdrawal and regroupment," but they can also become "bases and training grounds for agitational activities directed toward wider publics." What makes this transformation from an inward to an outward engagement possible is precisely the practices and discourses that a counterpublic has cultivated during its phase of "regroupment." Fraser's example of this process is the history of the nineteenth-century American "counter civil society of alternative, woman-only, voluntary associations," which "creatively used the heretofore quintessentially 'private' idioms of domesticity and motherhood precisely as springboards for public activity."[58] A more recent example comes from the 1980s, when many American fundamentalist Protestants transformed themselves, as Harding put it, from a "marginal, antiworldly, separatist people into a visible and vocal public force."[59]

From this perspective, Yusuf's pre-9/11 preaching was counterpublic and of the "withdrawal and regroupment" type. As he was making sense of his listeners' "condition," he spoke to them as a community, which emerged when they listened to and discussed his speeches collectively, in their homes, at conferences, and online. His critique of modern politics fashioned a counter-sense of "us," distinct from the official American, Canadian, or any other publics. It inculcated a practice of active distancing—but not complete dissociation—from secular life: he never called on his audiences to leave their secular studies or jobs, for example. By directing the energy of his message at their private lives, he spoke simultaneously from the grammar of their modern sensibilities and official public discourses. And then he subverted it through the Qur'an, through which he taught them how to re-member who they really were. Their practice of remembering the eternal was political because it cultivated an alternative, counter-modern mode of living. Their language was counterpublic because it subverted the grammar behind secular articulations of public life.

After 9/11 he began to make a different sense. This transformation reflected a dramatic change in the condition of American Muslims, who were his primary constituency all along. In the era of the War on Terror, withdrawal from public life and politics became a dangerous choice. It invited others, such as Skerry and Hughes, to define American Muslims as somehow foreign. (Remember how Hughes repeated Yusuf's trope as though it were foreign? It was something, she said, she had heard from "Muslims around the world" and not from an American speaker on the White House lawn.) In their everyday interactions with neighbors, coworkers, and government representatives, American Muslims now had to repeatedly prove that they too were American. Their heretofore marginal and largely ignored religious discourses became subject to scrutiny and surveillance. Even the participants of the explicitly nonpolitical RIS conferences could not escape the politics of the time: in the 2000s, dozens of American Muslims were detained, searched, and interrogated as they traveled to and from Toronto.[60] In response, increasing numbers of American Muslims became actively public: by the end of the decade, for example, 79 percent of American mosques were involved in interfaith activities, which was an officially *apolitical* way of entering American public life.[61] Their public engagements prompted them to become more fluent in the language of American politics, which, of course, is distinct from Canadian or other political dialects.

Under these conditions, Yusuf rearranged his language. He began to speak about American Muslims not as generic "Muslims in the West," but as "Americans and Muslims." Thanks to his dialectics of "us" and "them," as well as his customary critique of modernity, to most of his listeners his new formulations sounded like continuations of what he had preached before. This continuity was crucial because, by the powers of the Internet, what he had said in the past was a just click away from his listeners' present. In the domains of Google or YouTube—or their Muslim cousins, Halalgoogling and Halaltube—his recent lectures competed with the old. And he continued to preach in a counterpublic way, except that now he converted his rhetoric of withdrawal into a pedagogy of engagement with "wider publics." This was the sound of his new give-and-take, which was still "for God's sake."

··· VI ···

Yusuf's 2003 address was concise, just thirty-five minutes. He preached about American Muslims' involvement in their country's public life. For him, this message was somewhat new. He testified to this change constantly. "I cringe when I think about the things I said," he once told a journalist, and reiterated this confession repeatedly in Muslim gatherings.[62] His transformed rhetoric resonated with his listeners' experiences—partly because it spoke to the recent surge in their public activism but also because it reflected a more long-term American Muslim trend, upon which their post-9/11 efforts depended. Many African American Muslims, including W. D. Mohammed's community, had been politically active for decades. And many predominantly immigrant organizations, such as the Muslim Public Affairs Council, were carrying out political advocacy since at least 1980s. Even at ISNA and ICNA, which were officially apolitical organizations, Yusuf's 1990s articulations did not represent a consensus. What was new for such largely immigrant organizations was that, after 2001, they began to focus more on local, as opposed to international, concerns.[63] In addition to the post-9/11 realities, this shift was influenced by the generational change within these communities. The people for whom Yusuf preached in the 1990s were becoming older. Many of them were now young professionals, and their involvement in community life was different. For this generation of Muslims, most of whom were born and educated in the United States, American politics was closer to home. And for them, what their shaykh was now preaching was more than a message: it was the very language of their American politics, which he spoke with a Muslim conceptual accent.

Yusuf opened this speech on a distinctly post-9/11 note. "Brothers and sisters," he said, "friends, all the good people that have gathered here tonight, *in sha' allah,* I would like to talk here tonight about 'Give and Take for God's Sake.'"[64] His inclusion of "friends" and "all the good people" spoke to the realities of the new era, when many non-Muslim Americans reached out to their Muslim neighbors. I witnessed it firsthand, when before and after 9/11 I worked as a program director at the Interfaith Center of New York, the city's premier interfaith organization.

While Yusuf's acknowledgment of non-Muslim partners was new, his next step was customary—he proceeded to speak by remembering the Qur'an: "The Qur'an reminds us: 'Of the bounties of your Lord, We bestow freely on all, these as well as those.'[65] . . . The Qur'an also reminds us that Allah, *subhanahu wa ta'ala,* is self-committed to grace, to mercy— 'Kataba 'ala nafsihi ar-rahma . . . '66 Our Lord is a giving Lord, one committed to showering his servants, the good and the bad, the acceptors and the rejecters, the believers and the skeptics, with divine grace. For those who believe, Allah, *subhanahu wa ta'ala,* reminds them immediately in the Qur'an, 'alladhina' amanu 'bi-l-ghayb'—those who believe in the unseen, 'wa mimma razaqnahum yunfiqun'—'and from what we have given them, they give out.'"

These opening lines, which Yusuf delivered slowly, compressed three imperative notes. By remembering the Qur'an, he authenticated his message. By transforming "the divine grace," a Christian and colloquial American English phrase, into a Muslim expression, he demonstrated to his listeners how to speak in terms that would be understood by broader American publics. And through both of these moves, he introduced the central theme of his speech: the notion of God-conscious human generosity.

As always, he immediately connected the Qur'an to the Sunna: "The Prophet Muhammad, *salla-llahu 'alayhi wa sallam,* reminded us, 'kullukum 'iyal allah wa khayrukum 'anfa'ukum 'iyalihi'—all of you are the dependents of Allah, and the best of you are the best and the most beneficial to Allah's dependence." "And this," he interpreted, "is the nature of a believer: he gives—or she gives—out of the sense of gratitude for what they've been given; they desire to give back to Allah through the service to Allah's creation."

The phrasing of Yusuf's interpretation, which included the word "she" in his description of "a believer," was true to the scripture: the Qur'an often addresses believers as males and females. Yet, in the 1990s Yusuf's language was not as gender-inclusive. This change reflected his ability to hear and repeat his listeners' discourses, which by 2003 were steeped in gender politics. This resonance was crucial. It eliminated an obstacle, a dissonance, that would have made it more difficult for some of his listeners to hear his message, which was important because his reminder of their nature as believers contained in it an answer to the challenge they presently faced—the all-too-common public sense of their essential and values-based out-of-placeness in the "American body politic."

As before, the shaykh advanced his arguments dialectically. In this instance his description of "a believer" created a traditional-for-his-rhetoric dichotomy between "the best" and the rest among Muslims. Proper Muslims, he explained, were not materialistic: they "do not cling to their stuff and deem themselves independent of Allah and the needs of others." For his regular hearers this was a clear allusion to people like his teacher, Murabit al-Hajj. For all others he explained it Qur'anically, by speaking from Qur'an 36:47: "The Qur'an warns us from being like those, who 'when it is said to them, "spend from the bounties of Allah that He has provided," they say, "Should we feed who would Allah willed he would have fed them?" You are in nothing but manifest error!'"

Tellingly, Yusuf skipped the Arabic original of this verse and spoke it in translation, which was almost literal, except for the substitution of the Qur'anic phrase *"qala alladhina kafaru"* ("those who rejected said") with "they say." It is likely that he navigated around the verse's canonical Arabic phrasing on purpose, because it contains the verb *"kafaru,"* which is related to the noun *"kafir,"* a twin of the Christian term "infidel." Before 9/11 he used the word *"kafir"* regularly to describe the "others" who were completely consumed by the culture of materialism. It was a crude and frankly repulsive caricature, which he used, as he explained in "Making Sense," as a "discipline to the Muslims," to direct his listeners toward "giving up the life of *dunya,* returning to jihad, returning to *mujahada* of the self, [and] working on getting rid of the diseases of the heart." After 9/11 he erased *"kafir"* from his vocabulary—perhaps because Osama bin Laden and other extremists made it irredeemably toxic—and uttered "jihad" rarely.

Yusuf was not alone among religious people who adjusted their public language after 9/11. For example, one of the first words that President

George W. Bush said publically after that date was "crusade," a Christian synonym of "jihad." He used it to describe the nature of the new War on Terror.[67] Within days, however, he stopped using this word. Underneath Yusuf's and Bush's linguistic adjustments was a straightforward reality: meanings of words are shaped by their contexts. For Bush, a born-again Christian, "crusade" was not intrinsically problematic because he had learned its meanings from how it was used by his American Christian contemporaries, people like him, represented by such groups as the Campus Crusade For Christ. For him it was likely a routine expression that stood for values-based struggle, which possibly included a notion of a crusade of the self. Had he been an officially religious speaker addressing a like-minded religious community, his word choice would probably not raise an eyebrow. But he was the orator-in-chief, the supreme public speaker. For the broader American—and international—public of the time, "crusade" was drenched in the memories of medieval religious wars. It did not sound comfortably secular and therefore was not neutral. And so the president started to speak about "providence," a religious word that had been secularized by generations of politicians.[68] And Yusuf began consistently substituting "jihad" with "struggle."

This detail reflected a broader transformation of the sound of Yusuf's preaching. He now, for instance, began to say "God" just as often as "Allah." And after "Allah" he would occasionally omit the pious phrase, *"subhanahu wa ta'ala."* Sometimes he would even slip up and pronounce the Arabic word *"islam"* with his inborn American accent, by stressing its initial vowel—*"Ee*-slam." Such new pronunciations resonated with changing times. After 9/11 many American Muslim authorities, including traditionalists, began to emphasize that Islam had been an American religion all along, just like Christianity and Judaism. In 2004, one year after "Give and Take," for example, Umar Faruq Abd-Allah published an article, "One God, Many Names," that called on American Muslims to become more at ease about translating their religious articulations into English, the language they shared with other American publics. Abd-Allah's argument was in part defensive: it responded to the post-9/11 political realities. Yet it also reflected the practical work that the traditionalists had begun in the 1990s, when they established institutions, like Zaytuna, to train American Muslim scholars.

Of course, to continue their efforts after 9/11, they had to address the gnawing perception of a dichotomy between Muslim Americans and their non-Muslim fellow citizens. This is why the next step in Yusuf's speech was particularly timely. From the very first uttering, he had been planting the seeds for the eventual fusion of "us" and "the others." Now he proceeded toward this synthesis at full speed by speaking rapidly and responding directly to one of the most damaging anti-Muslim tropes of the time, the notion of a "clash of civilizations." His target was the book that made this concept famous, Bernard Lewis's 2002 bestseller, *What Went Wrong? The Clash Between Islam and Modernity in the Middle East.* "What I would like to say to Bernard Lewis," he declared, "is that the Muslims can ask the same question of the Western hemisphere." He continued, "We now, on this planet, are living in two completely dysfunctional hemispheres, the Northern and the Southern. The vast majority of wealth in the Northern hemisphere is accumulated through two industries, the arms industry and the industry of drugs, the intoxicants. These are the two primary money making industries in the Northern hemisphere, armaments and drugs—weapons of destruction and weapons of distraction."

This statement echoed Yusuf's traditional diagnoses of "the West." As before, it also sounded as if it could have been uttered by any Muslim critic of the generic "West." After 9/11, however, he had to address the realities of his American Muslim audiences more explicitly. Therefore, he immediately added, "And we, in the United States, have a unique historical position . . . we are neither of the East nor of the West. We are people living in a space that Allah, *subhanahu wa ta'ala*, has described as the space of the strangers—*al-ghuraba'*—people who neither feel they are of this or of that, because we are seeking to live a life committed to a spiritual path—'*wa inna ila rabbika al-muntaha*'—to your Lord is your end—in the midst of the cornucopia of nihilistic materialism, we are struggling to maintain our souls."[69]

This familiar note, which, as always, prioritized the jihad of the self, provided a deeper meaning to his listeners' current sense of marginality. They were "strangers," he implied, not really because of their secular identities, including their status as card-carrying Muslims, but because of their religiosity. And then, in a distinctly post-9/11 mode, he added that "we are not the only ones: there are many people in this society who are having the same struggle. And we have to recognize that."

Yusuf's articulation of this observation was markedly counterpublic, for the allies he urged his listeners to recognize were still "strangers." Like Muslims, they were religious, or at least spiritual, and struggled against the broader materialistic current of life. In this moment he seemed to be projecting yet another dichotomy: between religious and secular Americans. Yet, how could Muslims, and other religious "strangers," be anything but outcasts in this "cornucopia of nihilistic materialism"? How could they relate to more secularized Americans? And, how could they participate in American public life together with this secular category of "others"? The answer to this quandary lay in Yusuf's initial reminder about God's generosity and the true believers' service to "the needs of others." Bringing this message home, however, required yet another synthesis, which he presaged by redirecting Lewis's question—"What went wrong?"—toward his audience. "In the Muslim community," he preached, "in this country, we have very serious questions . . .

to ask . . . . why is it that so many Muslims have learned the worst of the Western civilization and failed to learn the best?"

New in this question was Yusuf's emphasis on "the best" of "the West." He delivered it in tandem with the already familiar dichotomy between the "best" and the rest of Muslims, and employed these two pairs of contradictions—between "the best" and the rest among "us" and "them"—to fuse "the best" of "us" with the "best" of "them." As in his pre-9/11 speeches, he reminded his listeners about the spread of the spiritual and material corruption in the Muslim world. But then he immediately asserted that American and other Western societies were "less corrupt" and that most non-Muslim Americans were more "ethical" in their everyday conduct than Muslims. Rhetorically, this was a repetition of his customary technique of generating insecurity among his listeners, which served to prompt them to hear his message. As before, he urged Muslims to be more religious. Yet, by inserting the word "ethical," he united them with most other Americans.

Yusuf's rhetorical synthesis of ethical Muslims and Americans relied on the common perception of ethics as something universal, which creates the impression that all it takes for us to really understand each other is a mere reminder of our essential commonality. From this common ground, the shaykh now spoke explicitly as an American public spokesperson, in the language of American public life: "This Muslim community is young, vibrant and filled with potential and a core of people that can literally change the landscape of this society. We are inheritors of the struggle in this country to keep this country in course with its founding principles. . . . Most of the people that preceded us suffered much more than we have ever suffered as a community . . . including the Hispanic peoples, the Chinese peoples, the Mexican peoples, the Native American people, the African-American people, the Japanese-Americans—they have all suffered greatly. And their suffering enabled so many of us to come into this country and be treated with respect, be treated with equality, because people put their lives on the line."

On the surface this statement was a mere reflection of what his listeners already knew. Their community was certainly young: in the 2000s over 70 percent of them were between the ages of eighteen and forty-four.[70] At a deeper level Yusuf was speaking from two uniquely American tropes. His assertion about his listeners' young character recalled the idea of "young America," which had been a mainstay of American public rhetoric since at least 1830s.[71] Just a few months before "Give and Take," Secretary of Defense Donald Rumsfeld relied on this notion to explain why some of America's European allies were lukewarm about invading Iraq: they were "Old Europe," he stated; they could not understand America's forward-looking ideas.[72] And now, as the war in Iraq was blazing, an American shaykh was appropriating this trope to teach his listeners how to speak and be heard by other Americans.

In a peculiar twist of tongue, Yusuf spoke about Muslims as though they were a race or an ethnicity, both secular categories. Perhaps he did it instinctually. For many of his listeners and maybe for him as well, it was a habitual way of speaking about their country's diversity. Like other Americans, they learned how to discuss it from their public institutions, such as the media and schools, which routinely portray America as a multiethnic and multiracial quilt.[73] Whatever the reason, by momentarily deemphasizing religion, the shaykh was able to speak about American Muslims in publically understandable terms, which, tellingly, were secular.

Yet his pronouncement was also—and simultaneously—religious, because it relied on the American trope of redemptive civic suffering. He evoked it fluently to describe the process of ensuring America's eternally young nature, which had kept "this country in course with its founding principles." This statement sounded commonsensical, neutral, and secular. Of course, the roots of this trope were religious, Christian, and African American. It had become publically commonsensical through the struggles of countless generations of Christian and other counterpublic agitators and through linguistic interjections of preachers such as Martin Luther King, Jr., and W. D. Mohammed. Yusuf's language embodied the American heritage of synthesizing religious and secular dialects. Religious critics of past American status quos such as slavery and Jim Crow had been able to speak to and be heard by broader publics precisely through such fusions of religious and secular vernaculars. That is how they "change[d] the landscape of this society." And this was what this American shaykh was now teaching in his "Give and Take": a method of synthesizing a new iteration of an American Muslim public language.

This deeper lesson of his speech became pronounced in its last minutes, when he fused his message of private jihad with the memories of American civic struggles and through this synthesis fashioned a notion of an American civic jihad. (Of course, given the restraints of the era, he called it "struggle.") To guide his listeners toward this way of articulating who they were, he resorted to yet another timely reminder:

> We are not only celebrating the 40th anniversary of the ISNA, we are celebrating the 40th anniversary of the march on Washington of Dr. Martin Luther King, Jr. And I do not believe that those two dates are fortuitous. I believe that there is a connection between these two great events. Because we are now in the position in this country to challenge once again the very thing that Dr. King challenged . . . to ask the question: Are you willing to live up to the truths of your formative declarations, that all people are created equal, that they are endowed by their creator with certain inalienable rights, among which are life, liberty and the pursuit of happiness? Are you willing

to live up to the words of Thomas Jefferson when he said that free-dom of religion is an essential right in this country and it is equal to the Christian and the Jew and the Mohammadan. And he mentioned the Mohammadan because that is providence, because that is the hand of providence that moved his hand to put Mohammadan in that great text, the Virginia Act of Religious Freedom. . . . And this is the message . . . we have to be willing to sacrifice and to struggle just as those who went before us sacrificed and struggled to improve this society. . . . And if you don't believe it, you do not recognize your historical purpose.

How was his message of an American civic jihad practical? And how was it, scripturally speaking, Muslim? Yusuf preemptively responded to such questions in his next declaration, where he blended texts of American civic memory with a hadith. He performed this fusion by reminding his audience that "dissent against the policies of the President during the time of war is a constitutional right," and recalling that this right had been put into practice by none other than Abraham Lincoln, who protested against the U.S.-Mexican War of the 1840s. At the same time, borrowing from the Cold War rhetoric of American Catholics, he proclaimed that "to call people who speak against misguided policies of this country anti-American is essentially anti-Ameri-can! It can be nothing other than Stalinist!"[74] And then he spoke from the scripture: "We are not anti-American! We are adhering to the finest principles of this country. And if we don't recognize those principles and recognize that they are Islamic principles and stand by them, then we have failed to live up to the historical task of this community. And that is the truth. And the truth is sometimes bitter. But our Prophet, may Allah's blessings and peace be upon him, said, *'qul al-haqq wa law [kana] murran,'* speak the truth, even if it's bitter. Speak the truth even if it's bitter. We must speak the truth. This is our right and our obligation." Judging by the reaction of his audience, this was the high point of the speech: the convention floor erupted with applause.

The "truth" of which Yusuf spoke, and which his audience endorsed, could be understood in at least two ways. It was public—and therefore, to an extent, secular—and religious as well. The synthesis of these two conno-tations came across in his merger of the secular and religious meanings of the notions of "right" and "obligation." His "right" was an obviously secular word, a part and parcel of the American public language. He made it reli-gious by connecting it with *"al-haqq,"* a scriptural word, which means the "truth," "right," and "obligation." On the immediate level his phrasing articu-lated what many of his listeners were already doing: as Americans, they were defending their civic rights and agitating against policies they deemed erro-neous. On a more subtle plain, however, his linking of the American concepts of "rights" with parallel, yet distinct, religious ideas hinted at a hierarchy of power, where religious authorities were still needed to guide American Muslim politics. Otherwise, why would ISNA invite a religious scholar to endorse its constituency's common sense?

What neither the shaykh nor ISNA explicitly stated was that he was delivering a religious opinion, a fatwa of sorts. Surely, he was a preacher and not officially a jurist. Like his *tafsir*, which was technically not a *tafsir*, his fatwa was officially not a fatwa. Those who needed official legal opinions could find them easily on the website of the Fiqh Council of North America or in the pronouncements of Yusuf's teacher, bin Bayyah, who was a leading authority in the relatively new branch of Islamic jurisprudence, *fiqh al-aqalliyyat*, the jurisprudence of Muslim minorities. Yet, Yusuf's opinion mattered more than a thousand fatwas, because he was America's most prominent Muslim preacher. In part his influence depended on his reputation of telling "it like it is," of being a values-based critic of the broader secular culture. At this juncture in his listeners' lives, however, his role was to testify that their sense of the natural affinity between their American and Muslim principles was religiously authentic. This, for him, was a new obligation. Therefore, in his concluding remarks, he made sure to respond to those who might have doubted the sincerity of his new articulations: "I want to say that we cannot spin our religion. . . . And by spin I mean that we cannot change our rhetoric because now the media is watching. We have to change because of principle. We have to recognize that we have made mistakes in the past. And . . . the people of God are those who repent from their mistakes and who change. This is the sign of the people of growth. . . . We are biological creatures [and we] must adapt to those things that are outside of us that are affecting us. This is the nature of life. If you don't respond, you're dead."

This was Yusuf's personal testimony of change, which he made collective by saying "we." Once again, he preached in a publically commonsensical mode. His phrasing echoed the language of the theory of evolution, an inescapably modern way of articulating change. Heard in this fashion, his declaration was comfortably secular and therefore publically acceptable. Yet it was also an elaboration on his religious theme of God-conscious generosity. His claim about "the nature of life" alluded to the Qur'anic concept of *fitra*, a naturally God-centered human disposition. This tacit reminder signaled that he was not endorsing a Machiavellian type of politics but teaching his audience how to be involved in public life while staying true to the "for God's sake" part of their nature.

As before, internal Muslim politics lay beneath the surface of his speech. The risk that Yusuf faced at this time was being misheard and perceived as yet another political spokesperson and a sellout. Some of the people who had listened to him before 9/11 could say, "What the heck happened to Hamza

Yusuf?" and turn to other authorities instead. In the overwhelming majority of cases, that would be a matter of taste: his new, explicitly public pronouncements might not have resonated with a person's search for more private lessons. Yet an impression of his "selling out" could, in some cases, add to the cynicism that some young Muslims undoubtedly felt toward American politics, with its War on Terror at home and abroad. Some such individuals could tune in, for example, to Yusuf's other Salafi competitor, the Yemeni American preacher Anwar al-Awlaki (1971–2011). In the mid-1990s and early 2000s, while serving as an imam in Colorado, California, and Virginia, al-Awlaki often orated about the clash between "Islam" and "the West"—and, in this sense, sounded like Bilal Phillips and Bernard Lewis. In 2002 he fled to the United Kingdom and, in 2004, to Yemen, where he went beyond Phillips's playbook and began promoting an armed jihad against Americans. One of the very few people who followed his call literally was Nidal Hasan, a U.S. Army psychiatrist who murdered thirteen people at the Fort Hood military base in Texas in 2009. This, as well as al-Awlaki's involvement in the failed attempt to down an American airliner on December 25, 2009, led to his assassination in 2011 by a CIA drone. Indeed, in the 2000s thousands of young American Muslims listened to al-Awlaki's Internet speeches. The fact that infinitesimally few of them translated his dictates into terrorist acts suggests that they heard him selectively, as audiences always do. What I heard from some of his listeners was that they were attracted to him because he reminded them of Malcolm X: he was a rebel who "told the truth." Some of them also shared that he sounded like the pre-9/11 "Shaykh Hamza."

To Yusuf's regular followers, the difference between him and al-Awlaki was obvious. They knew about the network of the authorities he represented. Many of them, for example, listened to the recording of bin Bayyah's 1999 lecture at Zaytuna, where he spoke about "obligations" that Western Muslims owed to their non-Muslim compatriots.[75] Some of them explained to me that Yusuf's post-9/11 rhetoric was a mere translation of his teacher's logic into an American political dialect. Yet, to Yusuf's less devout listeners, his change could be jarring. It helped that he continued to criticize modernity and interpret the Qur'an in a traditional mode. But at this juncture, to respond to some of his listeners' potential nihilism, this rhetorical continuity was not enough. His change had to come across as deeply and sincerely rooted in religion. It had to be heard and felt as authentic. This is why the sound of his speech was vital. This sound became pronounced in the last thirty seconds of "Give and Take," when Yusuf broke into tears right in the midst of delivering the final recap of his message of civic jihad:

> This is where the struggle is—it's stopping the proliferation of weapons, it's stopping the proliferation of drugs, condemning racism, it's

condemning the fact that in Rwanda 800,000 human beings can be massacred in our life time and the world stood by and watched it happen. And then everyone sheds tears for a few white people that die. We have to recognize that every life on this planet is sacred. And I will end this by saying this one thing: I reject President Bush's statement that you are either with us or against us as much as I reject Usama bin Laden's statement you're either with us or against us. We cannot turn this world into an insane dichotomy of those who support state terrorism and those who support vigilante terrorism. All terrorism is wrong. And bombing civilian populations is inflicting terror on those people. And I shake for the children's hearts—they were petrified as the bombs dropped on Baghdad. And I feel ashamed when I am in this country when things like this can happen in our life time. And we reject it. We reject it. And we will speak the truth. And we are Americans, and we are Muslims.

··· V I I ···

Much of what Yusuf said in 2003 was not new. He was, after all, a preacher, and preachers are not valued for their originality but for how well they make sense for those who hear them. Before and after 9/11, he made sense by speaking to the collective memories and senses of his listeners. One such example occurred at ISNA's 2004 convention, where he declared that "the question is not whether Islam can embrace democracy; the question is can democracy embrace Islam."[76]

This statement was an almost exact replica of the challenge John Courtney Murray, the American Catholic intellectual mentioned previously, issued in 1960 in response to the then-common allegation of Catholics' religious incompatibility with their country's public values. "The question is sometimes raised," Murray wrote in *We Hold These Truths: Catholic Reflections on the American Proposition,* "whether Catholicism is compatible with American democracy. The question is invalid as well as impertinent; for the manner of its position inverts the order of values." By "the order of values," the Jesuit priest meant his Catholic hierarchy of principles, where "the principles" of his "faith and morality" stood "superior to, and in control of, the whole order of civil life." And it was based on his community's religious values that he then gave "an affirmative answer" to the question of "whether American democracy is compatible with Catholicism."[77]

I do not know whether Yusuf echoed Murray intentionally; given his Catholic education, it was likely not a coincidence. What I do know is that his listeners responded to his assertion with a surge of applause. Most of them, perhaps like most of their Catholic contemporaries, did not remember

Murray. They did not applaud because they recognized a rendition of an American classic. Rather, their reaction signaled that this religious argument spoke to their current realities. Above all, to them it was a naturally American idiom of public speaking, a publically acceptable way of expressing their allegiance to America, while also challenging some of its culture, which some of them perceived as discordant with being religiously devout.

How did Yusuf and his listeners harmonize this discordance? He and they did it by recognizing and witnessing that "the finest principles of this country" are really religious. This message encapsulated the methodology of Yusuf's post-9/11 change, which he carried out by rearranging emphases. His post-9/11 linguistic remix followed the pattern of the post–World War II transformation in American Catholic discourses. Until that watershed event, many American Catholic authorities spoke about America as the prime example of the modern culture of secularism, in part because that is how mainstream non-Catholic intellectuals presented it as well. After World War II, Murray and others did not give up their critique of secularism. Instead, they adjusted their language and decoupled the idea of "America" from the notion of "modernity," a move that Yusuf echoed when he emphasized his country's "finest principles." As the historian R. Scott Appleby explained, this move allowed American Catholic authorities to acquit "the basic convictions and tendencies associated with Americanism" from the "charges of [its] guilt by association with modernism."[78] This modification marked a new American Catholic mode of public communication. It resonated with the changing realities of their diverse constituents, who by that time had become largely mainstream in terms of their socioeconomic status.

From the perspective of their economic and social standing, Yusuf's American Muslim audiences were not marginal either: in the 2000s, according to the 2007 Pew poll, their levels of education and income "generally mirror[ed] the U.S. public."[79] The groups that Yusuf addressed were typically middle class. One could hear this reality in "Give and Take," where his audience delivered their first applause nineteen minutes into the speech, when he reproached them for not yet establishing an American Muslim hospital. This reprimand was a specifically American Muslim meme, which I heard used by many speakers in the late 1990s and 2000s. It was resonant because organizations like ISNA included in their rosters many medical professionals. In "Give and Take," Yusuf spoke to this constituency when he reminded them that "there are over 20,000 Muslim healthcare workers" in this country and then retold a joke from David Letterman, whose Muslim doctor supposedly told him, "Turn to Mecca and cough!"

Yusuf's "Muslim doctor" meme highlights that his audience, before and after 9/11, was not limited to young people but included their middle-class parents as well. And his rebellious-sounding message was consistently middle class. Even when he spoke in terms that would make him "cringe" after 9/11, the counter-discipline he was preaching did not disturb his listeners' economic, social, and cultural integration. Otherwise, why would Sadaf's mother encourage her daughter to "hear this man"? And didn't Sadaf herself come up with the plan to study at Zaytuna while simultaneously pursuing a secular college education? Yusuf's "like it is" message urged young people to be religious, study, and stay away from consumerism. It was a sensible and quite middle-class form of youthful countercultural rebellion.

"Give and Take" was palpably different from "Making Sense," partly because Yusuf's primary constituency had changed: many of them were no longer teenagers, the classic subalterns.[80] In addition, ISNA and other Muslim organizations now invited him to speak to broader and not just youth-oriented concerns, and he reciprocated by preaching anew. As I interviewed his regular listeners, however, many of them, like Sadaf's friend, a student at Zaytuna, insisted that "Shaykh Hamza hasn't changed at all," noting, "The only difference that I see was that his tone changed." "What do you mean?" I asked. He explained that Yusuf "preach[ed] from the Qur'an," that the scriptural meanings he taught were eternal and always applicable: "The same tests and trials that were affecting those people [depicted in the Qur'an and Hadith] are affecting us now." I probed further: "Is there anything in his approach that is specific to his American audiences?" He paused and reflected: "Something that always struck me about him is that he has this uncanny ability to break down the language. He takes you into the world of symbols, and extracts meanings out of it for you. . . . And he looks at our condition. And he's able to make a bridge, [a] balance [between contemporary American Muslims and the Qur'an]. He does not deal with irrelevancies. He cuts right to the chase: what does it mean to me, now? He's able to strike that balance between fourteen hundred years ago and 2008 because the human condition hasn't changed, it's just that the forms have changed."[81]

I tend to agree and disagree with this characterization. On one hand the change in Yusuf's tone was significant. It marked his and some of his listeners' reorientation from an insular toward an outward type of counterpublic discourse. Yet, at the same time, the Qur'an did provide stability to what and how he taught. Vital here was the continuity in the cultural and conceptual grammar, the instinctual logic, embedded in Yusuf's preaching. The fact that my conversation partner did not pay attention to it is telling: native speakers rarely notice the grammar, linguistic or conceptual, of the languages they speak. Yusuf, after all, made sense of the Qur'an for him and other American Muslims through preaching, a genre of scriptural speaking that made his oral *tafsir* simultaneously flexible and stable. Its stability depended on his constant remembrances of the Qur'an. Its flexibility was derived from the fact that he "merely" spoke it. Through speaking, he constantly re-membered the language of the revelation and the language of his listeners, and then synthesized them anew. Such fusions wove the Qur'an into their everyday speech and collective memory.

How he performed such syntheses—how he culturally translated the Qur'an, and then, based on his Qur'anic rememberings, reshaped his listeners' common senses—was characteristically American all along. Before and after 9/11, Yusuf's lectures have been structured in a uniquely American style, reflecting the tradition of sermonizing that had been cultivated by generations of American religious and secular public speakers, beginning with the seventeenth-century Puritans. Sacvan Bercovitch, a Canadian Americanist, called it an "American jeremiad." According to Bercovitch, unlike the medieval and early modern European jeremiads, which traditionally amounted to lamentations over currently ungodly states of affairs, the "American jeremiads" have consistently relied on the trope of American hope: the notions of an American "promise" and "mission," linked to the ideas of America's exceptionalism and eternal "youth." "The American Jeremiad," Bercovitch explained, "posits a movement from promise to experience—from the ideal of community to the shortcomings of community life—and thence forward, with prophetic assurance, toward the resolution that incorporates (as it transforms) both the promise and the condemnation."[82] This was the internal logic of both "Making Sense" and "Give and Take." In both speeches Yusuf condemned "this culture" and its "nihilistic materialism," and then prophesied the arrival of a new dawn.

How and why he employed this logic was distinct in the two eras of his listeners' lives. In "Making Sense" he spoke in a "withdrawal and regroupment" mode. His promise of a new "intellectual renaissance" was directed at the generic "Muslims in the West." Yet it was based on the fact that they were young, like "young America," and lived not "back home," not in the world of their parents, but in a new space that was removed from the "corruption" of "the Muslim world." He did not say it explicitly, but what informed his promise was his and his listeners' location in the "New World," which assured a new beginning that would somehow break the regular pattern of decline and corruption.

The sound of Yusuf's "Give and Take" was more tangibly American. When he was called to teach the language of "agitational activities directed toward wider publics," the American grammar that undergirded his preaching all along became more pronounced, including his tropes of "young America" and American Muslims' "unique historical position." He now spoke these tropes explicitly. To his regular listeners, the change in his tone sounded harmonious, because to them it was a natural way of speaking and because, long before Yusuf, this style of synthesizing religious and civic dialects had become an American tradition, put into practice by countless other speakers such as John Winthrop, Martin Luther King, Jr., John F. Kennedy, Jeremiah Wright, and W. D. Mohammed.

Here it may be useful to remember that harmony, which is a musical concept, is always cultural: we do not notice just how unique our natural harmonies are until we run into compositions from other cultural settings. This explains why Sadaf tuned out so many other preachers and why, to her, Yusuf's preaching sounded "beautiful" and the Islam he taught did "not seem foreign." It was the very grammar of his speaking that made his cultural translation of the Qur'an resonant with her and many other American listeners' sensibilities. This was why it was important that Yusuf did not just preach from the Qur'an but spoke it as well. He took on the Qur'an's own characterization of its nature as a text of "remembrance" and translated it into how he spoke and synthesized it with his listeners' senses.[83] His preacherly techniques, like his didactic dichotomies, were helpful when he explained the Qur'an. But he harmonized—and rhapsodized—it at a much deeper level.

Yusuf's primary audience, the younger generation of Muslims who grew up as Americans, kept listening to him because to them his sound was natural. Yet why did their parents urge them to "hear this man"? And why did they applaud his uniquely American tropes? Most of them had lived in the United States for decades. Unlike their children, they were not native speakers of American English, and they could not sermonize as harmoniously as their American shaykh. But they heard him nonetheless. This was because the language they had learned later in their lives—and, as middle class professionals, spoke fluently—was not flat. It was saturated with local, American cultural meanings and memories, which by hearing and speaking they made their own. This, of course, highlights that being an immigrant is yet another way of being American and that the Qur'an as an American scripture is not a unique domain of subsequent generations of Muslims.

Still, where was the Qur'an in Yusuf's preaching? Certainly it was present in easily discernible places, such as his *tafsir* of "Qarun and Bill Gates." Yet explanations, no matter how culturally fluent, do not make a text American. The Qur'an of American Muslims must be embodied by them. It must be harmonious with their deeper common senses and cultural logics. It must be a natural part of their sensibilities. While typically imperceptible, such sensibilities come across in allusions that a speaker does not explain. In "Give and Take" two such elusive notes were infused in Yusuf's final declaration: one of them was political, another Qur'anic, and both were American. They were immersed in his tears, which began flowing down his face as he was sharing the shame over the 1994 genocide in Rwanda, most of whose victims were obviously non-Muslim but equally human. And they continued to flow as he testified to the physical shaking he felt as he witnessed the terror inflicted upon the mostly Muslim children of Iraq during the "Shock and Awe" of his country's latest war.

Yusuf, of course, was not the first American to cry while remembering Rwanda. By 2003 this testimony of an American shame became the standard "biggest regret" line of Bill Clinton's rhetoric (in 2002 I saw the former president publically weep about it at a fundraiser for my organization, the Interfaith Center of New York).[84] Yusuf's rendition of this American trope, which he delivered in a counterpublic mode, became tangibly Muslim when he connected it to the unfolding tragedy in Iraq. His tears, however, went beyond the secular language and politics of identities—Iraqi, Rwandan, American, or Muslim. Rather, they were a visceral reminder of the deeper politics he had taught all along: the practice of re-membering one's self by remembering the revelation, the discipline of embodying the scripture even when it is left unspoken. For many of Yusuf's American Muslim listeners, his tears were a palpable allusion to Qur'an 5:32, a verse many of them remembered repeatedly, in private and in public, after 9/11: it states that the murder of a single human being is an unspeakable evil, which God sees as equal to the genocide of the entire humanity.[85] For his more devout listeners, they also likely evoked the memories of his Sufi teacher, who personified "the spirit of Islam" when he cried while remembering the Qur'an. And now, at this juncture, Shaykh Hamza's tears embodied remembrance that was at once deeply American and Muslim—because it was Qur'anic.

AFTERWORD

In all the wonderful worlds that writing opens, the spoken word still resides and lives. Written texts all have to be related somehow, directly or indirectly, to the world of sound, the natural habitat of language, to yield meaning.

Walter Ong, *Orality*, 8

In the summer of 2014, I had a conversation with a Buddhist monk in New York City, Venerable Benkong Shi. Somehow I mentioned my book. He asked me what it was about. I said that it examined how the Qur'an becomes an American sacred text, that I analyzed the Qur'an's local written and oral interpretations, and that I approached such interpretations, found in books or sermons, as cultural translations. Then I said that my thesis "is that the Qur'an is an American scripture when Muslims speak it"; or, I may have said, "when it becomes an American spoken sacred text."

To Benkong Shi, this explanation sufficed—I did not need to spell out, for example, why I gave preference to sermons and other forms of scriptural speaking—because he was also an interpreter. He was a resident monk at a Buddhist temple in New York's Chinatown. With few exceptions, his congregation was entirely Chinese. He, however, was a convert, who had lived in China for a long time and spoke Chinese fluently, to the extent that his spoken English had Chinese intonations. Because of his cultural and linguistic fluency, he often served as a translator for his congregation: he made sense of documents and people who came their way. He was also one of their religious teachers, which is another way of being a translator. Every week, he held classes where he taught and explained Buddhist scriptures, the Sutras. These sessions were live; he spoke. And, by speaking, he carried out the Sutras' cultural translations: he related them to the experiences of the people in his community, in different moments of their lives. For those who had immigrated to the United States as adults, he explained the Sutras largely through Chinese cultural references. For their children, who grew up in this country, he spoke with an American conceptual accent. Therefore, when he heard what I told him about my book, he paused and then said, "Come to think of it, in a way, I speak Sutras."[86]

Learning to hear how people speak their texts takes time. This is a major reason behind some of my book's omissions. For example, I could have written more about people like Awlaki but chose not to proceed too deeply down this particular crevasse. Partly, it is because they represented extreme fringes of the discursive field I was surveying. Surely, as 9/11 and other tragedies demonstrated, their marginality did not make them benign. But for the purpose of this study, I decided not to spend thousands of hours engrossing myself in the minutia of their language. I think it was a sound choice. What I regret much more is that my case studies do not include explorations of American Shi'i discourses, which are certainly not marginal.[87] The reason behind it is that I had not spent enough time learning the conceptual language—and sensibilities—of these communities. Another important matter I did not examine in detail is the Qur'an as a cyber-text, although I touched upon it chapter 4. This subject deserves serious attention. Its exploration has to address the question of the Qur'an's embodiment by contemporary Muslims, increasing numbers of whom are, in a sense, cyber-humans: just as our sense of time is inseparable from clocks and other technologies that organize our lives, our engagements with texts have become increasingly intertwined with our cyber modes of living.

Of course, as Benkong Shi's story suggests, the topic of scriptures as living texts is wide-ranging. My book's broad inquiry is this: What happens afterward—after the words of scriptures are revealed, written down, and canonized? Do they become calcified, fixed forever? Or do they continue to speak and therefore live? My answer is that, to make sense in constantly changing contexts, sacred texts have to be spoken; they "have to be related somehow . . . to the world of sound." That is why most of this book's words are about words that were spoken. Sound is the "natural habitat of language" because it is embodied by people, not objects. And that is why, come to think of it, my thesis is that the Qur'an becomes an American scripture when it is embodied by its American faithful.

NOTES

······ ✗ ······

INTRODUCTION

1. Anonymous, interview with author, August 12, 2008. I spoke with this person under the auspices of a joint Duke University and University of North Carolina project, *Anti-Terror Lessons of Muslim-Americans*. The project's report is available at https://fds.duke.edu/db/attachment/1255 (accessed December 2, 2014).

2. Qur'an 80:1. There is disagreement among Muslims about the identity of the person who "turned away." The Egyptian teacher, like me, was Sunni. For most Sunnis it is common knowledge that the person reprimanded by God in this passage was the Prophet Muhammad. Many Shi'i exegetes remember the episode differently and teach that it was someone else. See, for example, Tabatabai, "Surah abasa 80, verses 1–16." (Many thanks to Jawad Bayat for reminding me about this detail.) On a different note, throughout the book, I adhere to a simplified version of the *International Journal of Middle East Studies* transliteration system. In chapters 3 and 4, the transliterations are often phonetic: when appropriate, they convey how transliterated Arabic words sounded when speakers uttered them, as opposed to how they are written.

3. My engagement with American Muslim discourses had begun earlier. A Muslim from Russia, I immigrated to the United States in 1993 and since then have been studying and working with American Muslims. This experience is one of the sources for this book.

4. Prager, "America, Not Keith Ellison."

5. Swarns, "Congressman Criticizes Election."

6. Kuo, "America's 'Holiest Book'?"

7. Spellberg, *Thomas Jefferson's Qur'an.*

8. In this book I employ the terms "the Hadith," "the hadith literature," and "hadith." By "the Hadith" and "the hadith literature," I mean collections of written-down memories of Muhammad's actions and words. The word "hadith" designates an individual record from such collections, one single record of a particular action, or an expression attributed to the Prophet.

9. Martin, "Inimitability," 526–36.

10. The same expression, "my Qur'an," can be found, for example, in Qutb, *al-Taswar,* 8, as quoted in Abu-Rabi', *Intellectual Origins of Islamic Resurgence,* 104.

11. Asad, *Formations of the Secular,* 17.

12. Alryyes, *Muslim American Slave.*

13. Loguen protesting the Fugitive Slave Law at the steps of Syracuse City Hall in 1851, as quoted in George, "Widening the Circle," 156.

14. Gade, *Perfection Makes Practice.*

15. Qur'an 94:5–6. In this instance I use T. B. Irving's translation, *The Noble Qur'an.* Elsewhere in the book, I employ translations that were used by the individuals whose

works I examine. In chapters 1 and 2, it is mostly the translation by Muhammad Marmaduke Pickthall. In chapters 3 and 4, it is the translation by Yusuf Ali. These translations are available online. See, for example, http://www.islamawakened.com/index.php/qur-an (accessed March 4, 2015).

16. Bakhtin, *Toward a Methodology*, 68.

17. Two notable American translations are Irving, *The Noble Qur'an*, and Bakhtiar, *The Sublime Qur'an*.

18. Eck, *New Religious America*.

19. See, for example, Schlund-Vials, *Modeling Citizenship*.

20. Nabokov, *Speak, Memory*, 275.

21. Rahman, *Major Themes of the Qur'an*, 59.

22. Rahman, *Major Themes of the Qur'an*, xii, 8.

23. This pattern is present, for example, in Qur'an 21, sura "Prophets."

24. Qur'an 3:110.

25. Donner, *Narratives of Islamic Origins*, 75.

26. Robinson, *Islamic Historiography*, 10.

27. Graham, *Beyond the Written Word*, 16.

28. Ricoeur, *Memory, History, Forgetting*, 494, 55.

29. Manguel, *History of Reading*.

30. Koselleck, *Futures Past*, 220.

31. When modernity began is not easy to say. Its origins are often traced to the invention of the printing press, the European conquest of the Americas in the fifteenth and sixteenth centuries, or the European Enlightenment of the seventeenth and eighteenth centuries. In many non-European settings, it is associated with the history of European colonialism and emergence of industrialized societies, which transformed the world most drastically in the nineteenth and the twentieth centuries. For a particularly informative discussion on the subject of modernity, see Giddens, *Modernity and Self-Identity*.

32. Koselleck, *Practice of Conceptual History*, 221–23.

33. Hadith Bukhari, vol. 3, bk. 48, no. 819.

34. See, for example, Friedmann, *Prophecy Continuous*.

35. Ernst and Lawrence, *Sufi Martyrs of Love*, 11–14.

36. Wadud, *Inside the Gender Jihad*, 205.

37. McAuliffe, "Tasks and Traditions of Interpretation," 181–210.

38. al-Suyuti, *Al-Itqan*, 191, as quoted in Ayoub, *Qur'an and Its Interpreters*, 1:5.

39. To be fair, Graham briefly reflected on how the Qur'an infuses Muslims' everyday speech. He also suggested that people who live in linguistic environments saturated with Qur'an-based discourses "absorb . . . more than a passing knowledge of scripture." His use of "absorb," however, is unfortunate, because the word deemphasizes the dialogical nature of Muslim engagements with the Qur'an. Graham, *Beyond the Written Word*, 114.

40. Abu Zayd, "Qur'an in Everyday Life," 80–98.

Chapter One: TIME

1. Rahman, "Some Islamic Issues," 285, as quoted in Berry, "Fazlur Rahman," 39.

2. On Rahman's international influence, see Saeed, *Approaches to the Qur'an* and Taji-Farouki, *Modern Muslim Intellectuals*.

3. Berry, "Fazlur Rahman," 37–48.

4. Sayyid M. Syeed, e-mail correspondence with author, March 22, 2009. Quoted with permission.

5. McGreevy, *Catholicism and American Freedom*, 191.

6. Webb, introduction, *Windows of Faith*, xi.

7. Barazangi, "Muslim Women's Islamic Higher Learning," 30–31.

8. Mattson faculty profile, Hartford Seminary website, http://reweb.hartsem.edu/pages/faculty/profiles/mattson.aspx (accessed April 20, 2014).

9. GhaneaBassiri, *History of Islam in America*, 267.

10. Abu-Rabiʿ, *Intellectual Origins of Islamic Resurgence*, 98.

11. See, for example: Nasr, *Young Muslim's Guide*.

12. GhaneaBassiri, *History of Islam in America*, 268.

13. Cadge, *Heartwood*, 9.

14. This project generated much press. See, for example, Curtis, "Islam Has Long History in Downtown."

15. GhaneaBassiri, *History of Islam in America*, 257.

16. Rahman, *Major Themes of the Qurʾan*, 1, 18, 10, 14.

17. Rahman, *Major Themes of the Qurʾan*, xii, xi.

18. Rahman, *Islamic Methodology in History*, 6.

19. For assessments of this theory and its impact on contemporary Qurʾanic interpretation, see Ebrahim Moosa, introduction, *Revival and Reform*, 1–29, and Hallaq, *A History of Islamic Legal Theories*, 241–53.

20. Moosa, introduction, *Revival and Reform*, 15.

21. Rahman, *Islam and Modernity*, 7.

22. A well-known example of *naskh* has to do with interpretations of the Qurʾanic passages that speak about wine. At one point in an earlier verse, the Qurʾan proscribes its audience from drinking it before prayers. Yet, in a verse revealed at a later point, it outlaws its consumption completely. For most Muslim exegetes, it meant that the later passage abrogated the earlier one. Hence, they ruled, no Muslim ever—even if she were to sober up before praying—could consume wine and, by extension, other intoxicants as well.

23. Mir, *Coherence in the Qurʾan*.

24. Rahman, *Islam and Modernity*, 7.

25. Rahman, *Major Themes of the Qurʾan*, 47. Emphasis on "the religious source" is Rahman's.

26. While Rahman stated that translations appearing in *Major Themes* were by Muhammad Marmaduke Pickthall, he also noted that he rendered them with "with some modifications." Typically, such modifications rephrased Pickthall dramatically.

27. United Nations, "Universal Declaration of Human Rights."

28. Rahman, *Major Themes of the Qurʾan*, 49. The translation of the verse is entirely Rahman's. In the Arabic text, in this particular portion of the verse, there is no corresponding word for "rights." Rahman took it as a grammatical continuation from a preceding phrase that has a similar word.

29. Rahman, *Major Themes of the Qurʾan*, 48.

30. Rahman, *Major Themes of the Qurʾan*, 49. Rahman relied here on Qurʾan 4:124, 40:40, 3:35 and a number of other verses.

31. Koselleck, *The Practice of Conceptual History*, 228. "Progress," of course, is an ideal behind our sense of history or, as Rahman would put it, its "normative" theme. We tend to feel betrayed when things fail to improve or when our progress is destroying our planet. But even when the problems we face are intertwined with our technological advancements, we keep trying to resolve them with more futuristic technologies. As moderns, we are stuck in the time of progress. See Latour, *We Have Never Been Modern*.

32. For a concise and insightful review of Iqbal's engagement with the Qur'an, see Lawrence, *The Qur'an: A Biography*, 151–62. For more in-depth studies, see Schimmel, *Gabriel's Wing*, and Mir, *Iqbal*.

33. Halbwachs, *On Collective Memory*, 175.

34. Schwartz, *Abraham Lincoln and the Forge*, xi.

35. On "pedagogic [uses of the] past," see Lowenthal, *Past Is a Foreign Country*, 371.

36. Schwartz, *Abraham Lincoln and the Forge*, x.

37. Rahman, *Major Themes of the Qur'an*, 22.

38. Rahman, *Islamic Methodology in History*, x.

39. McDonough, "Fazlur Rahman's Response to Iqbal," 68.

40. Iqbal's name appears in *Major Themes* once, in a tangential comment. Rahman, *Major Themes of the Qur'an*, 22.

41. Rahman, *Major Themes of the Qur'an*, 1.

42. Iqbal, *Reconstruction of Religious Thought*, 55, 14.

43. Iqbal, *Reconstruction of Religious Thought*, 56, 23.

44. Iqbal, *Reconstruction of Religious Thought*, 47.

45. Iqbal, *Reconstruction of Religious Thought*, 47.

46. Iqbal, *Reconstruction of Religious Thought*, 47–48.

47. Rahman, *Major Themes of the Qur'an*, 12, 15, 66, 34.

48. Rahman, *Major Themes of the Qur'an*, 68.

49. Rahman, *Major Themes of the Qur'an*, 67.

50. Iqbal, *Reconstruction of Religious Thought*, 96, 109, 56, 62, 6.

51. Rahman, *Major Themes of the Qur'an*, 13, 7.

52. Taylor, *Modern Social Imaginaries*, 62 and 194.

53. Fischer and Abedi, *Debating Muslims*, 109.

54. Latour, *We Have Never Been Modern*, 13.

55. As Talal Asad noted, most contemporary human beings embody this dilemma: they live their everyday lives in "secular time" and yet think that their "religions speak" from a different type of time, the time of eternity, "in light of which . . . [they] attempt to cultivate their bodies and souls." Asad, "Response to Connolly," 223.

56. This is how Taylor characterized eternity and "secular time." Taylor, *Modern Social Imaginaries*, 97. While groundbreaking, his writing sometimes comes across as more static than its overall dynamics suggest. He often expressed himself, quite naturally and unsurprisingly, through the very grammar of his and our modern sensibilities, which he attempted to change. (My hunch is that Taylor never read Iqbal.)

57. This insight was likely an outcome of Rahman's engagement with the works of the Persian philosopher Ibn Sina (d. 1037). See Rahman, *Prophecy in Islam*.

58. Iqbal, *Reconstruction of Religious Thought*, 126, 131, 49.

59. Iqbal, *Reconstruction of Religious Thought*, 15, 138.

60. Iqbal, *Reconstruction of Religious Thought*, vi.

61. On how routine this consensus was at the time, see Turner, *Orientalism, Postmodernism and Globalism*, 67–76.

62. Rahman, *Major Themes of the Qur'an*, 81.

63. Rahman, *Major Themes of the Qur'an*, 23, 80.

64. This precise phrase does not appear in the Qur'an. Variations of it can be found in many verses, such as 21:105, 39:74, and 44:28.

65. Rahman, *Major Themes of the Qur'an*, 59.

66. Rahman, *Major Themes of the Qur'an*, 12, 1.

67. Rahman, *Major Themes of the Qur'an*, 28, 37.

68. Rahman, *Major Themes of the Qur'an*, 28, 34.

69. Taylor, *Modern Social Imaginaries*, 194.

70. Rahman, *Islam*, 225–26.

71. al-Hibri, "Islamic and American Constitutional Law," 492–527.

Chapter Two: JUSTICE

1. Wadud, *Inside the Gender Jihad*, 126.

2. For an insightful study on the politics of Wadud's prayer and the issue of women's authority, see Hammer, *American Muslim Women*.

3. Wadud, *Inside the Gender Jihad*, 162.

4. Arkoun, *Unthought in Contemporary Islamic Thought*, 12.

5. Wadud, "Amina Wadud."

6. Wadud, *Qur'an and Woman*, xxii.

7. Later, Wadud noted that the book "reached number one on a best-seller list in *al-Qalam*, a Muslim newspaper" in South Africa. Wadud, *Qur'an and Woman*, xvi.

8. Wadud, *Qur'an and Woman*, 6, 52.

9. Wadud, *Qur'an and Woman*, 80.

10. Wadud, *Qur'an and Woman*, 94, xvii.

11. Weielandt, "Exegesis of the Qur'an," 124–42.

12. Wadud, *Qur'an and Woman*, xvii.

13. Brown, "The Triumph of Textualism," 55.

14. Wadud, *Qur'an and Woman*, xvii.

15. Wadud, *Qur'an and Woman*, xxii, 36.

16. Wadud, *Qur'an and Woman*, xii, 48, 63.

17. Wadud, *Qur'an and Woman*, 66.

18. Wadud, *Qur'an and Woman*, 69.

19. Wadud, *Qur'an and Woman*, 73.

20. al-Hibri, "Study of Islamic Herstory," 207–19.

21. Wadud, *Qur'an and Woman*, 73.

22. Wadud, *Qur'an and Woman*, xiii, 49, 91.

23. Wadud, *Qur'an and Woman*, x.

24. For reflections on the American and global legacy of Wadud, see Ali, Hammer, and Silvers, eds., *Jihad for Justice*, and Hammer and Spielhaus, eds., "Muslim Women and the Challenge of Authority," a special issue of the *Muslim World*.

25. Wadud, *Inside the Gender Jihad*, 102.

26. Wadud, *Inside the Gender Jihad*, 4.

27. See Wadud, *Inside the Gender Jihad,* 158–73, and Esack, *Qur'an, Liberation and Pluralism,* 246–48.

28. Haddad, Smith and Moore, *Muslim Women,* 122. This book provides an excellent survey of the early-twenty-first-century gender dynamics in American Muslim communities. An earlier excellent study that traces similar developments on a congregational level in the Shi'i community in Dearborn, Michigan, is Walbridge, *Without Forgetting the Imam.*

29. Cadge, *Heartwood,* 173.

30. See, for example, Nadell, *Women Who Would Be Rabbis.*

31. Schwartz, *The Rabbi's Wife.*

32. Wadud, *Inside the Gender Jihad,* 161.

33. For a parallel example from a sermon by a Jordanian preacher, see Antoun, *Muslim Preacher in the Modern World,* 67–106.

34. Wadud, *Inside the Gender Jihad,* 159.

35. Wadud, *Inside the Gender Jihad,* 159.

36. Wadud, *Inside the Gender Jihad,* 249–250.

37. Wadud, *Inside the Gender Jihad,* 251.

38. Shakir, "Examination of the Issue of Female Prayer Leadership," 244–46.

39. "Women Friendly Mosques," ISNA website, http://www.isna.net/Leadership/pages/Guidelines-Womens-Participation.aspx (accessed February 20, 2010).

40. Wadud, *Inside the Gender Jihad,* 79–80.

41. Turner, "God is a Negro," 347–48.

42. See Cone, *Risks of Faith;* Cone, *Martin and Malcolm and America;* and Jackson, *Islam and the Problem of Black Suffering.*

43. Wadud, *Inside the Gender Jihad,* 257.

44. Yuskaev and Stark, "Imam and Chaplain," 47–63.

Chapter Three: REDEMPTION

1. Mohammed, "National Imams' Meeting."

2. Cone, *Cross and the Lynching Tree.*

3. For estimates of the Muslim population in the United States, as well as African American affiliates of W. D. Mohammed's ministry, see Bagby, "Imams and Mosque Organizations," 19–36.

4. Nance, "Mystery of the Moorish Science Temple," 123–66.

5. King, "Letter from Birmingham Jail." This line of argument was not limited to King. Another example is Baldwin, *The Fire Next Time.*

6. See, for example, Ramirez and Brachear, "Imam's Views Created Rift."

7. Malcolm X and Haley, *Autobiography of Malcolm X,* 364.

8. Mohammed, "Interview with Imam W. Deen Mohammed."

9. On Elijah Muhammad's exegesis, see Berg, *Elijah Muhammad and Islam.*

10. Mohammed, as quoted in Lee, *Nation of Islam,* 83. On Mohammed's use of the term "resurrection," see Jackson, *Islam and the Blackamerican.*

11. Martin, "W. Deen Mohammed, 74, Top U.S. Imam, Dies."

12. This is a widely used phrase in W. D. Mohammed's community. One telling example is a thread devoted to the compatibility of the Qur'an and the U.S. constitution on the "Students of Imam W. Deen Mohammed" listserv: http://groups.yahoo.com/group/The-Students-of-Imam-W-Deen-Mohammed (accessed January 28, 2010).

13. Mohammed, "2003 Ramadan Session Transcript."

14. The CD sets became available for purchase in 2007 on Darnel Karim's website: http://islamicstudiesmaterials.com (accessed January 28, 2010).

15. Turner, *Islam in the African-American Experience.*

16. Muhammad Ali, *Translation of the Holy Quran.* Yusuf Ali's translation of the same verse reads: "The day when the Trumpet is blown. On that day we assemble the guilty white-eyed."

17. See, for example, Jackson, *Islam and the Problem of Black Suffering.*

18. Ayoub, *Redemptive Suffering in Islam.*

19. Rahman, *Major Themes of the Qur'an,* 63.

20. Raboteau, *Slave Religion,* Long, *Significations;* Lincoln and Mamiya, *Black Church in the African-American Experience.*

21. Mohammed, *Al-Islam,* 110. For an in-depth analysis of the concept of redemption in Elijah Muhammad and W. D. Mohammed's interpretations, see Yuskaev, "Redeeming the Nation."

22. Muhammad, "Savior's Day Address, 1975."

23. Mohammed, *Challenges That Face Man Today,* 86–87.

24. Mohammed, *Challenges That Face Man Today,* 55.

25. Mohammed, "Life: The Final Battlefield, Part 2." The audio recording of the speech is available at http://www.newafricaradio.com (accessed September 29, 2011).

26. Mohammed, "Live in Harlem."

27. Mohammed, "National Imams' Meeting."

28. Rosenberg, *The Art of the American Folk Preacher.*

29. Muhammad, *Supreme Wisdom,* 283.

30. This was the Nation's official policy. In practice, it was indeed involved in politics, as when it tacitly supported politicians such as Adam Clayton Powell.

31. See, for example, Mohammed, *Al-Islam,* 102, and "Live in Harlem."

32. Mohammed, "National Imams' Meeting."

33. The verses with the tone of lamentation are Qur'an 2:213, 5:48, 10:19, 11:118, 16:93, and 42:8. The exceptions are Qur'an 21:92 and 23:52, whose grammar Mohammed echoed when he said, at the end of his statement, *"ummatan wahida."*

34. Mohammed, *Al-Islam,* 102.

35. Mohammed, "Live in Harlem."

36. Mohammed, "National Imams' Meeting."

37. Ayoub, *Qur'an and Its interpreters,* 2:295.

38. Mohammed, *Challenge,* 36. He used similar lines in many of his subsequent speeches, such as his "Savior Day" address in 2002 in Charleston, South Carolina.

39. Mohammed, "National Imams' Meeting."

40. Mohammed, "National Imams' Meeting."

41. Mohammed and Mustafa, *Focus on Al-Islam,* 4.

42. Mohammed, "Life: The Final Battlefield, Part 2."

43. Mohammed, "The Day of Religion."

44. Mohammed, "National Imams' Meeting."

45. Mohammed, "The Temple of Islam."

46. Mohammed, "National Imams' Meeting."

47. Mohammed, "National Imams' Meeting."

48. Mohammed, "National Imams' Meeting."

49. Qur'an 32:30.

50. Mohammed, "Live in Harlem."

51. Mohammed, "National Imams' Meeting."

52. LaRue, *Heart of Black Preaching*, 72–82.

53. Shuaibe, "Response to 'Government Agent'"; Shuaibe, "Message to Those Who Condemn."

54. Faheem Shuaibe, telephone interview with the author, August 24, 2009. The emphasis on "this" and "that" was Shuaibe's.

55. For example, in 1987 Shuaibe set up the first "United Ta'leem," a teach-in for immigrant and African American Muslims. See Simon, "Interview with Imam Fahim Shuaib."

56. Ali translated this passage as, "If ye help not (your Leader) (it is no matter): for Allah did indeed help him; when the unbelievers drove him out: he had no more than one companion: they two were in the cave, and he said to his companion 'Have no Fear, for Allah is with us': then Allah sent down His peace upon him, and strengthened him with forces which ye saw not, and humbled to the depths the word of the Unbelievers. But the word of Allah is exalted to the heights: for Allah is Exalted in might, Wise."

57. In this section, unless otherwise noted, all of Shuaibe's quotes are from Shuaibe, *Fear Not for Allah Is with Us*.

58. See, for example, Mohammed, "How Islam Promotes Healthy Citizenship."

59. See Qur'an 15:26 and Mohammed, "The Day of Religion."

60. A parallel example is a sermon by Mozella Mitchell, pastor of Mount Sinai A.M.E. Zion Church in Tampa, Florida, who built one of her sermons around a contextually specific redefinition of the word "providence." LaRue, *Heart of Black Preaching*, 93–97.

61. Goldman, *Death and Life of Malcolm X*, 70.

62. Another interesting feature of both Shuaibe and Mohammed's sermons was their use of popular songs, which their audiences would immediately recognize. Such references—either implied or explicit—served to connect the language of the Qur'an, as the speakers presented it, to the everyday language of their audiences. In one 2006 speech, for example, Mohammed discussed the Qur'anic idea of human nature while illustrating it by referencing songs by Nat King Cole and Bill Withers. Shuaibe performed a similar move in a 2008 speech that promoted the diversity of Qur'anic interpretations and defended, through a wide selection of Qur'anic references and examples from the Hadith, the practice of indigenous, African American exegesis. The title of that sermon was "Different Strokes for Different Folks: The Universal and the Particular in Qur'anic Translation and Interpretation." For his audience it was an obvious reference to the song by Sly and the Family Stone.

63. On the practice of predatory lending targeting African American middle-class communities, see Coates, "The Case for Reparations."

64. Qur'an 3:104.

65. That book was Omar, *Dictionary of the Holy Qur'an*. Mohammed recommended it for his students during his 2007 Ramadan lectures.

66. For more standard translations of this word, see, for example, Penrice, *A Dictionary and Glossary of the Koran,* and Badawi and Abdel Haleem, *Arabic-English Dictionary of Qur'anic Usage.*

67. Yusuf Ali translated this verse as, "Because Allah will never change the Grace which He hath bestowed on a people until they change what is in their (own) souls: and verily Allah is He Who heareth and knoweth (all things)."

68. Faheem Shuaibe, interview with author, August 5, 2009.

69. Ong, *Orality,* 13.

70. For example, Thomas Carlyle, a witty nineteenth-century Scottish philosopher and historian, remarked that the Qur'an, which he read in translation, was a "toilsome a reading," filled with "endless iterations." Carlyle, *On Heroes, Hero Worship, and Heroic History,* as quoted in Ernst, *How to Read the Qur'an,* 22.

71. Mohammed, "Our Shared Freedom Space."

72. Mohammed, *As the Light Shineth,* 67.

73. Qur'an 49:1.

Chapter Four: POLITICS

1. Yusuf, "Give and Take."

2. ISNA's official incorporation was in 1982. Nineteen sixty-three was the date of the establishment of its precursor, the Muslim Student Association of the U.S. and Canada, which was also the antecedent of ICNA.

3. See, for example, Bayoumi, *How Does It Feel.*

4. For example, according to the 2000 and 2011 surveys of American mosques, in 2000, 86 percent of mosque leaders supported engagement in American politics; in 2011, this number increased to 91 percent. Bagby, *American Mosque 2011,* Report Number 1, 21.

5. Online discussion thread, "What the heck happened to Hamza Yusuf," Umma.com, http://www.ummah.com/forum/showthread.php?232275-What-The-Heck-Happened -To-Hamza-Yusuf (accessed September 09, 2014).

6. Schmidt, "Transnational Umma," 575–86.

7. Abdullah bin Hamid Ali, interview with author, July 26, 2008.

8. For example, as of February 12, 2010, one of Yusuf's speeches, "Changing the Tide," a 2006 address at ICNA's New Jersey symposium, accumulated 140,739 views. To the best of my knowledge, this was the most frequently listened-to online speech by any English-speaking preacher during the 2000s. In comparison, as of the same date, the most accessed speech by Siraj Wahhaj, "Muslim Women in Hijab," had 99,920 views. Siraj Wahhaj, "Muslim Women in Hijab," http://www.youtube.com/ watch?v=wRXm5ttFC_s (accessed February 12, 2010).

9. See, for example, Yusuf, "On Muslim Youth."

10. Yusuf, "Making Sense of Our Past." The statistics of online viewership on this speech are difficult to attain. Throughout the 2000s it had been repeatedly flagged as inappropriate by some viewers and removed by YouTube and other services. But then, as a sign of its persistent appeal, it would be immediately reposted, with each posting typically accumulating over ten thousand hits. Its popularity was corroborated through my interviews with his listeners, most of whom identified it as among his best-known recordings.

11. Skerry, "Problems of the Second Generation"; Pew Research Center, "Muslim Americans: Mostly Mainstream"; Pew Research Center, "Muslim Americans: No Signs of Growth in Alienation."

12. McGreevy, *Catholicism and American Freedom*, 167, 169. On the tradition of American anti-Catholicism, see Massa, *Anti-Catholicism in America*.

13. The phrase "completely opposed" is from Pope Pius X's 1910 "Oath Against Modernism." On American Catholic critiques of modernity, see Weaver and Appleby, *Being Right*, and O'Brien, *Public Catholicism*.

14. During Yusuf's time this was a global trend, exemplified by the "from the heart" style of Amr Khaled, an immensely popular Egyptian preacher. See Wise, "'Words from the Heart.'" For an insightful study of the gradual transformation of Muslim preaching styles in the twentieth century, see Antoun, *Muslim Preacher in the Modern World*.

15. See, for example, Messic, "Media Muftis," 310–22.

16. My observation is based on online recordings of the speech and its listeners' comments. In addition, I regularly played video recordings of the first minutes of "Give and Take" in my graduate courses at Hartford Seminary, where the majority of my students were well-versed Muslims. In five years of this informal experiment, the only person to notice Yusuf's misrecitation was a reciter of the Qur'an.

17. Yusuf, "Zaytuna Monthly Videocast: Episode 3—Broadening the Scope of the Pope."

18. At first, he was attracted to an idiosyncratic Muslim group, al-Murabitun, led by the Scottish Shaykh Abdulqadir as-Sufi (Ian Dallas). Within a few years, he separated from that community. As-Sufi's group belonged to the Traditionalist movement, which was distinct from what Yusuf would later call "tradition." On the Western Traditionalist network, exemplified by Seyyed Hussein Nasr's Maryamiyya Sufi order, see Sedgewick, *Against the Modern World*.

19. Yusuf, "True Spirit of Islam."

20. Zaytuna Institute, "Knowledge-Based Approach."

21. Zaytuna's initial claim of being the first American Muslim college was technically incorrect: three similar American Muslim institutions had been established before 2009. See Schmidt, *Islam in Urban America*, 84–135. Later, in the mid-2010s, Zaytuna's administration adjusted its language and began calling their institution "the first Muslim liberal arts college in the United States." Zaytuna College website, https://www.zaytuna.edu/about/ (accessed February 21, 2010, and December 23, 2015). For an informative outside perspective on the institution, see Korb, *Light without Fire*.

22. Brown, *Rethinking Tradition in Modern Islamic Thought*.

23. Kugle, *Rebel between Spirit and Law*. Zarruq's memory was incorporated into Zaytuna's institutional language, as in the "Perennial Faculty" page on its website: https://www.zaytuna.edu/about/perennial_faculty/ (accessed July 10, 2014).

24. Yusuf, "On Muslim Youth."

25. Yusuf, "True Spirit of Islam."

26. Abdullah bin Hamid Ali, interview with author, July 26, 2008.

27. http://www.sunnipath.com/about/ustadhanourashamma.aspx (accessed February 12, 2010). Later, SunniPath transformed into qibla.com (accessed July 11, 2014).

28. Abdullah bin Hamid Ali, interview with author, July 26, 2008.

29. This translation of the hadith comes from Murata and Chittick, *The Vision of Islam*, xxvi, as quoted in Kugle, *Rebel between Spirit and Law*, 11–12.

30. See Kugle, *Rebel between Spirit and Law*, 11, and Yusuf, Shakir, and Rhodus, "The Way Ahead."

31. Yusuf, "Reflections on al-Hujurat."

32. Anonymous, interview with author, August 7, 2008.

33. See, for example, "Muslim 'Rock Star.'"

34. Yusuf, as quoted in Leonard, *Muslims in the United States*, 23.

35. Hughes, "Move the New York City Mosque."

36. In this section, unless otherwise noted, all of Khan's quotes are from Sadaf Khan, interview with author, July 31, 2008.

37. Qur'an 16:125.

38. This is a key element in what Charles Hirschkind, after Walter Benjamin, called "effective audition": "an act that enables the integration of the narrative into the listener's own experience [and] requires a subordination to the authority" of a preacher. Hirschkind, *Ethical Soundscape*, 27.

39. Anonymous, interview with author, July 24, 2008.

40. See, for example, Rubenstein, *Aristotle's Children*.

41. By 2011 their attendance would rival ISNA's yearly conferences. "Canadian Islamic Convention."

42. See, for example: Yusuf, "Message to Humanity."

43. Qur'an 51:55.

44. In this section, unless otherwise noted, all of Yusuf's quotes are from Yusuf, "Making Sense."

45. Qur'an 10:57.

46. Qur'an 30:7.

47. This line of argument was not original. In large part it echoed the antimodern rhetoric of Seyyed Hossein Nasr and Yusuf's original Muslim teacher, Abdalqadir as-Sufi. See Nasr, *Young Muslim's Guide*, and as-Sufi, *Technique of the Coup de Banque*. It also had much in common with Catholic traditionalist rhetoric. See Sedgwick, *Against the Modern World*.

48. Tottoli, "Korah," 105.

49. Qur'an 28:79.

50. For example, one would find many parallels between Yusuf's articulations and those of Qutb, as in Qutb's *Dirasat Islamiyya*, a collection of articles from the early 1950s. See Abu-Rabiʿ, *Intellectual Origins of Islamic Resurgence*, 130–36.

51. GhaneaBassiri, *History of Islam in America*, 309–16.

52. Harding, *Book of Jerry Falwell*, 10.

53. See, for example: Giddens, *Modernity and Self-Identity*.

54. Fraser, "Rethinking the Public Sphere," 110, 117.

55. See Habermas, "Religion in the Public Sphere," 1–25; Casanova, "Civil Society and Religion," 1041–80; and Asad, "Response to Casanova," 207–10.

56. For example, after World War II, Catholics in the United States and other countries fostered a secular-sounding language of the church as a champion of human rights, which allowed its authorities to speak as partners in democratic political systems. See Casanova, "Civil Society and Religion," 1041–80.

57. Warner, *Publics and Counterpublics*, 121.

58. Fraser, "Rethinking the Public Sphere," 124.

59. Harding, *Book of Jerry Falwell*, ix.

60. The policy of surveillance is documented by, among others, the Associated Press's Pulitzer Prize–winning investigation of the New York Police Department's intelligence operations. See "AP's Probe Into NYPD Intelligence Operations." On the practice of detaining Muslims crossing the Canadian border, see Bloom, "Border Searches," 295–28.

61. Bagby, *American Mosque 2011*, Report Number 2, 9.

62. Yusuf, as quoted in Abdo, *Mecca and Main Street*, 5

63. See GhaneaBassiri, *History of Islam in America*, 350–78.

64. In this section, unless otherwise noted, all of Yusuf's quotes are from Yusuf, "Give and Take."

65. Qur'an 17:20.

66. Qur'an 6:12.

67. Bush, "Remarks by the President Upon Arrival."

68. Lears, "How a War Became a Crusade."

69. Qur'an 53:42.

70. Gallup and the Coexist Foundation, *Muslim Americans*, 22.

71. Widmer, *Young America*.

72. Rumsfeld, "Secretary Rumsfeld Briefs."

73. See, for example, "Diversity—In America" (CNN blog), and the Southern Poverty Law Center's K-5 curriculum on diversity, "Stitching It Together." For an analysis of American Muslim appropriations of such language, see Naber, "Muslim First, Arab Second," 479–95.

74. McNamara, *Catholic Cold War*.

75. bin Bayyah, "Muslims Living in Non-Muslim Lands."

76. Yusuf, "Message To Humanity."

77. Murray, We Hold These Truths, x–xi.

78. Appleby, "Triumph of Americanism," 40.

79. Pew Research Center, "Muslim Americans: Middle Class and Mostly Mainstream," 18.

80. Turner, "Betwixt and Between," 93–111.

81. Anonymous, interview with author, July 24, 2008.

82. Bercovitch, *American Jeremiad*, 16.

83. Qur'an 38:1; Sells, "Memory," 372–74.

84. Clinton, *My Life*, 167.

85. For numerous examples of post-9/11 evocations of Qur'an 5:32, see Kurzman, "Islamic Statements Against Terrorism."

AFTERWORD

86. Benkong Shi, conversation with the author, May 19, 2015.

87. An exceptional ethnographic study on the subject, which includes analysis of discourses, is Walbridge, *Without Forgetting the Imam*. For a useful overview of American Shi'i communities and their history, see Takim, *Shi'ism in America*.

BIBLIOGRAPHY

Abd-Allah, Umar Faruq. "One God, Many Names." Nawawi Foundation, Chicago, 2004. http://www.nawawi.org/wp-content/uploads/2013/01/Article2.pdf (accessed September 4, 2014).

Abdo, Geneive. *Mecca and Main Street: Muslim Life in America After 9/11*. New York: Oxford University Press, 2006.

Abdul Rauf, Feisal. *Islam: A Sacred Law*. New York: Threshold Books, 2000.

———. *Islam: A Search for Meaning*. Costa Mesa, Calif.: Mazda Publishers, 1996.

———. *Moving the Mountain: Beyond Ground Zero to a New Vision of Islam in America*. New York: Free Press, 2012.

———. *What's Right with Islam Is What's Right with America*. New York: HarperCollins, 2005.

Abu Zayd, Nasr Hamid. "Qur'an in Everyday Life." In *Encyclopaedia of the Qur'an*, edited by Jane Dammen McAuliffe, 2:80–98. Leiden, Netherlands: E. J. Brill, 2002.

Abu-Rabiʿ, Ibrahim. *Intellectual Origins of Islamic Resurgence in the Modern Arab World*. Albany: State University of New York Press, 1996.

al-Faruqi, Ismail Raji. *Toward Islamic English*. Herndon, Va.: International Institute of Islamic Thought, 1982.

al-Hibri, Azizah Y. "Islamic and American Constitutional Law: Borrowing Possibilities or a History of Borrowing?" *University of Pennsylvania Journal of Constitutional Law* 1:3 (1998–99): 492–527.

———. "A Study of Islamic Herstory: Or How Did We Ever Get Into This Mess?" *Women's Studies International Forum* 5:2 (1982): 207–19.

al-Suyuti, Jalal al-Din. *Al-Itqan fi ʿUlum al-Qur'an*. Vol. 2. Beirut: Dar al-Fikr, n.d.

al-Tabari. *Tarikh al-rusul wal-muluk*. Vol. 4, 48. http://www.yasoob.com/books/htm1/mo24/28/no2812.html (accessed February 19, 2015).

Ali, Kecia, Juliane Hammer, and Laury Silvers, eds. *A Jihad for Justice: Honoring the Work and Life of Amina Wadud*. Akron, Ohio: 48HrBooks, 2012.

Ali, Muhammad. *Translation of the Holy Quran*. Lahore, Pakistan: Ahmadiyya Anjuman Ishaat-i-Islam, 1951.

Alryyes, Ala. *A Muslim American Slave: The Life of Omar Ibn Said*. Madison: University of Wisconsin Press, 2011.

Antoun, Richard T. *Muslim Preacher in the Modern World: A Jordanian Case Study in Comparative Perspective*. Princeton, N.J.: Princeton University Press, 1989.

Appleby, R. Scott. "The Triumph of Americanism: Common Ground for U.S. Catholics in the Twentieth Century." In *Being Right: Conservative Catholics in America*, edited by Mary Jo Weaver and R. Scott Appleby, 37–62. Bloomington: Indiana University Press, 1995.

"AP's Probe Into NYPD Intelligence Operations." Associated Press website. http://www.ap.org/Index/AP-In-The-News/NYPD (accessed July 29, 2014).

Arkoun, Mohammed. *The Unthought in Contemporary Islamic Thought*. London: Saqi Books, 2002.

as-Sufi, Abdalqadir. *The Technique of the Coup de Banque*. Palma de Mallorca, Spain: Kutubia Mayurqa, 2000.

Asad, Talal. *Formations of the Secular: Christianity, Islam, Modernity*. Stanford, Calif.: Stanford University Press, 2003.

———. "Response to Casanova." In *Powers of the Secular Modern: Talal Asad and His Interlocutors*, edited by Scott and Hirschkind, 207–10. Stanford, Calif.: Stanford University Press, 2006.

———. "Response to Connolly." In *Powers of the Secular Modern: Talal Asad and His Interlocutors*, edited by Scott and Hirschkind, 220–24. Stanford, Calif.: Stanford University Press, 2006.

Ayoub, Mahmoud. *The Qur'an and Its interpreters*. Vol. 1. Albany: State University of New York Press, 1984.

———. *The Qur'an and Its interpreters*. Vol. 2. Albany: State University of New York Press, 1994.

———. *Redemptive Suffering in Islam: A Study of the Devotional Aspects of 'Ashura' in Twelver Shi'ism*. The Hague: Morton Publishers, 1978.

———. "The Speaking Qur'an and the Silent Qur'an." In *Approaches to the History of the Interpretation of the Qur'an*, edited by Andrew Rippin, 177–98. Oxford, U.K.: Oxford University Press, 1988.

Badawi, Elsaid M., and Muhammad Abdel Haleem. *Arabic-English Dictionary of Qur'anic Usage*. Leiden, Netherlands: E. J. Brill, 2008.

Bagby, Ihsan. *The American Mosque 2011*. Report Number 1. Hartford, Conn.: The Faith Communities Today Project, 2011. http://faithcommunitiestoday.org/sites/faithcommunitiestoday.org/files/The%20American%20Mosque%202011%20web.pdf (accessed November 1, 2014).

———. *The American Mosque 2011*. Report Number 2. Hartford, Conn.: Hartford Institute for Religion Research, 2012. http://www.hartfordinstitute.org/The-American-Mosque-Report-2.pdf (accessed October 27, 2014).

———. "Imams and Mosque Organizations in the United States: A Study of Mosque Leadership and Organizational Structure in American Mosques." In *Muslims in the United States: Identity, Influence, Innovation*, edited by Philippa Strum, 19–36. Washington, D.C.: Woodrow Wilson Center, 2006.

Bakhtiar, Laleh. *The Sublime Qur'an*. Chicago: Kazi Publications, 2007.

Bakhtin, Mikhail. *Toward a Methodology for the Human Sciences: Speech Genres & Other Late Essays*. Translated by Vern W. McGee. Austin: University of Texas Press, 1986.

Baldwin, James. *The Fire Next Time*. New York: Random House, 1963.

Barazangi, Nimat Hafez. "Muslim Women's Islamic Higher Learning as a Human Right." In *Windows of Faith: Muslim Women Scholar-Activists in North America*, edited by Gisela Webb, 22–47. Syracuse, N.Y.: Syracuse University Press, 2000.

Bayoumi, Moustafa. *How Does It Feel To Be A Problem? Being Young and Arab in America*. New York: Penguin Press, 2009.

Bercovitch, Sacvan. *The American Jeremiad*. University of Wisconsin Press, 1978.

Berg, Herbert. *Elijah Muhammad and Islam*. New York: New York University Press, 2009.

Berry, Donald L. "Fazlur Rahman: A Life in Review." In *The Shaping of an American Islamic Discourse,* edited by Earl H. Waugh and Frederick M. Denny, 37–48. Atlanta: Scholars Press, 1998.

bin Bayyah, Abdullah. "Muslims Living in Non-Muslim Lands." http://www.the modernreligion.com/world/muslims-living.html (accessed September 17, 2014).

Bloom, Robert M. "Border Searches in the Age of Terrorism." *Mississippi Law Journal* 78 (2008): 295–328.

Brown, Daniel W. *Rethinking Tradition in Modern Islamic Thought.* New York: Cambridge University Press, 1998.

Brown, Daniel. "The Triumph of Textualism: The Doctrine of Naskh and Its Modern Critics." In *The Shaping of an American Islamic Discourse,* edited by Earl H. Waugh, and Frederick M. Denny, 49–66. Atlanta: Scholars Press, 1998.

Bush, George W. "Remarks by the President Upon Arrival." White House, Office of the Press Secretary, September 16, 2001. *The White House: President George W. Bush.* http://georgewbush-whitehouse.archives.gov/news/releases/2001/09/2001 0916-2.html (accessed September 24, 2014).

Cadge, Wendy. *Heartwood: The First Generation of Theravada Buddhism in America.* Chicago: University of Chicago Press, 2005.

Callahan, Allen Dwight. *The Talking Book: African Americans and the Bible.* New Haven, Conn.: Yale University Press, 2006.

"Canadian Islamic Convention Attracts Record Breaking Attendance." *IQRA.ca,* December 26, 2011. http://iqra.ca/2011/canadian-islamic-convention-attracts -record-breaking-attendance (accessed August 10, 2014).

Carlyle, Thomas. *On Heroes, Hero Worship, and Heroic History.* London: James Fraser, 1841. Available online at *Project Gutenberg.* http://www.gutenberg.org/files/ 1091/1091-h/1091-h.htm (accessed February 19, 2015).

Casanova, Jose. "Civil Society and Religion: Retrospective Reflections of Catholicism and Prospective Reflections on Islam." *Social Research* 68:4 (2001): 1041–80.

Clinton, Bill. *My Life.* New York: Random House, 2005.

Coates, Ta-Nehisi. "The Case for Reparations." *Atlantic,* May 21, 2014. http://www.the atlantic.com/features/archive/2014/05/the-case-for-reparations/361631/ (accessed July 8, 2014).

Cone, James H. *The Cross and the Lynching Tree.* Maryknoll, N.Y.: Orbis Books, 2011.

——. *Martin and Malcolm and America: A Dream or a Nightmare?* Maryknoll, N.Y.: Orbis Books, 1992.

——. *Risks of Faith: The Emergence of a Black Theology of Liberation, 1968–1998.* Boston: Beacon Press, 2000.

Curtis, Edward E., IV. "Islam Has Long History in Downtown: Why the 'Ground Zero Mosque' Belongs in Lower Manhattan." *New York Daily News,* July 23, 2010. http://www.nydailynews.com/opinion/islam-long-history-downtown-ground -zero-mosque-belongs-manhattan-article-1.202169 (accessed February 14, 2014).

——. *Islam in Black America: Identity, Liberation, and Difference in African American Islamic Thought.* Albany: State University of New York Press, 2002.

"Diversity—In America." CNN Blog. http://inamerica.blogs.cnn.com/category/ diversity/ (accessed September 21, 2014).

Donner, Fred M. *Narratives of Islamic Origins: The Beginnings of Islamic Historical Writing.* Princeton, N.J.: Darwin Press, 1998.

Eck, Diana L. *A New Religious America: How A "Christian Country" Has Become the World's Most Religiously Diverse Nation.* New York: HarperCollins, 2001.

Ernst, Carl. *How to Read the Qur'an: A New Guide, with Select Translations.* Chapel Hill: University of North Carolina Press, 2011.

Ernst, Carl W., and Bruce B. Lawrence. *Sufi Martyrs of Love: Chishti Sufism in South Asia and Beyond.* New York: Palgrave Macmillan, 2002.

Esack, Farid. *Qur'an, Liberation and Pluralism: An Islamic Perspective of Interreligious Solidarity Against Oppression.* Oxford: Oneworld, 1997.

Fischer, Michael M. J., and Mehdi Abedi. *Debating Muslims: Cultural Dialogues in Postmodernity and Tradition.* Madison: University of Wisconsin Press, 1990.

Fraser, Nancy. "Rethinking the Public Sphere: A Contribution to the Critique of Actually Existing Democracy." In *Habermas and the Public Sphere,* edited by Craig Calhoun, 109–42. Cambridge: MIT Press, 1992.

Friedmann, Yohanan. *Prophecy Continuous: Aspects of Ahmadi Religious Thought and Its Medieval Background.* Berkeley: University of California Press, 1989.

Gade, Anna M. *Perfection Makes Practice: Learning, Emotion, and the Recited Qur'an in Indonesia.* Honolulu: University of Hawaii Press, 2004.

Gallup and the Coexist Foundation. *Muslim Americans: A National Portrait.* Washington, D.C.: Gallup, 2009.

Gardell, Mattias. *In the Name of Elijah Muhammad: Louis Farrakhan and the Nation of Islam.* Durham, N.C.: Duke University Press, 1996.

George, Carol. "Widening the Circle: The Black Church and the Abolitionist Crusade, 1830–1860." In *African-American Religion: Interpretive Essays in History and Culture,* edited by Timothy Earl Fulop and Albert J. Raboteau, 153–73. New York: Routledge, 1997.

GhaneaBassiri, Kambiz. *A History of Islam in America: From the New World to the New World Order.* New York: Cambridge University Press, 2010.

Giddens, Anthony. *Modernity and Self-Identity: Self and Society in the Late Modern Age.* Stanford: Stanford University Press, 1991.

Goldman, Peter Louis Goldman. *The Death and Life of Malcolm X.* Urbana: University of Illinois Press, 1979.

Graham, William A. *Beyond the Written Word: Oral Aspects of Scripture in the History of Religion.* New York: Cambridge University Press, 1987.

Grewal, Zareena. *Islam is a Foreign Country: American Muslims and the Global Crisis of Authority.* New York: New York University Press, 2013.

Habermas, Jurgen. "Religion in the Public Sphere." *European Journal of Philosophy* 14:1 (2006): 1–25.

Haddad, Yvonne Yazbeck, Jane I. Smith, and Kathleen M. Moore. *Muslim Women in America: The Challenge of Islamic Identity Today.* New York: Oxford University Press, 2006.

Halbwachs, Maurice. *On Collective Memory.* Edited and translated by Lewis A. Coser. Chicago: University of Chicago Press, 1992.

Hallaq, Wael. *A History of Islamic Legal Theories.* New York: Cambridge University Press, 1997.

Hammer, Juliane. *American Muslim Women: Religious Authority and Activism.* Austin: University of Texas Press, 2012.

Hammer, Juliane, and Riem Spielhaus. "Muslim Women and the Challenge of Authority." Special issue, *Muslim World* 103:3 (July 2013).

Harding, Susan Friend. *The Book of Jerry Falwell: Fundamentalist Language and Politics.* Princeton, N.J.: Princeton University Press, 2000.

Hirschkind, Charles. *The Ethical Soundscape: Cassette Sermons and Islamic Counterpublics.* New York: Columbia University Press, 2006.

Hughes, Karen. "Move the New York City Mosque, As a Sign of Unity." *Washington Post,* August 22, 2010. http://www.washingtonpost.com/wp-dyn/content/article /2010/08/20/AR2010082002124.html (accessed February 10, 2014).

Hutton, Patrick H. *History as an Art of Memory.* Hanover, N.H.: University Press of New England, 1993.

Iqbal, Muhammad. *Javid-Nama.* Translated by Arthur J. Arberry. London: Allen and Unwin, 1966.

———. *The Reconstruction of Religious Thought in Islam.* Lahore, Pakistan: Muhammad Ashraf, 1962.

Irving, T. B. *The Noble Qur'an: The First American Translation and Commentary.* Brattleboro, Vt.: Amana Books, 1992.

Jackson, Sherman. *Islam and the Blackamerican: Looking Towards the Third Resurrection.* New York: Oxford University Press, 2005.

———. *Islam and the Problem of Black Suffering.* New York: Oxford University Press, 2009.

Kahf, Mohja. "Men Kill Me." In *E-mails from Shaherazad,* 61. Gainesville: University Press of Florida, 2003.

King, Martin Luther, Jr. "Letter from Birmingham Jail." May 1, 1963. Available online at the King Center website. http://www.thekingcenter.org/archive/document/letter -birmingham-city-jail-0 (accessed July 1, 2014).

Korb, Scott. *Light without Fire: The Making of America's First Muslim College.* Boston: Beacon Press, 2013.

Koselleck, Reinhart. *Futures Past: On the Semantics of Historical Time.* Translated by Keith Tribe. New York: Columbia University Press, 2004.

———. *The Practice of Conceptual History: Timing History, Spacing Concepts.* Translated by Todd Samuel Presner. Stanford, Calif.: Stanford University Press, 2002.

Kugle, Scott. *Rebel between Spirit and Law: Ahmad Zarruq, Sainthood, and Authority in Islam.* Bloomington: Indiana University Press, 2006.

Kuo, David. "America's 'Holiest Book'?" *Huffington Post,* May 25, 2011. http://www .huffingtonpost.com/david-kuo/americas-holiest-book_b_35462.html (accessed February 17, 2014).

Kurzman, Charles. "Islamic Statements Against Terrorism." Charles Kurzman website. http://kurzman.unc.edu/islamic-statements-against-terrorism/ (accessed November 12, 2014).

LaRue, Cleophus J. *The Heart of Black Preaching.* Louisville: Westminster John Knox Press, 2000.

Latour, Bruno. *We Have Never Been Modern.* Translated by Catherine Porter. Cambridge, Mass.: Harvard University Press, 1993.

Lawrence, Bruce B. *The Qur'an: A Biography.* New York: Atlantic Monthly Press, 2006.

Lears, Jackson. "How a War Became a Crusade." *New York Times,* March 11, 2003. http://www.nytimes.com/2003/03/11/opinion/how-a-war-became-a-crusade.html (accessed September 27, 2014).

Lee, Martha. *The Nation of Islam as a Millenarian Movement.* New York: Mellen House, 1989.

Leonard, Karen Isaksen. *Muslims in the United States: The State of Research.* New York: Russell Sage Foundation, 2003.

Lewis, Bernard. *What Went Wrong: Western Impact and Middle Eastern Response.* New York: Oxford University Press, 2002.

Lincoln, C. Eric. *The Black Muslims in America.* 3rd ed. Grand Rapids, Mich.: William B. Eerdmans, 1994.

Lincoln, Eric C., and Lawrence H. Mamiya. *The Black Church in the African-American Experience.* Durham, N.C.: Duke University Press, 1990.

Long, Charles H. *Significations: Signs, Symbols, and Images in the Interpretation of Religion.* Philadelphia: Fortress Press, 1986.

Lowenthal, David. *The Past Is a Foreign Country.* New York: Cambridge University Press, 1985.

Mackay, Harvey. *Swim with the Sharks without Being Eaten Alive: Outsell, Outmanage, Outmotivate, and Outnegotiate Your Competition.* New York: Morrow, 1988.

Malcolm X and Alex Haley. *The Autobiography of Malcolm X.* New York: Ballantine Books, 1992.

Manguel, Alberto. *A History of Reading.* New York: Penguin, 1996.

Martin, Douglas. "W. Deen Mohammed, 74, Top U.S. Imam, Dies." *New York Times,* September 9, 2008. http://www.nytimes.com/2008/09/10/us/10mohammed.html (accessed October 10, 2008).

Martin, Richard C. "Inimitability." In *Encyclopaedia of the Qur'an,* edited by Jane Dammen McAuliffe, 2:526–36. Leiden, Netherlands: E.J. Brill, 2002.

Massa, Mark S., S.J., *Anti-Catholicism in America: The Last Acceptable Prejudice.* New York: The Crossroads Publishing Company, 2003.

McAuliffe, Jane Dammen. "The Tasks and Traditions of Interpretation." In *The Cambridge Companion to the Qur'an,* edited by Jane Dammen McAuliffe, 181–210. New York: Cambridge University Press, 2006.

McDonough, Sheila. "Fazlur Rahman's Response to Iqbal." In *The Shaping of an American Islamic Discourse,* edited by Earl H. Waugh and Frederick M. Denny, 67–88. Atlanta: Scholars Press, 1998.

McGreevy, John T. *Catholicism and American Freedom: A History.* New York: W. W. Norton, 2003.

McNamara, Patrick. *A Catholic Cold War: Edmund A. Walsh, S.J., and the Politics of American Anticommunism.* New York: Fordham University Press, 2005.

Messic, Brinkley. "Media Muftis: Radio Fatwas in Yemen." In *Islamic Legal Interpretation,* edited by Khalid Masud, Brinkley Messick, and David Powers, 310–22. Cambridge, Mass.: Harvard University Press, 1996.

Mir, Mustansir. *Coherence in the Qur'an: A Study of Islahi's Concept of nazm in Tadabbur-i Qur'an.* Indianapolis: American Trust Publications, 1986.

———. *Iqbal.* London: I. B. Tauris, 2006.

Mohammed, Warith Deen. *Al-Islam: Unity and Leadership.* Chicago: The Sense Maker, 1991.

———. *As the Light Shineth from the East.* Chicago: WDM Publishing, 1980.

———. *Challenges That Face Man Today.* Vol. 2. Chicago: W. D. Muhammad Productions, 1985.

———. "The Day of Religion: Address at the Educational Weekend presented by Clara Muhammad School and Masjid Muhammad of Washington, D.C., on Sun., Jan. 14,

2007." *New Africa Radio,* reprinted from the *Muslim Journal,* March 23, 2007, and April 13, 2007. http://www.newafricaradio.com/articles/41307.htm (accessed June 23, 2009).

——. "How Islam Promotes Healthy Citizenship." New Africa Radio, reprinted from the *Muslim Journal,* May 5, 2003, and May 16, 2003. http://www.newafricaradio .com/articles/050903.html (accessed July 24, 2009).

——. "Imam W. Deen Mohammed's Address at 'Savior Day'—February 26, 2002, in Charleston, SC." *New Africa Radio,* reprinted from the *Muslim Journal,* May 3, 2002, and May 17, 2002. http://www.newafricaradio.com/articles/05-03-02.html (accessed June 21, 2009).

——. "An Interview with Imam W. Deen Mohammed and the British Broadcast Corporation." *Muslim Journal,* November 12, 1993.

——. "Life: The Final Battlefield, Part 2," *Muslim Journal,* May 9 2008.

——. *Live in Harlem, NY. New Africa: A New Mind, A New Life, A New Beginning for Black People in America.* Calumet City, Ill.: WDM Productions, 2003. Compact disc.

——. *National Imams' Meeting: Yusuf Analogy.* Calumet City, Ill.: WDM Productions, 2008. Compact disc.

——. "Our Shared Freedom Space: First Sunday Lecture recorded September 7th 2008," *New Africa Radio* audio. http://www.newafricaradio.com/audio/wdm/ october2008_5.ram (accessed June 15, 2009).

——. "The Temples of Islam." *Muslim Journal,* June 27, 2008.

——. "2003 Ramadan Session Transcript, November 23, 2003." Unpublished. Copy in possession of author.

Mohammed, Warith Deen, and Ayesha K. Mustafa. *Focus on Al-Islam: A Series of Interviews with Imam W. Deen Mohammed in Pittsburg, Pennsylvania.* Chicago: Zakat Publications, 1988.

Moosa, Ebrahim. Introduction to *Revival and Reform in Islam,* by Fazlur Rahman, 1–29. Oxford: Oneworld, 2000.

Muhammad, Elijah. *Supreme Wisdom.* Atlanta: Messenger Elijah Muhammad Propagation Society, n.d., ca. 1995.

Muhammad, Wallace. "1975 Savior's Day." Video. https://www.youtube.com/watch ?v=cmKkVzk2oP0 (accessed October 24, 2016).

Murata, Sachiko, and William Chittick. *The Vision of Islam.* New York: Paragon House, 1994.

Murray, John Courtney, S.J. *We Hold These Truths: Catholic Reflections on the American Proposition.* New York: Sheed and Ward, 1960.

"Muslim 'Rock Star' on Terrorism: A Leading American Islamic Cleric is Visiting Wales to Examine the Fight Against Terrorism." *BBC News,* April 26, 2004. http:// news.bbc.co.uk/2/hi/uk_news/wales/south_east/3659683.stm (accessed February 19, 2015).

Naber, Nadine. "Muslim First, Arab Second: A Strategic Politics of Race and Gender." *Muslim World* 95:4 (2005): 479–95.

Nabokov, Vladimir. *Speak, Memory: An Autobiography Revisited.* New York: Vintage International, 1989.

Nadell, Pamela. *Women Who Would Be Rabbis: A History of Women's Ordination, 1889–1985.* Boston: Beacon Press, 1998.

Nance, Susan. "Mystery of the Moorish Science Temple: Southern Blacks and American Alternative Spirituality in 1920s Chicago." *Religion and American Culture* 12:2 (2002): 123–66.

Nasr, Seyyed Hossein. *A Young Muslim's Guide to the Modern World.* Chicago: Kazi Publications, 1993.

O'Brien, David J. *Public Catholicism.* 2nd ed. Maryknoll, N.Y.: Orbis Books, 1996.

Omar, Abdul Mannan. *Dictionary of the Holy Qur'an.* Hockessin: Noor Foundation, 2005.

Ong, Walter J. *Orality and Literacy: The Technologizing of the Word.* New York: Routledge, 2002.

Penrice, John. *A Dictionary and Glossary of the Koran.* New York: Biblo and Tannen, 1969.

Pew Research Center. "Muslim Americans: Middle Class and Mostly Mainstream." Pew Research Center, Washington, D.C., 2007. http://www.pewresearch.org/2007/05/22/muslim-americans-middle-class-and-mostly-mainstream/ (accessed November 16, 2014).

———. "Muslim Americans: No Signs of Growth in Alienation of Support for Extremism." Pew Research Center, Washington, D.C., 2011. http://www.people-press.org/2011/08/30/muslim-americans-no-signs-of-growth-in-alienation-or-support-for-extremism/?src=prc-headline (accessed November 16, 2014).

Pius X. "Oath Against Modernism." September 1, 1910. Available at *Papal Encyclicals Online.* http://www.papalencyclicals.net/Pius10/p10moath.htm (accessed October 30, 2014).

Prager, Dennis. "America, Not Keith Ellison, Decides What Book a Congressman Takes His Oath On." *Townhall.com,* November 28, 2006. http://www.townhall.com/Columnists/DennisPrager/2006/11/28/america,_not_keith_ellison,_decides_what_book_a_congressman_takes_his_oath_on (accessed February 16, 2014).

Qutb, Sayyid. *al-Taswar al-Fanni fi-l-Qur'an.* Cairo: Dar al-Ma'rif, 1962.

———. *Dirasat Islamiyya.* Cairo: Dar al-Fath, 1967.

Raboteau, Albert J. *Slave Religion: The "Invisible Institution" in the Antebellum South.* New York: Oxford University Press, 2004.

Rahman, Fazlur. *Islam.* 2nd ed. Chicago: University of Chicago Press, 1979.

———. *Islam and Modernity: Transformation of an Intellectual Tradition.* Chicago: University of Chicago Press, 1982.

———. *Islamic Methodology in History.* Islamabad: Islamic Research Institute, 1965.

———. *Major Themes of the Qur'an.* 2nd ed. Minneapolis: Bibliotheca Islamica, 1994.

———. *Prophecy in Islam: Philosophy and Orthodoxy.* Chicago: University of Chicago Press, 1979.

———. "Some Islamic Issues in the Ayyub Khan Era." In *Essays on Islamic Civilization, Presented to Niyazi Berkes,* edited by Donald P. Little, 284–302. Leiden, Netherlands: E. J. Brill, 1976.

Ramirez, Margaret, and Manya A. Brachear. "Imam's Views Created Rift with Black Nationalists." *Los Angeles Times,* September 10, 2008. http://articles.latimes.com/2008/sep/10/local/me-mohammed10 (accessed October 1, 2009).

Ricoeur, Paul. *Memory, History, Forgetting.* Translated by Kathleen Blamey and David Pellauer. Chicago: University of Chicago Press, 2004.

Robinson, Chase F. *Islamic Historiography.* New York: Cambridge University Press, 2003.

Rosenberg, Bruce A. *The Art of the American Folk Preacher.* New York: Oxford University Press, 1970.

Rubenstein, Richard E. *Aristotle's Children: How Christians, Muslims, and Jews Rediscovered Ancient Wisdom and Illuminated the Middle Ages.* San Diego: Harvest Books, 2003.

Rumsfeld, Donald. "Secretary Rumsfeld Briefs at the Foreign Press Center." U.S. Department of Defense, January, 22, 2003. http://www.defense.gov/transcripts/transcript.aspx?transcriptid=1330 (accessed September 20, 2014).

Saeed, Abdullah, ed. *Approaches to the Qur'an in Contemporary Indonesia.* Oxford, U.K.: Oxford University Press, 2005.

Schimmel, Annemarie. *Gabriel's Wing: A Study into the Religious Ideas of Sir Muhammad Iqbal.* Leiden, Netherlands: E. J. Brill, 1963.

Schlund-Vials, Cathy. *Modeling Citizenship: Jewish and Asian American Writing.* Philadelphia: Temple University Press, 2011.

Schmidt, Garbi. *Islam in Urban America: Sunni Muslims in Chicago.* Philadelphia: Temple University Press, 2004.

——. "The Transnational Umma—Myth or Reality? Examples from the Western Diasporas." *Muslim World* 95:4 (2005): 575–86.

Schwartz, Barry. *Abraham Lincoln and the Forge of National Memory.* Chicago: University of Chicago Press, 2000.

Schwartz, Shuly Rubin. *The Rabbi's Wife: The Rebbetzin in American Jewish Life.* New York: New York University Press, 2006.

Sedgwick, Mark. *Against the Modern World: Traditionalism and the Secret Intellectual History of the Twentieth Century.* New York: Oxford University Press, 2004.

Sells, Michael. "Memory." In *Encyclopaedia of the Qur'an,* edited by Jane Dammen McAuliffe, 3:372–74. Leiden, Netherlands: E. J. Brill, 2002.

——. "Sound, Spirit, and Gender in Surat al-Qadr." *Journal of the American Oriental Society* 111:2 (1991): 239–59.

Shakir, Zaid. "An Examination of the Issue of Female Prayer Leadership." In *Columbia Sourcebook of Muslims in the United States,* edited by Edward E. Curtis IV, 239–46. New York: Columbia University Press, 2008.

Shuaibe, Faheem. *Fear Not for Allah Is with Us.* Oakland: A Clear Understanding, 2009. Compact disc.

——. "A Message to Those Who Condemn Imam Mohammed's Position on Christianity, the Trinity and Islam in America." Unpublished. Copy in possession of author.

——. "A Response to 'Government Agent': The Truth Regarding Warith Deen Mohammed." Unpublished. Copy in possession of author.

Simon, Nuri Muhammad. "Interview with Imam Fahim Shuaib." *Muslim Journal,* April 10, 1987.

Skerry, Peter. "Problems of the Second Generation: To Be Young, Muslim, and American." *Weekly Standard,* June 24, 2013. http://www.weeklystandard.com/articles/problems-second-generation_735247.html (accessed October 5, 2014).

Southern Poverty Law Center. "Stitching It Together." *Teaching Tolerance: A Project of the Southern Poverty Law Center.* http://www.tolerance.org/lesson/stitching-it-together (accessed September 21, 2014).

Spellberg, Denise A. *Thomas Jefferson's Qur'an: Islam and the Founders*. New York: Alfred A. Knopf, 2013.

Swarns, Rachel L. "Congressman Criticizes Election of Muslim." *New York Times*, December 21, 2006. http://www.nytimes.com/2006/12/21/us/21koran.html (accessed February 16, 2014).

Tabatabai, Allamah Muhammad Hussein. "Surah abasa 80, verses 1–16." In *Tafsir al-Mizan*, 2014. http://www.almizan.org (accessed September 24, 2015).

Taji-Farouki, Suha. *Modern Muslim Intellectuals and the Qur'an*. New York: Oxford University Press in association with the Institute of Ismaili Studies, 2004.

Takim, Liyakat. *Shi'ism in America*. New York: New York University Press, 2009.

Taylor, Charles. *Modern Social Imaginaries*. Durham, N.C.: Duke University Press, 2004.

Tottoli, Roberto. "Korah." In *Encyclopaedia of the Qur'an*, edited by Jane Dammen McAuliffe, 3:104–5. Leiden, Netherlands: E. J. Brill, 2002.

Turner, Bryan S. *Orientalism, Postmodernism and Globalism*. New York: Routledge, 1994.

Turner, Henry McNeal. "God is a Negro." In *Preaching with Sacred Fire: An Anthology of African American Sermons, 1750 to the Present*, edited by Martha Simmons and Frank A. Thomas, 347–48. New York: W. W. Norton, 2010.

Turner, Richard Brent. *Islam in the African-American Experience*. Bloomington: Indiana University Press, 2003.

Turner, Victor. "Betwixt and Between." In *The Forest of Symbols*, 93–111. Ithaca, N.Y.: Cornell University Press, 1967.

"The Universal Declaration of Human Rights." December 10, 1948. Available online at the United Nations website. http://www.un.org/en/documents/udhr/ (accessed May 3, 2014).

Wadud, Amina. "Amina Wadud." *Nederlandse Moslim Omroep* video. http://www.nmo.nl/67-Amina_Wadud.html (accessed February 3, 2010).

———. *Inside the Gender Jihad: Women's Reform in Islam*. Oxford, U.K.: Oneworld, 2006.

———. *Qur'an and Woman: Rereading the Sacred Text from a Woman's Perspective*. New York: Oxford University Press, 1999.

Wahhaj, Siraj. "Muslim Women in Hijab." YouTube video. Posted by "Islam on Demand," November 21, 2006. http://www.youtube.com/watch?v=wRXm5ttFC_s (accessed February 12, 2010).

Walbridge, Linda. *Without Forgetting the Imam: Lebanese Shi'ism in an American Community*. Detroit: Wayne State University Press, 1997.

Ware, Rudolph T., III. *The Walking Qur'an: Islamic Education, Embodied Knowledge, and History in West Africa*. Chapel Hill: University of North Carolina Press, 2014.

Warner, Michael. *Publics and Counterpublics*. New York: Zone Books, 2002.

Weaver, Mary Jo, and R. Scott Appleby, eds. *Being Right: Conservative Catholics in America*. Bloomington: Indiana University Press, 1995.

Webb, Gisela. Introduction to *Windows of Faith: Muslim Women Scholar-Activists in North America*, edited by Gisela Webb, xi–xx. Syracuse, N.Y.: Syracuse University Press, 2000.

Weielandt, Rotraud. "Exegesis of the Qur'an: Early Modern and Contemporary." In *Encyclopaedia of the Qur'an*, edited by Jane Dammen McAuliffe, 2:24–42. Leiden, Netherlands: E. J. Brill, 2002.

Widmer, Edward L. *Young America: The Flowering of Democracy in New York.* New York: Oxford University Press, 1999.

Wimbush, Vincent L., ed. *Theorizing Scriptures: New Critical Orientations to a Cultural Phenomenon.* New Brunswick, N.J.: Rutgers University Press, 2008.

Wise, Lindsay. "'Words from the Heart': New Forms of Islamic Preaching in Egypt." M.Phil. thesis, Oxford University, 2003.

Yuskaev, Timur R. "Redeeming the Nation: Redemption Theology in African-American Islam." *Studies in Contemporary Islam* 1 (1999): 29–61.

Yuskaev, Timur, and Harvey Stark. "Imam and Chaplain." In *The Oxford Handbook of American Islam,* edited by Yvonne Y. Haddad and Jane I. Smith, 47–63. New York: Oxford University Press, 2014.

Yusuf, Hamza. "Changing the Tide." YouTube video. Posted by "Faith, Submission, & Beauty," July 20, 2006. http://www.youtube.com/watch?v=WfEIGw8NtNA (accessed February 12, 2010).

——. "Give and Take for God's Sake." YouTube video. Posted by "IslamTrueReligionTV," April 29, 2013. https://www.youtube.com/watch?v=NFQbcF87qoE (accessed November 20, 2014).

——. "Making Sense of Our Past." YouTube video. Posted by "Mo987665," September 26, 2011. https://www.youtube.com/watch?v=t6p8kuoNnkM (accessed October 11, 2014).

——. "A Message To Humanity (ISNA 2004)." YouTube video. Posted by "Mo987665," October 8, 2011. https://www.youtube.com/watch?v=ih-Zto_HkBk (accessed February 19, 2015).

——. "On Muslim Youth," YouTube video. Posted by "thikr," April 22, 2006. http://www.youtube.com/watch?v=Xl6d2bC6lco (accessed June 5, 2007).

——. *Reflections on al-Hujurat, the 49th Chapter of the Sacred Qur'an.* Southwest Ranches, Fla.: Sandala Productions, 2008. Compact disc set.

——. "True Spirit of Islam." YouTube video. Posted by "thikr," April 22, 2006. http://www.youtube.com/watch?v=locjog_9frc (accessed June 6, 2007).

——. "Zaytuna Monthly Videocast: Episode 3—Broadening the Scope of the Pope." Zaytuna College video. http://www.zikrcast.com/podcast/VidStream/ZVCast_Ep3Strm.mov (accessed June 11, 2007).

Yusuf, Hamza, Zaid Shakir, and Yahya Rhodus. *The Way Ahead: Effective Muslim Responses to Contemporary Challenges.* Berkeley, Calif.: Zaytuna Institute, 2008, compact disc set.

Zaytuna Institute. "Knowledge-based Approach of Zaytuna Institute." YouTube video. Posted by "Zaytuna College," July 31, 2006. https://www.youtube.com/watch?v=E7Mq6TYic1w (accessed February 20, 2015).

INDEX

······ ✄ ······

www.ingramcontent.com/pod-product-compliance
Lightning Source LLC
Chambersburg PA
CBHW022317250925
33121CB00002B/72